LIVING WITH
STAR TREK

LIVING WITH STAR TREK

AMERICAN CULTURE AND THE *STAR TREK* UNIVERSE

LINCOLN GERAGHTY

I.B. TAURIS

LONDON · NEW YORK

Published in 2007 by I.B.Tauris & Co Ltd
6 Salem Road, London W2 4BU
175 Fifth Avenue, New York NY 10010
www.ibtauris.com

In the United States of America and in Canada distributed by
Palgrave Macmillan, a division of St Martin's Press
175 Fifth Avenue, New York NY 10010

ISBN 978 1 84511 265 3 Paperback
ISBN 978 1 84511 421 3 Hardback

A full CIP record for this book is available from the British Library
A full CIP record for this book is available from the Library of Congress

Library of Congress catalog card: available

Typeset in Quadraat by Steve Tribe, Andover
Printed and bound in Great Britain by TJ International Ltd, Padstow

CONTENTS

ACKNOWLEDGEMENTS

To start, I must thank those in the School of American and Canadian Studies at the University of Nottingham for helping to create a stimulating and supportive environment that provided a suitable setting in which to undertake the research for my PhD, which forms the basis of this book. For providing travel expenses for a research trip to Los Angeles, I would like to thank BAAS for their support and the staff of the Arts Special Collection Library at UCLA for their help and priceless knowledge of the Gene Roddenberry archive. Special mention must also go to Majel Barrett Roddenberry, who allowed me access to the collection. I want to also thank my colleagues in the School of Creative Arts, Film and Media at the University of Portsmouth for welcoming me into their department. Special thanks go to all those in the Film and Media teams who helped me settle in while completing this book. Particular thanks go to Eithne Quinn and Mark Jancovich, who were my supervisors for the PhD, and Julian Stringer and Tim O'Sullivan, my PhD examiners. To Philippa Brewster, my editor, and all those at I.B.Tauris who supported the publication of this book, I offer my sincere thanks and appreciation.

My deepest gratitude and affection are reserved for the following: Laurence and Kathy Janicker, who have been incredibly supportive throughout; my parents, Malcolm and Diane Geraghty, whose support and love were priceless throughout the entire project; and finally my partner, Rebecca Janicker, who not only helped proofread the manuscript in all of its varying stages, but has also had to put up with me wittering on about *Star Trek* for the past six years. Rebecca has remained a source of continual inspiration and encouragement. It is for all these reasons, and for many more, that this book is dedicated to her.

NOTE

Since this book is partly drawn from my PhD thesis, components have also been published elsewhere in different forms:

Chapter One as '"Carved from the rock experiences of our daily lives": Reality and Star Trek's Multiple Histories', *European Journal of American Culture* 21.3 (2002): 160–76;

Chapter Two as 'Telling Tales of the Future: Science Fiction and Star Trek's Exemplary Narratives', *Reconstruction: Studies in Contemporary Culture* 3.2 (Spring 2003);

Chapter Three as 'Creating and Comparing Myth in Twentieth Century Science Fiction: Star Trek and Star Wars', *Literature/Film Quarterly* 33.3 (2005): 191–200;

Extracts from Chapter Four as 'The American Jeremiad and Star Trek's Puritan Legacy', *Journal of the Fantastic in the Arts* 14.2 (2003): 228–45;

Chapter Six as '"Help When Times are Hard": Bereavement and Star Trek Fan Letters', *Refractory: A Journal of Entertainment Media*, Volume 5 (2004).

LIVING WITH STAR TREK

'Without freedom of choice there is no creativity.
Without creativity there is no life.'
Kirk to Landru, 'Return of the Archons' (1967)

Is *Star Trek* dead? Some might wonder why I ask such a question at the beginning of a book called *Living with Star Trek*, but with *Star Trek: Enterprise*[1] no longer being produced and plans for an eleventh movie being hotly contested by fans wishing producers would stop interfering with *Star Trek*'s back story, people might be right in assuming that this is the end for the world's most famous, and once most popular, science fiction franchise. On the one hand, this can be seen as a devastating blow to the millions of fans who continue to watch *Star Trek* in syndication around the world; on the other, the current predicament is not new to *Star Trek* or its fans. In 1967, when the original series was entering its second season, it too was facing cancellation. Only after a successful fan-led campaign did it go on to complete a third and final season. What the contemporary situation really reminds us is that *Star Trek* has had a history of cancellations and problems with image: *Enterprise* is not the first series to face criticism and commercial failure.

HISTORY

Gene Roddenberry, an ex-pilot and Los Angeles police officer from El Paso, Texas, created *Star Trek* in response to his increasing lack of success in securing long-term television show writing contracts.

After reading Arthur C. Clarke, he decided to write and pitch a science fiction series that would allow him 'to talk about love, war, nature, God, sex', and one that the censors would pass 'because it all seemed so make-believe.'[2] In 1964, NBC let him begin production on the first of three pilot scripts; 'The Cage' was to be the first in a series of programmes charting the missions of the Starship Enterprise and her crew. After negative feedback from the network, Roddenberry was persuaded to make another pilot, a more action-orientated adventure where the audience could see a brave captain heroically command his ship. As a result, 'Where No Man Has Gone Before' was aired in 1966 with William Shatner as Captain James T. Kirk. The controversy over the direction Roddenberry had to take with the pilot alludes to the conflicting themes that remain at the heart of *Star Trek*'s ethos. The network wanted to emphasise the rugged individualism of the captain, he was supposed to be a role model for America's New Frontier.[3] Roddenberry wanted to emphasise diversity within a community, he had a female first officer and an alien science officer working together and alongside more typical WASP characters. Instead of cancelling each other out, these dichotomous interpretations of humanity's future became the main focus of the original series: It was to be a series that promoted individual success and achievement through space travel as well as promoting diversity and equality within a utopian future. Even after eventual cancellation and many years absent from television-screens, *Star Trek* continued to stand for those apparently incompatible attitudes and, as a result, its fans understood the series to be about the individual and communal pursuit of utopia.

When Kirk and Uhura shared the first televised inter-racial kiss in the episode 'Plato's Stepchildren' (1968), *Star Trek*'s reputation as a liberal science fiction series was sealed. Nichelle Nichols, the African-American actress who played the beautiful communications officer, remembers in her autobiography how much her character helped to address and critique racism just by her presence on the bridge. A true story, one which has become as much a part of the *Star Trek* mythos as Uhura herself, describes how Dr Martin Luther King Jr. told her not to leave the show because she had become a role model for black people everywhere. Nichols quotes King as saying:

You must not leave. You have opened a door that must not be allowed to close. I'm sure you have taken a lot of grief, or probably will for what you are doing. But you changed the face of television forever. For the first time, the world sees us as we should be seen, as equals, as intelligent people – as we *should* be. There will always be role models for Black children; you are a role model for everyone.[4]

Both the kiss and this story mean a lot to fans and critics. In her autobiography, Nichols goes on to describe how a white Southern gentlemen wrote to her and said that he did not agree with the mixing of the races but, because she was so beautiful, no one could resist kissing her, especially the red-blooded Kirk.[5] Whenever Nichols attends a convention or gives an interview, fans eagerly anticipate her story; it has become part of the mythical retelling of franchise history. As much as anything, the continued retelling or rehashing of Star Trek history speaks to the fans' passion for the text and its continual influence on their daily lives. The same can be said of the famous letter campaign that was organised by fans to help save the show from being axed in 1967.[6] For some critics, however, these examples of Star Trek's liberalism are all too often relied upon as guides to what Roddenberry was trying to mediate in the 1960s. They point out that the inter-racial kiss was actually forced upon Kirk and Uhura as torture by a malevolent alien being, and that their lips never really touched. For critics, this probably says more about Star Trek's attitude towards race than anything else does: It never went far enough; it did not live up to its promise. The same can be said of the letter campaign; the promise of a better third season, with more action and character-orientated stories, meant network executives were always going to commission more episodes. The influx of fan mail was not the deciding factor.

The original series lasted three seasons, from 1966 to 1969 and, after a second letter campaign failed to save the show, fans were left to rewatch and relive the seventy-nine episodes on syndicated television. The ten-year period after Star Trek's cancellation was a defining moment both in franchise history and the history of audience studies. More and more fans came to watch the series for the first time in the early 1970s, expecting a supply of new episodes when the seventy-nine ran out. Unfortunately, this was not the case and only a short-lived animated series in 1974 kept them entertained. What did emerge from this period in *Star Trek* history are fanzines – featuring fan-written stories – and organised conventions, the first of which was held in New York in 1972, where fans could, for the first time, meet up with other fans from around the USA to discuss their favourite episodes and buy merchandise. It was also at this time that Susan Sackett, Roddenberry's production assistant from the original series, began to compile letters that had been sent to Roddenberry regarding the fans' love of *Star Trek*. Alongside Sackett's project of collecting together fan correspondence, there was a real drive to create a fan culture centred on the series' and Roddenberry's liberal humanism.[7] Out of this fan culture grew a renewed call for more *Star Trek*. Initial ideas for a second series starring most of the original cast grew into *Star Trek: The Motion Picture* (1979), released as a big-budget movie to counteract and feed off the hype created by *Star Wars* (1977). During the early 1980s, the almost yearly big-screen versions of *Star Trek* kept fans absorbed and helped the franchise remain ever-present in the American media.

In 1987, *Star Trek: The Next Generation* (TNG) was introduced to the world, with Rick Berman as Producer and Gene Roddenberry now acting as Executive Producer. This series was initially received with some trepidation, because fans were unhappy that a new crew was aboard the famous Enterprise. In narrative terms, it was also set two hundred years after the original series, which meant there was no possibility that the original cast could appear further down the line (apart from dabbling with the timeline). It is interesting to note that, after its first two seasons, TNG was also under pressure to be cancelled; it did not seem that there was an audience for the adventures of a new ship and crew. After the screening of 'The Best of Both Worlds' (1990) as a season cliffhanger, however, fans became more enthusiastic and began to realise the possibilities TNG offered in the way of fictional narrative. New stories meant not only that they could see what the future looked like after Kirk's time, but also that there would be more back-story in which to immerse themselves. The series went from strength to strength as the characters were allowed to develop and interact with others in ways which were denied to the original crew. As the seasons progressed, the franchise built upon its fanbase by continuing to release movies starring Shatner, Nimoy and the rest, as well as having a weekly series.

In 1993, this was extended further with the creation of *Star Trek: Deep Space Nine* (DS9). Unlike the continued adventures of the original and new Enterprise, DS9 was set on a space station. Producers broke the mould by having an African-American actor play the lead role and it offered a third dynamic setting in which a core group of characters could learn and grow as friends. Even without Roddenberry's involvement – he died in 1991 – DS9 continued to espouse the original themes of individualism and self-improvement within a supportive community. TNG came to an end in 1994, after seven successful seasons, with the promise of a new series of movies that would follow *Star Trek VI: The Undiscovered Country*. DS9 did not remain alone for long because a fourth *Star Trek* series, *Star Trek: Voyager*, began in 1995 with the pilot episode 'Caretaker'. Again producers made 'history', this time by making a woman the captain of the Starship Voyager. Both series regularly suffered criticism, DS9 in particular from fans, because they were seen as being too dissimilar from the *Star Trek* format where a ship's crew explores space, meeting different alien species week after week. Nevertheless, evident in all of the *Star Trek* sequels is Roddenberry's utopian future, a depiction of what humanity will achieve if it fulfils its potential and stops destroying itself. *Enterprise*'s ethos was no different. In fact, with the series set only a hundred years in the future, viewers were able to see how humanity made that leap to the utopian future first seen by audiences in 1966.

Despite *Enterprise*'s cancellation after only four seasons, failing to match the seven each of TNG, DS9, and *Voyager*, what is significant is that the patterns of possible cancellation, concern and fan activity continue to characterise the entire franchise. If one can say that *Star Trek* is losing audience appeal on American television, not a new occurrence, then one could also theorise that it is in fact enlarging its audience and fanbase internationally. Fans around the world number in their millions, episodes still air in syndication, and more recent franchise developments have helped secure its popularity. *Star Trek* has gone on the road with world tours to Edinburgh, Berlin, London's Science Museum and Hyde Park that combine the latest in digital technology and interactive gaming with the props and costumes from the various series and movies. These 'experiences' bring the Star Trek franchise, and Roddenberry's original message, to millions of people around the globe, giving them the opportunity to see pieces of 'future history' not ordinarily available to them.[8] Star Trek has also moved into the theme park genre by opening up walk-through experiences in the Las Vegas Hilton Hotel that cater for the fans' desire to get closer to their favourite show.[9] As the series continues to change and adapt for a new audience in the twenty-first century, so too does the franchise. One would be justified in thinking that this may be a trend that goes against Roddenberry's ethos, but it also corresponds to certain themes and images that he wanted to promote. He believed the individual communities of the world should forget their differences and live together in peace. As Star Trek begins to transform into a global franchise, albeit primarily concerned with profit, new fans are being introduced to his vision of a utopian future. Consequently, the fictional text is becoming more and more of a template for how fans might achieve that utopia, and, as I will argue throughout this book, its binary nature as an open and closed text is becoming increasingly contested in the work of those who study its devoted audience.

NARRATIVE

George Lipsitz describes mass communication within popular culture as an embodiment 'of our deepest hopes' and an engagement with 'some of our most profound sympathies'. Popular commercialised leisure pursuits such as jazz, film, and television are modes of history – in that they form a 'repository of collective memory that places immediate experience in the context of change over time'.[10] Television in particular performs as a 'therapeutic voice ministering to the open wounds of the psyche' through its vocabulary of 'emotion and empathy ... ritual and repetition'. Lipsitz believes television addresses the inner life by 'maximising the private and personal aspects of existence'.[11] As such, one can see Star Trek as speaking to the inner life – addressing the individual on a personal and private level allowing them to relate to its overall utopian message. The fan letters examined in this book suggest that there is definite attention paid to the individual possibilities that Star Trek's fictional text provides its audience. However, Lipsitz is cautious in discussing the prominence of TV in American culture because he believes it helps and hinders public life. Television both nurtures and excludes the individual; giving the opportunity to empathise with people and characters on-screen but also focusing attention inwards, undermining 'the psychic prerequisites for a public life'.[12] This turn to the inner-self is not a new development in American culture and it is most definitely not an argument reserved for scholars of popular culture and American Studies. In order to understand the central themes and issues that emerge from within the *Star Trek* text and fan letters we must appreciate their position within American history at large. Notions of utopia, community and self-improvement are themes that exemplify the disputed nature of America's national identity and, therefore, it would be helpful here to briefly flesh out these particular themes within the contexts of American culture.

For the Puritans, travelling to America was part of their divine mission to establish a utopia on God's Earth in preparation for the Second Coming of Christ. Of course, once they arrived in the New World, the Puritan experience with the land and the native 'Indians' would go on to transform their particular mission from a community-driven enterprise to one centred on the individual pursuit of happiness. Regardless of this transformation, however, utopia remained the focus for early Americans as it spoke to their desire for change under exceptional circumstances. For some, America was a utopia – created from a savage wilderness and civilised for the benefit of God's chosen people. For others, America was far from the utopian world for which the Puritan forefathers had risked their lives. The dichotomous nature of America as realised and failed utopia continued to influence those who held power and was influential in the creation of the American nation after the Revolution and the forming of the United States of America in 1783. Thomas Jefferson, Benjamin Franklin and the like began to envision America as an exceptional nation, one that the world could look to as an example of the successful transition from feudal commonwealth to independent democracy.[13]

During the nineteenth century, those who believed that America did not embody their religious and social values, and subsequently felt estranged from society, began to form their own communities.

These communal organisations saw themselves as agents for their own creation of utopia in America and often totally withdrew from normal life so as to set up their own villages and communes based on their unique belief systems.[14] Utopia could be achieved through balancing the needs of the individual and the community. One can imagine that during this period there were hundreds of 'utopias' within America and each one was envisioned by a community dedicated to preserving and prolonging their utopia in fulfilment of their divine mission. What these communities did share was 'a faith in the perfectibility of mankind and a belief that the millennium was at hand'. Whether these communities disavowed drinking or promoted free love, they all desired 'to bring heaven on earth'.[15] Consequently, the utopian nature of American culture in the nineteenth and early twentieth centuries continued to propagate, eventually resulting in the kinds of utopian fiction offered by Edward Bellamy's *Looking Backward* (1888), L. Frank Baum's *Oz* stories (1900–1920) and early science fiction literature.[16] *Star Trek*'s vision of an American utopia is part of this tradition and therefore shares many of the same themes associated with bringing 'heaven on earth' and having faith 'in the perfectibility of mankind'. However, one must remember that Roddenberry's utopia is also determined by humanity's willingness to change for the better and the desire for self-help.

Living with Star Trek considers to what extent *Star Trek* fan letters can be seen as evidence for a supportive community, where fans' hopes, desires and traumatic experiences can be expressed, shared and utilised. This community, or what I term 'network of support', relies on the fictional utopian television text as a common frame of reference; relevant *Star Trek* episodes and characters are used as markers for specific emotional and physical experiences. If mass communications mediate the boundaries between the public and the private, then they not only provide images of the world around us and places with which we are not familiar but they can also provide us with the practices and beliefs for a sense of 'imagined community'.[17] Within this community, the text is a therapeutic aid for fans' daily lives. However, the act of writing and sharing their letters with other fans – getting them published in a public sphere – is perhaps of greater therapeutic benefit. Realising that other fans within this community share similar thoughts and experiences is the driving force behind the individual's emotional, physical and personal self-improvement. Notions of the supportive community are again not new in American culture, therefore I want to emphasise how Star Trek's communal appeal is part of wider trends in society.

THE AUDIENCES OF STAR TREK

Studies such as Ann Gray's 'Behind Closed Doors: Video Recorders in the Home' (1987) or Dorothy Hobson's work on Crossroads (1964–1988) intimate that the places and spaces for watching one's favourite television programmes, particularly soap operas, become centres of relaxation and escape from the daily routine of family and domestic life.[18] In television studies, the physical location of reception and how a text is consumed is just as important to the understanding of the audience as studying how they interpret it. Television is by its very nature a polysemic text; its popularity, the making or breaking of any particular show, therefore depends on it reaching a wide audience – it must be open. As John Fiske identified in his examination of television detective series Hart to Hart (1979–1984), we cannot predict the meanings audiences take but we can identify the polysemic characteristics and theorise the relation between text and social context. The polysemy of meaning is as much a power struggle as that of economics or politics, yet TV fails to control meaning just as social authority attempts and fails to control oppositional voices.[19] Consequently, a large proportion of recent and famous ethnographic audience studies have focused specifically on the oppositional/cult fan and especially the active fan of Star Trek.[20] The field of fan studies can be seen as a result of what Mark Jancovich and Lucy Faire describe as cultural studies' tendency 'to divide the public rather too neatly into two distinct groups – the conformist and the resistant'. The 'activity, interest and creativity was to be found in the usually subcultural groups who composed the latter position', therefore they were the ones who were analysed.[21] However, Ien Ang's work on the fans of Dallas (1978–1991) and David Morley's famous study of the Nationwide (1969–1983) audience showed us the diverse nature of TV's audiences and, as with Christine Geraghty's Women and Soap Opera (1991), the television text's capacity to represent the boundless personal space of utopian possibility.[22] Many audiences attempt to resist the dominant ideology of the text, what Morley would call the 'oppositional audience', yet there are those that 'inflect the preferred meaning ... by relating the message to some concrete or situated context which reflects' their own personal interests; these are described as the 'negotiated audience'.[23] It is this type of audience – the non-oppositional – that best exemplifies those fans of *Star Trek* I look at in this book.

One can say that those fans of *Star Trek* who were seen as active and creative participants in the 'textual poaching' of the text were the type of fan that routinely formed the basis for fan studies.[24] Nicholas Abercrombie and Brian Longhurst observe that these studies 'were concerned to examine the way in which sectors of the audience were *active* in response to dominant forms of mass media'. Fan activity 'represented a form of resistance to the dominant messages contained in texts which on the face of it represented forms of dominant ideology'.[25] The inactive or passive (for want of better words) fans, those who did not openly transform the text in a recognised fashion by writing stories, singing songs, dressing up in costume or drawing artwork, became less important to the study of fan culture and were therefore never included in a comprehensive study of *Star Trek* fandom. This book is an attempt to bring those fans, so often overlooked, into the spotlight. This does not mean I want to divide *Star Trek* fans into the active and passive categories. Instead, I want to separate what one can call their 'activities' into those types of grouping. This means that the fans I look at may or may not participate in documented cult practices such as dressing up and attending conventions, what is important is that they felt the need to convey their thoughts and feelings about *Star Trek* in letter form and share them with other fans. The practice of letter writing thus becomes the activity and it is what the fans say about the so-called 'dominant ideology' of the text and how it impacts on their lives that will remain important to this study. Similarly, Sara Gwenllian-Jones and Roberta Pearson have noted that the popularity of the cult television text 'stems not from resistance to capitalism but rather from an imaginative engagement with cult television programmes encouraged by' their generic and textual characteristics: internal logics, realistic and archetypal characters, seriality and fictional worlds where ethical issues can be explored free from the banal problems of everyday life.[26]

The following chapters redress the imbalance found in Star Trek fan studies, since they do not exceptionalise those fans who are more visibly active or are members of distinct fan clubs. Instead, I concentrate on what all types of fan have to say about the text and how they engage with it on a more personal and emotional level. The act of writing letters is in itself an activity that demarcates boundaries between types of fans; however, I feel that by examining these letters one can get a sense of how Star Trek is used within fans' daily lives and what it means to them more personally. This is far beyond what previous studies have attempted to do, since they primarily deal with what remains in the public spotlight. Fan costumes and conventions are routinely exposed and discovered in the media and are taken as representative of the totality of Star Trek fan culture. I focus on letters that are not so much in the public gaze and therefore do not correspond to established publishing and media constraints; fans can speak to other fans in an atmosphere of shared textual knowledge and self-awareness. Therefore, there are no boundaries set up between different fans, as there might be at a convention, because all the fans are writing their personal feelings and experiences and sharing in each others' correspondence. Their letters are both illustrative of Star Trek fandom's continued cultural and social work and a new area of fan study: the epistolary of Star Trek.

A STAR TREK EPISTOLARY:
FAN LETTER WRITING AS SOCIAL PRACTICE

For David Barton and Nigel Hall, letter writing should be viewed 'as a social practice, examining the texts, the participants, the activities and the artefacts in the social contexts'.[27] Letters have always provoked discussion and resulted in response, whether verbal or written, and can therefore be described as open texts. In this sense, they are not products of solitary experience but are instead significant community practices. The content of the letter is often personal and reflects individual lives, and, as in the case of the letters I have looked at, the content is dependant on a Star Trek text that is open to millions of fans worldwide; reciting through that text, people can share similar experiences and emotions. Reading these letters 'requires acts of imagination and empathy' whereby we recognise the contexts in which the 'vulnerability, sorrow, folly, and crudity, as well as the invention, eloquence, and lyricism, that such conditions bring out'.[28] William Merrill Decker's study of letter writing in America before the age of mass telecommunications is a unique study of how the act of writing and reading letters created a space for communication desperately required by people living in a large and, above all, still untamed nation. Epistolary writing, he quotes Bruce Redford as saying, 'fashions a distinctive world at once internally consistent, vital, and self-supporting'.[29] Letters are a social genre that enables people to organise and cultivate relations and provides a space to imagine 'the ways in which one may exist in reciprocity with others'.[30] Thus *Living with Star Trek* shows how much the utopian fictional text enables organisation and cultivation of relationships within the fan community and, as a result, its epistolarity provides fans a space within which they can share experiences and emotions analogous to a narrative of self-help and social betterment.

Unlike previous studies of the *Star Trek* audience, this book will look at what fans have to say about the text and how they use it in their daily lives. It is important to remember that the letters I look at were often written to Gene Roddenberry since he was the man whose vision of the future offered inspiration to fans. Later letters, received after his death, often speak of Roddenberry's vision as still relevant to their own lives; in some senses, therefore, he has not really died. Fans now send their mail to magazines and fan publications instead. The readership for these letters changed from a personal correspondence with Roddenberry to one that incorporated other fans with numerous experiences and opinions. Overall, the collected letters I have examined signal the development of a *Star Trek* community that works in parallel with the franchise and helps to support other fans who feel affected by the themes and messages contained within the text.

CONTENT

Part One examines the historical, narrative, and mythic roots of the *Star Trek* text, highlighting the themes of utopia, community and self-improvement that are important to the study of the fan letters. More specifically, Chapter One includes a short history of Star Trek fandom and how the fictional text has become a form of alternative reality for its fans. This reality is founded on a 'history of the future' that to all intents and purposes has become a verifiable prediction of what the future will be like. Of course, this vision of a utopian future is the blueprint so often referred to by fans in their letters examined in Chapter Five. Chapter Two examines the literary roots of Star Trek's storytelling, in that the series make much use of common cultural narratives to communicate their own form of historical discourse. Using Hayden White's work on the typology of rhetorical figures of speech, I analyse the types of narrative Star Trek uses for its representation of history and the theoretical underpinnings that form the basis of its popularity and diverse appeal.[31] Moving on from the literary to the mythical, in Chapter Three I compare Star Trek's use of American myth in relation to another science fiction phenomenon, Star Wars. Using, building upon, and updating the work done on Star Trek and myth in texts such as Jewett and Lawrence's The American Monomyth, I posit that the franchise applies myth in a different way to Star Wars by setting its narrative in the future rather than the past.[32] This makes myth relevant to the audience, turning the series into the enabling fiction that, as I investigate in Chapters Six and Seven, fans adapt and use in their daily lives.

Chapter Four is a detailed textual analysis of a specific American foundational narrative: the American Jeremiad. I concentrate on how both the literary form of the Jeremiad and the Star Trek text refer back to the past in order to prophesy a better future. Promoting a particular kind of American history, I maintain that the Puritan experience is replicated in three of the Star Trek movies made in the late 1980s. Notions of self-improvement and self-help become increasingly important to both the Puritan errand and Star Trek's utopian message and I want to contextualise this trend in the Star Trek text in order to highlight how and where fans recognise similar themes when they write their letters. Using Sacvan Bercovitch's analysis of the Jeremiad in his seminal work The American Jeremiad (1978), I posit that Star Trek acts as a marker for Americans, just as the Jeremiad did for the Pilgrim Fathers and their descendants, providing them with guidance and encouragement in their lives.[33]

Part Two focuses on fan letters, investigating the ways in which American fans talk about and use the themes of utopia, community and self-improvement. These letters create a 'network of support' that offers a nurturing atmosphere through which fans can express their feelings, emotions and experiences interpreted through the universal framework of the *Star Trek* text. Chapter Five on utopia and social change examines letters that describe Gene Roddenberry's depiction of utopia and how fans feel his vision was and still is an attainable goal in their own lifetimes. Fans define the series as a blueprint for solving existing social problems in America such as racism, poverty, and war. In their letters, fans see the series as representing a utopian future that exists in contrast to the dystopian future to which existing social problems will lead. I use and adapt Richard Dyer's model of utopia in entertainment to contextualise the contents of these letters.[34] The concept of communal achievement is carried further in Chapter Six, where I look at the various ways fans use and decipher the *Star Trek* text to help cope with traumatic experiences in their lives, in particular bereavement, illness, and disability. These stressful, momentous, yet often inevitable, life experiences are dealt with by a close personal affinity with the fictional text; often specific episodes speak to individual needs. I maintain that fans who have written about their traumatic experiences do so to find a voice. This voice articulates the level of grief suffered and is typically hard to share in public. With so many similar stories in circulation, however, people write these letters in an attempt to become part of a special community, one that offers support through a common dialogue based on the *Star Trek* fan experience. Introducing and adapting the work of Robert Putnam and Robert Wuthnow in relation to the decline of community in America will be integral to my analysis of the merits of *Star Trek*'s community of support.[35] If Chapter Six uncovers an environment where fans are beginning to get over troubled periods in their lives, then Chapter Seven looks at fans who recount how *Star Trek*, and even individual characters such as Data, Seven of Nine or Captain Janeway, provided inspiration for a personal change for the better. I compare and contrast the letters in a framework of self-help narratives and draw particular attention to how these letters perform similar tasks to the talk show. Finding a public voice is a hard yet rewarding goal for fans who believe that

Star Trek has inspired them and that Roddenberry's utopian vision is achievable. Fans who believe that the text provided inspiration are careful to point out that they themselves instigated the change in their lives, yet Star Trek was always there to offer support. These self-improvement narratives speak to specific traditions of self-help in American history and to an increasingly common trend in television programming: the confessional talk show.

Finally, Part Three provides an analysis of two exclusive texts: Enterprise and the science fiction comedy Galaxy Quest (1999). I explore in more detail the future history of the Star Trek narrative and the fan culture surrounding the interpretation and reception of a cult movie outside of the franchise. In Chapter Eight, I compare DS9 with Enterprise, arguing that the former provides an historical narrative where possibilities of the future remain open and the latter reinforces a history that has already happened and cannot be changed. Enterprise's reinvention of and reverence for the Star Trek past is representative of the fictional text's reliance on historical narrative and the fans' investment in the potentialities of Roddenberry's future. However, I have also found that both international and American fans are acutely aware of the dangers that such a reliance on American history entails, and they respond to this by emphasising in letters that Star Trek is meant to be about a universal utopia. In an analysis of Enterprise's opening titles, I shall be revisiting some of the issues discussed in Chapter Four with regard to American exceptionalism and the theory of America's frontier destiny. Like the fans in Chapter Five, fans in this chapter who engage with the title sequence do so because they believe Star Trek's utopia is not confined to a select few but is instead open to all people. Chapter Nine looks at the positive portrayal of cult fandom offered by Galaxy Quest. The film is a comedic homage to the Star Trek phenomenon, looking at the potential empowerment a cult text can offer its fans and how those fans use the text as an enabling fiction in their daily lives. The realisation of the fans' individual potential is a recurrent theme throughout this book and, by analysing Galaxy Quest, we will see how the concept of learning to improve and help oneself is intertwined with the fans' belief in the reality of the fictional text and how they live with that text on a daily basis. In effect, these two particular case studies not only look at how fans live through Star Trek day to day, but also draw attention to how they live with Star Trek as part of a supportive and culturally integrated group.

1

'CARVED FROM THE ROCK EXPERIENCES OF OUR DAILY LIVES'

HISTORY, MYTH, AND *STAR TREK*'S EXEMPLARY NARRATIVES

'Just words.'
'But good words. That's where ideas begin.'
Kirk and David, Star Trek II: The Wrath of Khan *(1982)*

'A dream that became a reality and spread throughout
the stars.'
Captain Kirk, 'Whom Gods Destroy' (1969)

Many studies have attempted to demonstrate the connections Star Trek has with American culture through its representations of society in all five series and ten feature films. What I seek to establish is what lies at the bottom of all this interest. When the façade of twenty-fourth-century gadgetry is peeled back, what is at the root of Star Trek's storytelling? Following on from that, what makes it so long-lasting and popular?

Star Trek is history; it is more than just good televisual entertainment. Star Trek is a historical, narrative discourse that not only feeds our passion for what the future might bring but also forms a relationship with the past, mediated not through written discourse, as Hayden White has suggested regarding history, but through television and film.[1] Star Trek acts as a canonical reference to what makes America American, and what will make Americans more human. Its roots, or tropics of discourse, were perhaps formulated in the 1960s but they originated when the first white settlers arrived in the New World claiming America as the Promised Land. This reliance on such an exceptional and wholly white male historical narrative is probably why so many critics, Daniel Bernardi, Jan Johnson-Smith and Robin Roberts amongst others, have studied Star Trek's racial, national, and gender interpretations.[2] But I want to analyse beyond those issues and examine the tropic connections between the American past and the American present and how they are used in Star Trek to posit an American future. To that end, I analyse the assemblage of tropes and metaphors that such a task relies upon to mediate those messages to an American audience.

How does the creation of a fictional narrative which encompasses the visual text on-screen and the fans' own productivity off-screen affect *Star Trek*'s aim of showing a future that is no longer exclusive or prejudiced? Ultimately, the fictional universe in which so many fans immerse themselves represents something entirely exclusive and totally at the mercy of what the producers and creators decide is appropriate. The *Star Trek* canon, the episodes and films, is in effect rather more constrictive and bound to set values than fans and audiences might expect. As Daniel Bernardi previously theorised, the *Star Trek* canon as a shared fan mythology is susceptible to the same flaws as America's own mythology.[3] For example, in 1991, Arthur Schlesinger Jr. wrote the book *The Disuniting of America: Reflections on a Multicultural Society*. In it, he criticised multiculturalism and its attempts at revising American history taught in schools, emphasising the supposed harm it did to the country and its children of all races. His solution was to reunite America by making minorities who wanted to become more culturally independent conform to its so-called liberal historical and political traditions. He focused on documents of note such as the Constitution and the Declaration of Independence and work by authors such as Emerson, Jefferson, de Tocqueville and Lincoln. In the 1998 edition, Schlesinger even went as far as to offer his own version of an American canon called the 'Baker's Dozen Books Indispensable to an Understanding of America',[4] in which he lists thirteen works of major importance to Americans, some by the authors I have already mentioned. What he failed to notice was that his entire list comprised white males, bar one: Harriet Beecher Stowe. The only non-white representation was also Stowe, through her book *Uncle Tom's Cabin* (1852). Because *Star Trek* perpetuates 'a final frontier that is explored and domesticated for a dominantly white imagination', Bernardi warns that it is important to be aware of the varied meanings of race that can be found in the mega-text since it is informed by public mythology.[5] The canon is rooted in real-time events so the image of the mega-text is realistic not fantastic. However, just like all forms of realism, *Star Trek* is prone to naturalising rhetoric, thus perpetuating the 'white only' myth.

In analysing literature based on western conceptions of the Orient, Edward Said posited that 'texts can create not only knowledge but also the very reality they appear to describe.'[6] *Star Trek*'s reality, influenced by the exclusive rhetoric described by Bernardi, is seen as real by many fans. Its text has literally created the fictional reality in which fans enjoy living and participating. Their active involvement with the ever-increasing text continues to make its fictional narrative even more real; as more people believe in the message and ethos of Star Trek, its future history seen in films and episodes becomes a legitimate prophecy of things to come. Star Trek as a franchise has an enormous amount of cultural power because it has become another way of living for many of its fans. I draw attention to some of those fans in Chapter One and go on to further emphasise how Star Trek's various histories have created new realities for many of them. What is more, these new realities would seem to have a destabilising effect on Bernardi's theory of Star Trek, continuing to perpetuate an exclusive view of the future, since they provide fans with unlimited freedom for their imaginations, fulfilling their own dreams, desires, and fantasies. The once constrictive and absolute mega-text is at the same time a suitable vehicle to release fans' creativity and create a sense of personal identity.

Initially, I investigate Star Trek and the exemplary narrative; examining what makes it so understandable and transmutable to a modern audience. Following on from this, I examine the role myth plays in Star Trek's exploration of human nature and life experiences. Then, using this research as a stepping stone for Chapter Four, I identify the people America looks to as its forefathers: the Puritans. Specifically, I examine their form of rhetorical and polemical narrative called the Jeremiad.

1

A LOOK TO
THE PAST

REALITY AND *STAR TREK*'S
MULTIPLE HISTORIES

Star Trek creates a future world where the glories of
the past are pristine and the failures and doubts of the
present have been overcome. It gives us our past as
our future, while making our present the past which,
like any historical event for the future-orientated
American, is safely over and forgotten.[1]

The many interpretations of *Star Trek*'s meanings have themselves
merged into a very diverse and flexible framework within which
students and academics can dip for reference. By interpretations,
I mean the many academic and non-academic studies of *Star Trek*
published each year in journals and by independent publishers. Not
only do the many analyses of the television phenomenon enable
us to understand its overall cultural significance, they also provide
us with a language that helps to express our attitudes towards *Star
Trek*. Even if some texts are critical of the series they are still paying
it a certain amount of reverence – they recognise its mythic and
figurative underpinnings.[2]

This reverence resembles what Audre Lorde would call 'poetry as
illumination' – a way of forming the ideas by which we live in order
to pursue our magic and fulfil our dreams: 'It is through this that
we give name to those ideas which are – until the poem – nameless
and formless, about to be birthed, but already felt.'[3] Fans and critics
alike have used *Star Trek* as a means by which they can express their

hopes and fears for the future; it is their poetical reverence for the series that enables them to write about many other issues that concern them. The audience, made up of die-hard fans and those less enthusiastic, have used the creative springboard that *Star Trek* provides to write their own short stories, novels, poems, essays and fanzines, representing their own form of 'poetry as illumination'. For example, at present there have been published nine volumes of collected short stories written by fans and set in the *Star Trek* universe, not all necessarily including any of the main characters. The series entitled *Star Trek Strange New Worlds* (1998–2006) is advertised as being made up of work by some of *Star Trek*'s most talented fans; its editors are proud to report that the universe of writers just keeps on expanding.[4]

There has been a poetry anthology published called *Star Trek The Poems* (2000), which not only features fan appreciation for the show but also includes first-time poets, hate poems and poems that combine unlikely locations and situations with the *Star Trek* phenomenon. In 'Bred to Boldly Go', for example, Mandy Coe describes her memories of a Butlins holiday, growing up as a teenager coping with menstrual cramps and high heels, and how *Star Trek* provided the hope of revolution for many women not happy with the unequal society in which they lived. Other poems pose some quite unusual questions such as how would the *Star Trek* crew cope with the miners' strike or a simple request for the toilet. These are real people writing about real issues of which they have experience, but they are also people who recognise *Star Trek*'s impact upon them and want to use that cultural impact to exhibit their personal poetry.[5] Henry Jenkins uses the term 'textual poaching', taken from Michel de Certeau's *Practice of Everyday Life* (1984), to describe this process by which fans embrace and transform the original text – in this case, *Star Trek* and its characters – which then becomes a catalyst for a network of new elaborate interpretations and meanings resulting in a 'common point of reference [that] facilitates social interaction amongst fans'.[6] In other words, those fans who earnestly pursue their interest in *Star Trek* through fan clubs, fanzines, novels, and conventions become active participants in the production and preservation of the fictional universe of *Trek*. In Part Two, I shall be examining at length the world of the *Star Trek* enthusiast and investigating what sort of identities they construct from the text of the series and how they use that identity in the day to day living of their lives. For now, I just want to draw out the sort of fictional realities Star Trek has created for those fans using history, narrative and myth, and how they might find their own niche within its ever expanding sphere of influence.

Another important way fans have expressed their 'poetry of illumination' is through the fanzine. This form of collected fan writing grew extensively after the original three-year run of Star Trek had finished and included short stories, novel serialisations, poetry, technical writing and artwork; sometimes these were pornographic in nature and often focused on just one character. For the fans, writing stories about or drawing pictures of their favourite characters was the next best thing to watching them on-screen. It had, and still has, such a diverse and wide-ranging audience fanbase that no other television programme can begin to compare in popularity. 'The power of Star Trek,' according to director David Carson, 'is its ability to jump off the screen and say things to you which you maybe wouldn't accept in a naturalistic drama.' It was pure entertainment on one level, keeping the network temporarily happy by winning in the ratings war, but on another there was something special about the ethos behind the stories, something with which fans could connect: 'It has an ability to raise itself poetically above the more mundane things. It appeals across the board poetically and philosophically to so many people in a way that [most naturalistic dramas] haven't a hope of ever doing.'[7]

With the publication of Star Trek Lives! by Jacqueline Lichtenberg, Sondra Marshak and Joan Winston in 1975, fans of the series were identified for the first time as creative participants in the Star Trek phenomenon. This book recognised the numerous clubs and fanzines that people from all walks of life had started in order to demonstrate the appeal Star Trek held for budding writers, artists, and those with only a minimal talent for the creative arts. Theoretically they distinguished two effects that they said accounted for the series' popularity: 'The Discovery Effect' and 'The Tailored Effect'. The first effect described how people originally 'discovered' Star Trek after it had started to be shown as syndicated reruns in the early 1970s; this preliminary contact triggered fans' creative urges because they wanted more of Star Trek but had to create new stories to fulfil their desires. The second outlined the individuals who picked their own favourite parts of Star Trek because it was 'tailored' to suit everyone's own tastes and interests. These fans concentrated on the specific characters and themes with which they most identified; their stories therefore became popular in their own right thanks to the fanzines that published them and like-minded fans who wanted to read them.[8]

Stories and art that have included a high sexual content are referred to by fans as *slash fiction*; instances where fans and amateur writers have 'ingeniously subverted and rewritten Star Trek to make it answerable to their own sexual and social desires'.[9] In some cases, particularly with the characters of Kirk and Spock, writers (mostly women) have 'recognised that there was an erotic homosexual subtext there, or at least one that could easily be *made* to be there'.[10] The fact that such themes and issues have been read into Star Trek and written about in such numbers proves that it provided a framework open to interpretation and poetic licence; it had something for everybody and everybody had something to say about it. They just said it in many different ways.

Star Trek is often quoted as a way of expressing one's dreams and how they can be fulfilled; especially a nation's dreams in the 1960s when political freedom and enfranchisement were so desired by those excluded that they would risk all to achieve them. In the post-liberal age, and at a time of increased national anxiety, it is no surprise that Star Trek has remained as a symbol of those struggles and still endures as a form of 'poetry as illumination', because Star Trek as a text allows America to dream. Albeit, according to Jay Goulding, in an attempt to 'ground a turbulent American culture which is challenging its own roots in the 1960s because of the horrors created in the Third World by American imperialism'. Star Trek, in some senses, uses its future frontier setting to critique and theorise about America's social problems from a safe distance, dislocating the 'viewers' attention from present dilemmas', allowing 'them to dream about American heritage'.[11]

Nevertheless, no one would be inspired by it if they could not see it as a means by which they could fulfil their dreams. David Gerrold sees Star Trek as being about 'the *sense of wonder*'. A term used to describe science fiction of the Golden Age, *sense of wonder* concerns the enthusiasm for a combination of gadgets (technophilia) and the future (progress), for Gerrold, 'that is the seed of [Star Trek's] power to move us.'[12] Lorde's application of poetry mirrors that of Star Trek's inasmuch as it provides a rich figurative language – or poetry – to describe or imagine fans' desires: 'The farthest horizons of our hopes and fears are cobbled by our poems, carved from the rock experiences of our daily lives.'[13]

Star Trek's ability to inspire peoples' innermost desires stems from its perception of reality; fans would not be inspired by it if they did not believe it to be a real version of things to come. By rewriting and reworking the original text, fans of Star Trek make it more real, in a sense they incorporate it into their lives and use it in their own particular lived experiences. However, as Henry Jenkins observes in his work about how texts become real, this does not mean the original text changes in any significant way, rather it 'becomes something more than what it was before, not something less'.[14] For example, Barbara Adams, a reserve juror in the 1996 Whitewater trial, attended every day dressed in Starfleet uniform complete with phaser and tricorder. Her reason was that she wanted to promote the programme's 'ideas, messages and good solid values' and, not surprisingly, she received a great deal of media attention.[15] So much so that she had to be relieved from duty because the judge believed her talking to the press about her love of Star Trek was a breach of confidentiality. Adams took it upon herself to represent Star Trek's ideals in court because she saw them as entirely appropriate in that real-life situation. The ridicule and public interest stirred up by the national press only brought more attention to her actions, so the judge had to intervene. As a result, Adams was promoted within her 'ship', her local fan club, because she had upheld and defended the ideals of Star Trek's Federation. Heather Joseph-Witham states that 'fans who wear Star Trek apparel to public events attempt to actualize the ideals of the show's creator, Gene Roddenberry, and the Star Trek universe,'[16] a point emphasised by Adams' recollection of why she wanted to wear the uniform to court:

> It's not that it's an obsession or something that totally consumes my life but certainly the ideals of *Trek* are ideals

that I live by and so I'll stand up for those every day, twenty-four hours a day.[17]

Examining Star Trek's knack for telling good stories might seem rather easy if one were to take Brent Spiner's explanation of its popularity at face value:

The reason Star Trek **is so popular is that I honestly think [creator] Gene Roddenberry came up with what is the single greatest formula for a TV show ... It never ends, because travelling the galaxy offers thousands of stories to explore.**[18]

This statement is partly true, Star Trek does have a great formula which was shared by many other popular television series such as The Fugitive (1963–1967) and Quantum Leap (1989–1993) to name just two, but that does not fully explain its popularity. Spiner, who played the character Data in The Next Generation, has got it only half right because he thinks the show's popularity relies on there being thousands of episodes revealing countless things about aliens and the universe. I believe that Star Trek is so popular because it is the exact opposite of Spiner's theory: it offers only a handful of stories through which the audience can explore the universe, and, at the same time, explore themselves. What is more, I believe that Star Trek relies so much on the fact it uses the same stories, only slightly different each time, that if it were to change its approach and produce stories too far from the norm it would lose audience appeal and fade from popularity.

Rick Berman, the man who took over the mantle of maintaining Star Trek's image following Roddenberry's death in 1991, explained that he was taught how to understand Star Trek; how to write stories that kept within the boundaries of the original concept. In an interview with TV Guide to celebrate the final season of TNG in 1994, Berman explained that he had had to become fluent in a language created by Roddenberry in order to continue his vision. Also, rules were in place to keep Star Trek on course with its mission to promote liberal humanism in an entertaining fashion. Berman's choice of words hints at there being a formula or blueprint to which Star Trek must stick lest it departs from Roddenberry's vision and loses its ability to entertain the audience. It also hints at the strong connection to narrative which will be extrapolated further in Chapter Two. Star Trek's credo discussed by Berman is, for many fans and critics, all that defines it:

> **Gene taught me a new language, and now I have become relatively fluent. We've bent his rules a little, but we haven't broken them.** *Star Trek: The Next Generation* **is not a series about my vision of the future or Patrick Stewart's or anybody else's. It's a series about Gene's vision of the 24th century. As a result, I will continue to follow his rules as long as I'm connected with** *Star Trek* **in any way.[19]**

Star Trek has been described as a *space opera*, implying that it emphasises the character's representative rather than realistic qualities and that its plot structure can be equated to the traditional formats used in Greek and Shakespearean drama.[20] *Space opera* was also a term used about the Golden Age of sci-fi; it usually described traditional adventure stories where the audience was expected to know the plot or at least recognise some of its familiar themes. Shakespeare's use of familiar plots and traditional stories enabled him to garner a popular audience because people were already accustomed to the themes and plots of his work. The same is true for Star Trek, although in a different league from Shakespeare, it uses familiar and traditional stories to devise its own form of anecdotal storytelling on a weekly basis. At times it even goes so far as to borrow famous quotes from Shakespeare's plays and sonnets to use as episode titles or parts of scripted dialogue, thus highlighting the connections between literature, foundational narratives and Star Trek which I will be making in the next few chapters. Larry Kreitzer points out that Star Trek borrows and quotes from literature, music, and images from a wide range of sources. In doing so, these cultural references have given Star Trek 'a veneer of cultural sophistication, helping to create the impression that its world is a well-read one', and they also 'provide a level of respectability which might not otherwise be forthcoming to a science fiction series'.[21] Star Trek's status as a topic for academic debate relies on there being some form of underlying intellectualism beneath its popular culture front. Its pseudo-philosophical tropes and invocation of literature offers the veneer that Kreitzer talks of but also, crucially, is detachable from that veneer by virtue of a supreme anti-intellectualism embedded within fan culture. This is seen in instances where fans become annoyed at the level of criticism directed at Star Trek by academics who can read too much into episodes and thereby spoil the fictional elements that allow fans to believe in a positive outlook for the future.

These observations go some way toward explaining how the series follows a rigid screen arrangement but they alone cannot account for why Star Trek is so popular with a diverse and cross-generational audience. That particular and integral role goes to narrative; specifically the way it is continually used to offer the same types of stories, characters and events by employing the same symbols, figures, and metaphors in every episode. The only differences are visual: one week the audience might be faced with a 350-year-old genetic experiment seeking revenge; the next week by an omnipotent non-corporeal being onboard a starship. Whatever the scenario, the story is always the same because Star Trek relies upon a minimum number of familiar foundational narratives to provide the thousands of stories Brent Spiner believes Star Trek offers when exploring the galaxy.

If there are only a few stories that make up the many thousands that Star Trek offers, what are they, and what makes them so important to an American audience? If it were so obvious that Star Trek relied on the same old tales of exploration and good versus evil, why did it not fade out of favour forty years ago when the original series was cancelled after three seasons? These are undeniable points of enquiry that permeate Star Trek criticism. Vivian Sobchack describes the Star Trek films as backward-looking, nostalgic, and basically old-fashioned:

> Despite all their 'futurist' gadgetry and special effects, then, the *Star Trek* films are conservative and nostalgic, imaging the future by looking backward to the imagination of a textual past.[22]

If we see Star Trek as such a historical pastiche of the future, then we can also view its stories, its fictional narrative, as some sort of history – albeit a history set in the fictional representations of a contemporary American reality. My 'Star Trek is history' statement not only makes more sense thanks to Sobchack's remarks but it also would seem to promote Star Trek as an alternative historical narrative that critics such as Hayden White, Northrop Frye, and Kenneth Burke have analysed in the sphere of literary criticism. This historical narrative, as described by White below, provides a connection between the past and the present (in Star Trek's case the future as present) that not only makes history more identifiable for the people studying it, but also makes it intrinsically valuable for contemporary society. This is because it uses metaphors and symbols culturally familiar both in history and to modern day readers:

> Historical narratives are not only models of past events and processes, but also metaphorical statements which suggest a relation of similitude between such events and processes and the story types that we conventionally use to endow the events of our lives with culturally sanctioned meanings. Viewed in a purely formal way, a historical narrative is not only a *reproduction* of the events reported in it, but also a *complex of symbols* which gives us directions for finding an *icon* of the structure of those events in our literary tradition.[23]

Star Trek's clever use of familiar symbols and tropes not only reproduces a historical narrative then, but it also gives viewers and fans a framework through which they can learn about their history and seek to understand their American cultural identity. Critics have understood historical narratives as didactic approaches forming links with the past in a literary arrangement. I am saying that Star Trek achieves the same thing through the visual media of television and film. To refer back to Sobchack, Star Trek looks 'backward to the imagination of a textual past' and projects that 'history' forward through the depiction of a utopian, futuristic version of modern-day America.

Another scholar of literary criticism was Erich Auerbach, who analysed western literature and its delineation of what is real and what is fiction in his book *Mimesis: The Representation of Reality in Western Literature* (1953). His work concerned the whole scope of classical western literature and its connections with the real world that surrounded it. He observed that, through *figuration*, literatures could be imitated, reproduced and then adapted to embody stories in which people could be bound up and believe to be true – in effect alter reality so that fiction could symbolise what people thought was real in their lives. *Star Trek*'s representation of a reality through its fictitious future has not only been entrenched as a possible outcome for society; it has become reality for some people who want to believe that it is true, or, as David Gerrold states, 'it represents a future we would like to make real.'[24] Its connections to history only add legitimacy to its figuration of the future; they have both become inseparable from each other, making *Star Trek* a signifier of the future and a signifier of the past. It acts as a certified history of the real past and a proper history of the soon-to-be-real future. Figural interpretation:

> establishes a connection between two events or persons in such a way that the first signifies not only itself but also the second, while the second involves or fulfils the first. The two poles of a figure are separated in time, but both, being real events or persons, are within temporality. They are both contained in the flowing stream which is historical life, and only the comprehension, the *intellectus spiritualis*, of their interdependence is a spiritual act.[25]

Star Trek uses 'history' in three distinct but not so isolated ways to comment on society. It recounts famous events to help frame its episodic storylines: for example, in the *Star Trek: Voyager* two-part episode 'The Killing Game' (1998), the crew are held hostage in a holodeck recreation of occupied France during the Second World War. Being completely immersed in their respective roles as French Resistance fighters, soldiers and villagers, the crew have to combat the aggressive Hirogen who have taken on the persona of Nazis. *Star Trek* also changes narrative 'history' altogether and sets up an alternative historical reality grounded in its perception of the future: Each episode brings yet another small detail that will potentially help fill in the gaps in *Star Trek*'s future history. For instance, the *Voyager* episode 'One Small Step...' (1999) recounted the mission of the first manned space flight to Mars in 2032; the film *Star Trek: First Contact* (1996) revealed how humans achieved warp flight and encountered the Vulcans in 2063; and, most significantly, the series *Enterprise* is set in 2151 between *First Contact* and the voyages of Captain Kirk, allowing viewers to see how the Federation was born and how humans became the technologically advanced species synonymous with *Star Trek*'s view of humanity. Finally, *Star Trek* places historical events and contemporary issues into a science fiction format so that its stories are understood by the audience as fictitious but the social messages conveyed can be digested without resentment. For example, the ongoing conflict between the Klingons and the Federation in the original series reflected the USA's cold war with the Soviets, and the fiftieth anniversary of the dropping of the atomic bomb on Hiroshima provided the occasion for *Voyager*'s allegorical treatment of its consequences in the episode 'Jetrel' (1995). All three plot devices serve to ingrain *Star Trek* as a culturally aware television series that uses history and narrative to dramatise its stories and bring about a new social awareness. However, while *Star Trek* is in tune with the American Zeitgeist, it also relies upon multiple histories for its critical, but ultimately utopian, look to a possible future.

Steve Anderson has observed that *Star Trek* has often used narrative plot devices such as 'encountering worlds that have developed like Earth' in order to try and change the 'fictional' history for the better because the chance was missed in the 'real' history on Earth. This not only establishes the series as a morally correct and consummate disseminator of history to the public, it also promotes it as a benchmark for what Americans should strive to achieve in their short lives. *Star Trek* keeps returning to this plot paradigm because it feels a sense of urgency in trying to make things better for the audience. The need to 'learn from the mistakes of the past' has been an integral part of coming to grips with issues such as 'who we were', 'what we have now become' and 'where will we end up in the future', both for history and for those who might still be suffering from the traumatic effects of past events. As Anderson asserts, 'in various corners of the galaxy, Captain Kirk succeeds in reforming a 1920s-style Chicago crime syndicate, ousting a corrupt Roman proconsul, dethroning a despotic Greek emperor, and overthrowing a proto-Nazi regime,' all in the name of doing what is right.[26] What history lesson could be better than having the chance to relive entire eras and be able to take part in the actual events knowing you had the opportunity to do the right thing?

However, contrary to the view that *Star Trek* uses history to teach America about right and wrong, Jay Goulding contends that famous episodes such as 'Tomorrow is Yesterday' (1967) and 'The City on the Edge of Forever' (1967) establish *Star Trek* as a purveyor of 'a false sense of power'. To be able to 'put things right' and 'see the future', Goulding argues, 'generates a static vision where democracy triumphs over all time dimensions', making *Star Trek* just as oppressive and imperialistic as the society it was trying to expound upon in the politically turbulent 1960s. Goulding recognises that the dichotomy which characterises *Star Trek*'s use of historically motivated stories comes from its attempts to correct American history for the better and sanctify whatever mistakes may have happened in the past in the name of democracy: 'It promises an omniscience and omnipotence which is an horrific concept, but necessary for the mythology which prides itself on the craft of changing what has happened.'[27]

To some extent, Goulding does have a point about *Star Trek*'s need to sanitise history, but what he did not recognise was that *Star Trek* only allowed for the possibility of change through the interventions of Kirk and his crew rather than changing history itself. The narrative of the series offered those alien worlds the chance to redeem their own mistakes since the Enterprise would always leave orbit and let the inhabitants choose to take action, giving them a chance to change history for themselves. In 'The Omega Glory' (1968), Kirk teaches a tribe of 'Yang' warriors, who had misinterpreted the preamble to the Constitution as an order to exclude their 'Kohm' enemies, that the words 'must apply to everyone or they mean nothing'. Spock declares his idealistic action a breach of the Prime Directive, but Kirk replies: 'We merely showed them the meaning of what they were fighting for ... I suggest we leave them to discover their history, and their liberty.' This sequence embodies the series' optimism in view of the fact that the future was not set in stone, it was up to the aliens – and likewise us – to take control of destiny.

Star Trek's pilgrimages into US and world histories do not just depict our past but also give the audience a definitive guide to the history of the future. Four series are set in and after the twenty-third century, with *Voyager* finishing late in the twenty-fourth. The gaps between our time and theirs, and between the original series and its later incarnations, have been filled by the writers and producers with many 'historic' events: World War Three, the discovery of alien life, scientific advancement in space travel (to name but a few). In effect, the series have mapped out a chronology within which fans can further engross themselves, a fictional universe complete with its own documented history ripe for Jenkins' 'textual poaching'. This evolution is highlighted by *The Star Trek Encyclopedia: A Reference Guide to the Future* (1997) and *Star Trek Chronology: A History of the Future* (1993), both routinely revised and updated. Here, everything from the forty years of *Star Trek* is cross-referenced and recorded in minute detail to give the fans absolute insight into the ever-expanding universe. In effect, much of this desire to record the history of the future flows from what Daniel Boorstin has termed the 'effort to catalogue the whole creation', whereby since the dawn of time humanity has toiled to record and catalogue its discoveries in order to provide a lasting description of life itself.[28] Likewise, the psychologists Rom Harré and Paul Secord have argued that, in order to understand any area of phenomena in a scientific way, it is necessary to construct a classificatory and analytical scheme plus an explanatory scheme. The former consists of the systematic division of a field of phenomena into distinct types, the classification of these types into taxonomy.[29] Of course, with regard to *Star Trek* the record or phenomena is not real; everything included in the taxonomic publications from alien planets to their subsequent indigenous wildlife is fictional and, what is more, will probably never exist to the extent that they do in many fans' imaginations.

However, the attempts to document a *Star Trek* history of the future, essentially fashioning the 'taxonomy of *Star Trek*', encompassing everything that has ever existed in its world and will ever exist in ours, is similar to Jorge Luis Borges' short story 'The Library of Babel', in which he describes a library collection comprised of the entire knowledge of the universe (a fictional one) from 'the minute history of the future' to 'the veridical account of your death'. The library is infinite, 'limitless and periodic', allowing the reader a lifetime of searching for what they desire, just as the *Star Trek* fan endeavours to pursue their dreams and desires through the fictional but documented and limitless universe compounded by books such as *The Star Trek Encyclopedia* and *Star Trek Chronology*.[30] What is more, as Michael Jindra states, 'this universe is much larger and more complex than any other fictional universe', including that of J. R. R. Tolkien's Middle Earth novels and the game loosely based on it, *Dungeons and Dragons*.[31]

Many episodes deal with fictional events in the past which are still set in our future, literally going 'back to the future' to create an original historical narrative. The main plot of *Star Trek: First Contact* concerns events intrinsic to the creation of Starfleet and the Federation along with the discovery of warp drive (one of the series' key catchphrases), yet these developments are still potentially in advance of our time period – even set after a third world war! Nevertheless, because they have been eulogised by *Star Trek*'s chronology of the future, fans are well aware of these events and see them as part of their 'history'. The plethora of official and unofficial short stories and novels (the majority written by fans) also provides a narrative background to many of the popular characters and stories at the same time 'filling in the syntagmatic gaps in the original narrative'.[32] Greg Cox's *Star Trek: The Eugenics Wars* (2001) describes itself as *Volume One* in the history of Khan Noonien Singh – a favourite with fans – and it recounts how he rose to power in the late twentieth century. The author intertwines contemporary figures from history and incidents from the *Star Trek* mythos with real historical events such as the fall of the Berlin Wall, creating a story that endorses *Star Trek*, both accurately and historically. It constantly enhances and reintegrates its own details into its own history of the future. It has been followed up by *Volume Two* (2002), charting Singh's life right up until his eventual demise seen in *Star Trek II: The Wrath of Khan*. The editor of the official *Star Trek* magazine highlights the balance the series strikes between fact and fiction and how the fans respond to its future history:

> For continuity freaks, a show like *Star Trek* is a godsend.
> Each new episode brings yet another small detail that will

potentially help fill in the gaps in *Star Trek*'s labyrinthine
future history. There are, of course, entire books devoted
to mapping the *Star Trek* timeline, but books can only get
you so far in the search for previously unknown little titbits.
Only new episodes can provide that extra thrill derived
from learning something new about *Star Trek*'s chronology,
reinforcing the show's status as a living, breathing,
developing entity, fleshing out and colouring in its past as it
moves ever forward.[33]

It is interesting to note that, as an officially licensed publication,
the monthly *Star Trek* magazine helps to maintain the illusion of
an accurate historical *Star Trek* timeline. There are often special
articles highlighting the continuities and connections *Star Trek*'s
fictional events have with real life; these articles help to 'reinforce',
as the above quote states, 'the show's status as a living, breathing,
developing entity' and project an image of a coherent and unerringly
comprehensible 'history' which real-time world events lack. For
example, in every issue there is a section called 'Treknology', devoted
to reporting new inventions and scientific achievements that can
be related to the futuristic technologies seen in the series. In the
February 2002 issue, an article entitled 'Parallel Universes' applied
an historical perspective to *Star Trek*'s space-travel back-story and
compared it to humanity's real-world 'cosmic exploits'.[34] It charted
the evolution of 'man's' journey into space from Sputnik and Apollo
11 through Einstein's theories about the speed of light and stopped
at the Mars Orbiter mission launched in April 2001. These events
were shown in contrast with *Star Trek* episodes that used them as
stepping stones to future developments such as first contact with
aliens, warp drive and the human colonisation of Mars and made
sense of them through extrapolating their historical significance
in a possible future timeline. Perhaps the most telling example of
Star Trek's obsession with its own narrative and our history was its
newest and most eager project to date: *Enterprise*.

In fact, fans were so concerned with getting the 'history' right
that the co-creators, Rick Berman and Brannon Braga, told the
American press at the time of its release that they knew that they
were 'looking for trouble from the hardest of the hardcore' fans if

they got anything wrong.[35] One observer for the *Radio Times* pointed out that *Enterprise* would 'inherit a history more detailed and more catalogued than that of some small countries'.[36] There are, however, limits to what *Star Trek* does with its history. As Berman and Braga have intimated, there was a lot of 'history' they had to consider when producing the new series, as it was set before much of what had already appeared on-screen and therefore was already part of the canon. They could not possibly cater for every fan who wants to see stories retold and past plots returned to, because they were dealing with a series that was in production thirty-five or more years after the original series. Many of the stories and fictional history laid out previously and set in stone by fans had to be readjusted or even written out in order for *Enterprise* to tell its own entertaining stories. Once Berman and Braga said that changes had to be made to the historical canon, there was immense interest from concerned fans on the Internet, with evidence of a growing tension between fans and producers over what is considered important in the *Star Trek* canon. Berman himself highlighted the official stand on what is considered important and what position fans really occupy in relation to the canon:

> **Fans discussing the past, present, and future of *Star Trek* is something that has gone on forever ... We are conscious of it. We are respectful of it. We have people who are in touch with it and who keep us abreast of what the feelings of the fans are. But we have to eventually do what we think is best. That's not to say that some of the things that we hear don't influence us to some degree, but we can't let the fans create the show.[37]**

Everything that appears on the television series or on the movie screen is deemed by producers as officially canonical within the fictional *Star Trek* universe. Literature such as the technical manuals and fact files produced under license to Paramount are also seen as canonical because they expand upon material aired on-screen and are used as points of reference for further episodes and movies. However, the novels and fan literature are not seen as canonical because the stories they tell have not 'happened', they have not taken place on-screen and are therefore unofficial.[38] Some are produced as officially licensed books by Paramount, which 'has decreed that anything that's televised as Star Trek is "Star Trek fact", whereas anything that's printed is "Star Trek fiction".'[39] Nevertheless, however much the dichotomy between official and unofficial is loathed by fans, it is necessary to have such a divide to ensure that the integrity of the series does not weaken and its popularity does not diminish. As Michael Jindra intimates, Star Trek's fictional reality is entirely based on fans believing it to be true, or at least it being a possible version of the truth. Without an official canon, fans would no longer be able to maintain their belief in the reality of Star Trek's future history:

> Star Trek, like many other shows, actively encourages a 'suspension of disbelief' and sets itself up as a 'reality' in which fans can exist. The reality of this universe is important to many people ... The coherence of this alternate universe must be maintained in order for fans to continue their 'suspension of disbelief'. As a result, there is a Star Trek 'canon'.[40]

Both official and fan literatures have attempted to fill in the gaps between storylines and character backgrounds originally aired on-screen. The expansion of the fictional universe outside of the studios – characterised by novels, technical manuals, encyclopaedias, conventions, comics, graphic novels and fanzines – has made Star Trek into what can only be described as an alternative world. One in which most fans would dearly love to live or at least look upon as the ideal. This utopian vision reflects that of the Puritans at the beginning of the seventeenth century and one that was continually expressed through the American Jeremiad. I shall explore these connections with Star Trek's version of utopia in greater depth in Chapter Four. What is important to remember is that in the last ten years, since its fanbase multiplied as a result of four synchronised television series, Star Trek's own fictional historical narrative has given credence to its prognosis of future human endeavour. Licensed novelisations, fan culture, and Star Trek's dramatisation of a history of humanity that has yet to emerge have cemented it as a certified cornerstone of American culture. It gives Americans a legitimate identity with which they can sympathise, and assume, in order to make *Star Trek*'s vision of the future seem more real.

2

TELLING TALES OF THE FUTURE

STAR TREK'S EXEMPLARY NARRATIVES

> Narrative focuses our attention on to a story, a
> sequence of events, through the direct mediation of a
> 'telling' which we both stare at and through, which is
> at once central and peripheral to the experience of the
> story, both absent and present in the consciousness of
> those being told the story.[1]

If one were to take Robert Scholes and Robert Kellogg's view that
'to be a narrative no more and no less than a teller and a tale are
required,' then *Star Trek* seemingly does not represent a narrative
because there is an absence of a teller.[2] There are many stories
played out week after week but who is telling them? J. Hawthorn
also points out that the 'telling' focuses our attention on the story
so much that it itself can become central to the experience of the
story; it can become part of the story and part of the recipient of
the story. It is obvious from these analyses of narrative that the
narrator is important, but it does not necessarily rule out *Star Trek*
as a narrative. For example, *Star Trek*'s most famous line, 'space,
the final frontier', comes from the opening narration first used in
the episode 'The Corbomite Maneuver' (1966). Every episode began
with Kirk speaking to the audience, 'telling' them that what they
were about to see was a true and correct account (or *history*) of the
voyages of the crew aboard the Enterprise. There was a story about to

be told and those immortal words were a harbinger of the wondrous tales about to unfold on-screen. The tradition of the opening narration continued on TNG, which highlighted the importance of the 'telling' aspect at the beginning of Star Trek episodes and the fact that people were totally engaged in the telling of these stories and the way in which they were told. How every episode began with this narration was, as Hawthorn suggests about narrative, both 'central and peripheral to the experience of the story', and 'both absent and present in the consciousness of those being told the story':

> **Space, the final frontier. These are the voyages of the *Starship Enterprise*. Its five-year mission: to explore strange new worlds, to seek out new life and new civilisations, to boldly go where no *man* has gone before.[3]**

Just as Star Wars begins with the line 'A long time ago in a galaxy far, far away...', Star Trek also uses a narrative opening to begin its stories on-screen. Children have all been read stories that start 'once upon a time', knowing that they are about to be told something; with Star Trek it is no different. This was Gene Roddenberry's way of telling the audience his story, one which he had battled to get on television, so that they too could be enthused by and engaged in what he believed was the most important story of all: the human story. For David Carson, if Star Trek 'dealt with racial tensions and tried to preach to the masses, the masses would not watch'. However, placing those issues in a science fiction drama set in the future extinguishes its 'preachiness' and allows 'a storyteller, be you a writer or director, the opportunity of telling a story that has something to say'.[4] To a large degree, this statement is a valid one, but we should be aware of how much other forms of television programming such as comedy or animation can relate to and comment on politically charged issues without being too obvious or lacking in sincerity.

The opening narration has entered popular imagination just like the characters of the shows, it was inevitable that it would be used on TNG but only once it had been updated. Star Trek's mission statement was modernised to suit an age that recognised women were not just there to support the men as they explored the galaxy, but were there to do the exploring themselves. This was not fully validated until Kate Mulgrew became the first woman to command a starship and take the lead role in *Star Trek: Voyager*:

> **Space. The final frontier. These are the voyages of the Starship *Enterprise*. Its continuing mission, to explore strange new worlds, to seek out new life and new civilisations, to boldly go where no *one* has gone before...[5]**

As I have already mentioned, *Star Trek* makes much use of the common cultural narratives to communicate its own form of historical discourse, and even then there are only a handful of them. In this chapter, I will outline the types of narratives *Star Trek* uses for its representation of history and the theoretical underpinnings that form the basis of its popularity and diverse appeal. According to the historian Kerwin Lee Klein, '[Hayden] White followed the lead of formalist literary critics Northrop Frye and Kenneth Burke, arguing that a limited number of plot forms and tropes characterised historical narratives'.[6] For Frye, this meant that there were four archetypal plot modes, or *mythoi* as he liked to call them, that characterised western literature. Klein lists them as the romance, the tragedy, the comedy and the satire. In *Anatomy of Criticism*, Frye uses different terminology, also breaking up the *mythoi* into specific forms such as 'scriptural play' and irony: Epos, Prose, Drama, Lyric.[7] There were many other categories that could be filtered out through the original, but Frye considered the main four to be of paramount importance. Kenneth Burke analysed the existence of common literary genres, or modes of thought that characterised the human understanding of history, determining the four tropes that White went on to unpack in his later work.[8] What these two scholars ultimately suggest is that our understanding of the past – and therefore our understanding of ourselves – is inseparable from the manner in which we broadcast our history. This conclusion is mirrored in Marshall McLuhan's aphorism 'The Medium is the Message',[9] and it is the conclusion that White comes to in *The Content of the Form*:

> **Narrative, far from being merely a form of discourse that can be filled with different contents, real or imaginary as the**

case may be, already possesses a content prior to any given actualization of it in speech or writing.[10]

Following on from Frye's and Burke's analyses of literary plot forms, Klein recognises that White reads the usage of plots as a form of historical explanation. Historians had no experience or empirical evidence of what actually happened in history so they inadvertently borrowed from the common plots and narrative forms already present in literature to help manifest a coherent discourse from their material – this leads to the creation of politically and ideologically biased histories. This appropriation of literary methods to construct history is exactly what *Star Trek* does when it uses culturally significant metaphors and tropes to symbolise its own futuristic take on American history and society.

Klein goes further in his breakdown of White's theories by recounting the four master tropes described in *Metahistory* (1973), White's first and most influential piece. There is a typology of rhetorical figures of speech made up of four tropes, they in turn govern the way we operate language: metaphor, metonymy, synecdoche, and irony.[11] It is obvious here that White based much of his work on Burke and the premise that language, and therefore history, was reliant upon only a minimum number of narrative modes of production. The larger differences between White and his predecessors are accounted for by the fact that White was dealing with the nature of writing history, whereas Frye and Burke were concerned with literature. However, White's work does provide a link between the two fields thanks to his utilisation of a common literary typology; again this is something that *Star Trek* employs to bridge the gap between telling good stories and mediating history, only its form of storytelling is mediated visually.

Metaphor is a trope of resemblance, replacing one object with another object that is taken to mean the same. Future America is a metaphorical representation of the present, with the Federation taking the place of the USA or the UN: in the 1960s, the Klingons were the Russians; the Romulans were the Chinese. On DS9, the Cardassian enslavement of the Bajorans can be seen as a metaphor for the German treatment of the Jews during the Second World War. Some scholars have criticised *Star Trek* for slotting in ethnic minorities and alien stereotypes, claiming that they are token gestures; however, such sublimation was necessary when Star Trek first aired. Gene Roddenberry had to make one thing stand for another so that he could get stories about racism or prejudice past the television censors. On a slightly different level, the various crews made up of the main characters for each Star Trek series are interpreted as being representative of American society. The crew of the original series was created to symbolise America in the 1960s – encompassing different races and ethnic backgrounds – even though mainstream white society at that time denied the cultural diversity that actually characterised America. Further developments to the composition of the crews signify the transformation of a pluralist American society to the multi-ethnic and multiculturally minded society that is synonymous with the mid-to-late 1990s. On board TNG, there were female doctors, a blind pilot and children in command positions; later, on DS9, we were introduced to an African-American single parent who had to command a space station; and, in Voyager, the crew had a female captain. Through the allegorical representations that the separate crews offer the series – allegory is a narrative mode based on metaphor – Star Trek is able to act out its own social fantasies and still comment on the inequalities present in modern society.

In his essay 'The Nautilus and the Drunken Boat', taken from the collection Mythologies (1993), Roland Barthes recognises that Jules Verne's fictional ship may be a symbol for departure, but it is also a symbol for closure. Similarly, one could equate Star Trek's consistent use of a ship on which to set its stories with the departure/closure dichotomy. Just as Verne's ships have been used to cross great distances so too have the USS Enterprise and Voyager. But as Barthes' work intimates, these ships represent not only travel but also a habitat: 'All the ships in Jules Verne are perfect cubby-holes, and the vastness of their circumnavigation further increase the bliss of their closure, the perfection of their inner humanity.'[12] Star Trek uses the ship as a vessel for enclosing humanity; each crew is but a microcosm of contemporary America. It encapsulates cross-sections of society within the boundaries of a ship or, in DS9's case, a space station, using the miniaturised representation of society as a metaphor for humanity's own failings and successes.

Metonymy is the trope of contiguity, part-part relationships, where a single event may provide a causal link in a chain of events. With this trope, there is no determined end but rather an incomplete and continuous series of events that form an unfinished narrative. Some *Star Trek* episodes have not only stood on their own as individual one-hour shows, they have also been part of larger story arcs that have typified entire series. This particular trait is best identified in DS9, where the last season in particular was devoted to the culmination of a war that was first brought to attention at the end of the second season.[13] DS9 was created to be different from the more explorative ethos of the original *Star Trek* and its later offspring TNG. What characterised DS9 were the inner conflicts and social turmoil found on the space station that could also then be found in the different alien societies encountered in every episode. The larger story arcs concerned the religious, cultural, and political ideologies of entire empires and the personal conflicts initiated when races collided in war. But individual episodes would also be concerned with those issues on a smaller scale – perhaps looking at certain key characters and their backgrounds – enabling the audience to fully understand the complexities of the larger storylines and become familiar with 'who's who'.

What is important to bear in mind when looking at DS9 is that it is metonymic because some of its story arcs were not finalised and completed when the last episode, 'What You Leave Behind', was aired in 1999. The war may have ended but many plotlines remained unfinished, and the audience was left wondering what would happen to some of their favourite characters. For example, Captain Benjamin Sisko left the station to pursue his destiny as religious Emissary to the people of Bajor. Originally, he was very wary of assuming this important religious role and, throughout the seven years DS9 aired on television, the very secular character was shown to be at odds with his religious duties. In the last episode, however, Sisko decided to continue as Emissary and live with the Wormhole Prophets that all Bajorans looked to for spiritual guidance; they would teach him how to lead his new-found people to salvation. In undertaking this spiritual quest in a non-corporeal universe, Sisko had left his son Jake and pregnant wife Kasidy on board the station wondering whether he would ever return – it also left the fans wondering if he would ever return to the screen. This was a first for Star Trek because both previous series captains, Kirk and Picard, remained in Starfleet and their characters continued as they had left off; Kirk appeared in several movies and Picard is slowly doing the same. It is because DS9 was designed as something slightly different from the franchise norm that Sisko's character was written with less confidence and determination for the future. Sisko's metonymic exploration of spirituality reflects how DS9 in general viewed America's unfinished journey towards a totally free and democratic nation at the beginning of a new century (see Chapter Eight). The audience was unsure of what would happen to him just as Americans are unsure of what will happen to them entering the second millennium as the world's only financially and culturally dominant superpower. It also highlighted the postmodern tack that Star Trek had taken with DS9, searching for a new definition of life and the reaffirmation of humanity at the centre of its stories.[14]

Synecdoche is the trope of integration, whereby the whole of a subject can be symbolised by a small part because it has some of the inherent qualities found in the former. Take, for example, the cartoon comedy series South Park (1997–) and The Simpsons (1989–). Both are set in archetypal and stereotypical American towns where the viewer can more than likely identify with the characters they watch because they recognise them as their neighbours, friends or even themselves. The communities that the cartoons parody not only represent 'small-town America', but they can also be seen as sophisticated goldfish bowls where the viewer can scrutinise the daily occurrences of American life whilst maintaining a fictional safe distance. Whereas in reality the viewer has probably tired of getting involved with community life and can no longer see the lighter side of their daily tedium:

> The Simpsons **takes up real human issues everybody can recognize and thus ends up in many respects less 'cartoonish' than other television programs. Its cartoon characters are more human, more fully rounded, than the supposedly real human beings in many situation comedies. Above all, the show has created a believable human community: Springfield, USA.**[15]

The Simpsons is set in the fictional town of Springfield, which could be anywhere in the country, proving that the show not only represents the small-town version of America but also the bigger one. The poignancy of the name Springfield is even more significant considering there is at least one town in every US state called Springfield – Illinois, Massachusetts, Ohio, Missouri to name but four – but *The Simpsons* never identifies the specific Springfield in which the series is set. *South Park* is set in Colorado, a small mountain community where everyone knows everybody else. The main characters are four young boys who could each be any young boy in America; their families and friends are just the same. This series differs slightly from *The Simpsons* because it illustrates the stereotyped characters such as the American youth, bureaucratic power-seekers and a prejudiced WASP lower class in hyperbole. It draws attention to the familiar stereotypes but also makes them look farcical and burlesque because of the way they have been animated and also because of the way that they act.

In *Star Trek*, it is possible to see synecdoche quite easily, each episode on its own is a small example of the overall humanistic message that the franchise tries to mediate. The ten feature films also provide a snapshot of what lies beneath *Star Trek*'s science fiction veneer, only transposed onto the big screen they tend to concentrate on one issue and form the action and plot around it. However, taken as a whole, the *Star Trek* feature films from *The Motion Picture* (1979) to *Star Trek VI: The Undiscovered Country* (1991) represent a completed story – one that concerns the famous crew from the original series. The use of synecdoche in *Star Trek*'s narrative suggests the whole 'thing' described is a totality – a system.

The big-screen saga started in 1979 with Kirk as an admiral tired of not being in command of the Enterprise. In 1982, with *The Wrath of Khan*, Kirk has regained the captain's chair only to lose his closest friend Spock when the crew came up against an old adversary first seen in 'Space Seed' (1967). As a sequel to Spock's death, both *The Search for Spock* (1984) and *The Voyage Home* (1986) showed Kirk and his crew disobey orders and try to rescue Spock after they find out he was not dead. Then, as fugitives, they try to return home to twenty-third-century Earth after saving two humpback whales from the twentieth century. In what was touted as *Star Trek*'s last film with the original crew, *The Final Frontier* (1989) shows Kirk, McCoy and Spock close to retirement asking questions about life and mortality. Yet, when Spock's half brother Sybok commandeers the Enterprise to seek God, the three friends along with Chekov, Uhura, Sulu and Scotty arrive at an understanding that there is much to come in life. Following on from this new-found zeal, *Star Trek VI* sees Kirk and the Enterprise on their last mission before retiring, trying to save the fragile peace between the Klingons and the Federation. It is the last time fans can see most of these characters on-screen, but the story brings closure to the epic voyages that had started twenty-five years earlier. The six films resurrect, continue, and conclude the story of the Enterprise through the use of a synecdochic narrative and, as an appendix to that, Kirk dies in *Star Trek Generations* (1994), drawing the curtain on the most famous and popular *Star Trek* era.

In *Star Trek: Voyager*, there were a number of episodes where contemporary newsworthy topics such as capital punishment, genetic engineering and organised healthcare provided a suitable allegorical basis for stories. In the episode 'Repentance' (2001), the crew encounter a prison ship returning to its home world. The convicts are being transported to their deaths, returning home to be executed. This causes problems for those on board Voyager who do not agree with such a harsh form of punishment. In 'Lineage' (2001), lieutenants Torres and Paris get the chance to see their baby in the mother's womb. Torres, who is half Klingon, sees that the baby will be born with the distinctive Klingon head ridges and so decides to have the Doctor change its DNA to be born without. Torres' own childhood experiences dictate how she wants her child to be born. 'Critical Care' (2000) sees the Doctor having to administer treatment to an alien race infected with a curable disease; however, the cure is only available to the rich upper class who can afford the drug. The Doctor takes it upon himself to treat all those infected, even those who have not been designated as worthy. This concern for current affairs is not a new plot device for *Star Trek*, but it does tend to characterise *Voyager*'s ethos more than past series. DS9 finished its run in 1999 and, since *Voyager* was left as the stand-alone series on the relatively new UPN network, it took the lead in addressing issues important to Americans at that time; not least because 2000 was an election year where those issues proved to be important battlegrounds for the presidential candidates. It could be argued that Enterprise did not rely so much on the sort of contemporary issue stories that characterised *Voyager*'s final two seasons; returning instead to a more simplistic adventure format reminiscent of the original series. However, in *Voyager*'s entirety, the aforementioned episodes contribute to the series' concentration on an inner humanity and the individual's search for the meaning of life.

Klein and White deem irony the hardest to pinpoint due to its intrinsic ability to negate the meanings of the other three tropes. Irony seeks to bend the rules and has a tendency to make a mockery of the complexities of language. Out of this trope comes a criticism of the other three, especially metaphor, because it broadens the horizons of language to include scepticism, satire, and cynicism.[16] *Star Trek*'s irony comes in the form of its more comedic episodes, wherein the familiar characters and their recognisable traits are slightly out of tune with what the audience has come to expect. Also irony becomes apparent in episodes where the crew and/or storyline pay homage to the original series, both recognising the historical narrative created by *Star Trek*, and appeasing fans' desires for meta-narrative.

Self-recognition is a common feature in *Star Trek*. There are times when characters from different series swap over and intermingle with members of the other crews. Fans enjoy this because it allows them the chance to see their favourites from different series interact with each other. The best-known coming together was in the film *Generations*, where the two captains of the Enterprise, James T. Kirk and Jean-Luc Picard, meet and join forces to stop an evil nemesis. The fictional time gap between the two characters was conveniently written out so that the film could provide the fans with what they had wanted to see since TNG had first aired in 1987.

The joining together of two or more of the series can work in two opposite ways. Firstly it could be of benefit to the fictional reality that *Star Trek* has created because it legitimises the narrative universe in which the series are set. If different characters appear on other series then it indicates that both series in question are contemporary to each other, both series represent a larger fantasy through which the audience can 'dream'. This trait is not unique to *Star Trek* and can be found in comic-book superhero narratives. Richard Reynolds defines the super-ness of superheroes such as Batman, who incidentally does not possess gifted superpowers like other comic-book characters such as Spider-Man or the Hulk, in terms of their interaction with the Superman crowd. Therefore, the integrity of the characters depends upon the existence of a 'universe' in which all the characters owned by a particular company inhabit the same fictional world.[17] In *Star Trek*'s case, the larger stories that have the Federation on the brink of destruction are made more urgent for the audience because other members of other crews become involved; the threat is not restricted to just one series.

On the other hand, character integration can undermine the fictional reality created because it admits to the audience that the characters are not real – this may be obvious to some but it can come as quite a shock to more engrossed fans. For example, if a favourite character is advertised to appear on another *Star Trek* series then some might cynically say that it is only to boost the ratings. This happened when Michael Dorn was hired to play his popular TNG character Worf on DS9 from Season Four onwards. Some critics implied that it was not a move to improve stories but a move to improve the viewer ratings that were lagging behind competition such as *Hercules: The Legendary Journeys* (1994–1999) and *Xena: Warrior Princess* (1995–2001). Crossover episodes are hard to judge and sometimes do fail to attract good press, but some of the most successful episodes have contained crossover plots and have been some of the most entertaining.

In 1996, *Star Trek* celebrated its thirtieth anniversary, and both DS9 and *Voyager* aired special commemorative episodes in honour of this. In 'Trials and Tribble-ations', the crew of DS9 has to go back in history to save the life of Captain Kirk. They do this by becoming members of the famous Enterprise crew first seen in the 1960s. The producers managed to integrate the actors into the story 'The Trouble with Tribbles' (1967) by splicing their film with the original and recreating many of the older sets. This gave the audience the chance to see what the modern characters looked like against the 1960s version of the *Star Trek* universe. The new plot centred on the original, in which Kirk and his crew square up to the Klingons; at the same time, Tribbles (small furry animals) infest the ship. A plot to blow up the ship by using a bomb disguised as a Tribble is undertaken by a Klingon posing as a human but in the DS9 episode the future version of the bomber tries to influence history by helping himself in the past. Sisko and his crew become members of Kirk's crew in order to prevent the bomb going off and save Kirk's timeline from changing. Not only did the episode recognise the popularity of the original 'The Trouble with Tribbles', but it also highlighted how much the audience appreciated a comedic embellishment of a previously aired episode. Star Trek's own history was used as a basis for a plot, taking advantage of its popularity and treating itself with a little humour. The 1996 episode had recognised the cultural impact that the original 1967 episode had had and used that to tell a new story. At the same time as this negated the previous narrative, it also emphasised the culturally significant place Star Trek still holds in American society.

For Thomas M. Disch, the ability to poke fun at oneself was something that science fiction was not capable of; it took itself far too seriously and suffered as a result. In The Dreams Our Stuff is Made Of, Disch criticised television science fiction as being rather overused and clichéd, the sense of wonder was no longer present. However, Star Trek was different but not because of its liberated approach to a multi-ethnic crew; Disch saw its popularity inadvertently grow out of the aesthetic quality of the series, specifically the colourful pyjamas the actors wore as uniforms. The uniform 'taught that conformity will be the order of the day in the future even more than in the present', and that all we had to aspire to was working in an office (the Enterprise) 'disguised as the future'.[18] This cock-eyed view of Star Trek's impact not only makes a mockery of the series but also disregards the serious attempt at change that Roddenberry tried to make with it. By concentrating on its visual look, Disch was trying to point out that too much austerity and gloominess prevented science fiction series, including Star Trek, from having fun with what could be an exciting and adventure-filled format. However, Star Trek is much more than a visual series, hence the vast amount of fan literature and the success of printed word material.

Taking into account the views of Thomas Disch, one can see Star Trek has recently tried to have a laugh with itself, especially after having celebrated forty years at the pinnacle of television science fiction. In 'Trials and Tribble-ations', Odo pokes fun at the odd-looking older version of the Klingons, lacking the visible forehead ridges synonymous with the more modern Klingon look. Klingons from the 1960s were painted with shoe polish and wore long thin moustaches to make them look alien; the budget could not stretch to anything more imaginative. Today, Star Trek has updated the look so as to make Klingons more menacing but, of course, this drew attention to the fact that they were originally ridgeless. Worf in the episode had to hide his ridges and explained the discrepancy between old and new looks by saying it is something that Klingons do not like to discuss with others. The audience watching could laugh at this, because Star Trek chose to recognise the visual difference between the old and new series and decided to explain it in a humorous and ironic fashion.

Voyager's birthday episode, 'Flashback' (1996), also used a previous Star Trek story. On this occasion, it was based on the feature film The Undiscovered Country and was specifically concerned with the popular original series character Sulu. In this episode, the audience discovers that Voyager's Tuvok was originally a member of Sulu's crew, therefore linking him with the famous original series and timeline. Both Janeway and Tuvok have to confront his forgotten past by assuming roles on what fans recognise as the USS Excelsior, whilst not changing the past. What both special episodes represent is a similar reverence for the Star Trek phenomenon that I have already said is distinguished by Audre Lorde's 'poetry as illumination'. Through this reverential recognition of past episodes, the audience is further absorbed into the fictional reality of the Star Trek universe, believing more and more that 'it represents a future we would like to make real'. But reverential recognition does not just occur in the episodes; there have been countless comedy sketches, TV shows, and films that have made a joke out of Star Trek and also paid it homage. The US comedy series Saturday Night Live (1975–) has on numerous occasions satirised Star Trek, even going as far as having William Shatner take part in a sketch, famously telling freakish fans to 'Get a Life!' The Simpsons has also mocked Star Trek by showing the old crew as geriatrics aboard the Enterprise in Star Trek IX: So Very Tired, when Sulu says 'Sir, there are Klingons on the starboard bow', Kirk replies 'Again with the Klingons!' Practically every episode of the cartoon Futurama (1999–2003, created by The Simpsons' Matt Groening) had visual and thematic links to the classic series, no doubt partly due to the fact it was set in the future and Star Trek is notorious for promoting its own version of the future. Given that its central character, Fry, is transplanted from New York in the twentieth century to New York in the thirty-first, he brings these historic cultural references forward with him to the future where they are ironically laughed at by his friends because they represent a future that is archaic compared to their advanced timeline. In the episode 'Where No Fan Has Gone Before' (2002), Fry determines to retrieve Star Trek episode tapes that were banished to a forbidden planet: 'The world needs Star Trek to give people hope for the future,' Fry declares. Leela replies 'But it's set 800 years in the past!' The film *The Cable Guy* (1996) – a dark satire on the power of television – pays tribute to the famous scene from 'Amok Time' (1967), when Spock challenges Kirk to a death match. It does this by placing the characters played by Jim Carrey and Matthew Broderick in a similar situation with the same music and weapons as used in the original. Even Kate Mulgrew (Captain Janeway) has taken part in a comedy sketch with the cast from *Frasier* (1993–2004) as her crew on board *Voyager* for the television special *Star Trek: Thirty Years and Beyond* (1996). What these examples suggest is that, whether Star Trek is mocked or idealised, people have been affected by it and use its phenomenal appeal to express their own desires and highlight Star Trek's idiosyncrasies in a humorous and comical way.

The 'multiform story', recognised by Janet H. Murray as a term that describes 'a written or dramatic narrative that presents a single situation or plotline in multiple versions, versions that would be mutually exclusive in our ordinary experience', was another way in which the series was able to tell its stories.[19] Many of its films and episodes are based on the premise that there is more than one alternative timeline. In the original episode 'Mirror, Mirror' (1967), Captain Kirk is accidentally transported onto an alternate version of the Enterprise where the normally peace-loving Federation is a war-mongering barbaric empire. He tries to persuade the opposite version of Spock to change in order for that timeline to be more like his own. This obviously brings about a short-term improvement for the alternate Enterprise, but in the long-term Kirk's message of change proves to be the downfall of the Federation. We see the results of this in DS9 crossover episodes where humans have become galactic slaves to the Klingon, Bajoran and Cardassian alliance: 'Crossover' (1994), 'Through the Looking Glass' (1995), 'Shattered Mirror' (1996), 'Resurrection' (1997), 'The Emperor's New Cloak' (1998). These episodes play out separate plotlines in which familiar characters are somewhat different to the originals and provide an equivalent but upside-down version of the *Star Trek* universe in which the normal characters can be exchanged to accommodate an exciting story.

The multiform story is also used in such episodes as TNG's 'Parallels' (1993), where Worf shifts through a number of alternative timelines. These range from having a family with his crewmate Deanna Troi to realising that his friends have been killed in the battle with the Borg from 'The Best of Both Worlds'. 'Yesterday's Enterprise' (1990) also involves a multiform story, only this time it deals with *Star Trek* lore. The crew of Picard's Enterprise is transported into another time where they are at war with the Klingons, this is because a previous incarnation of the famous ship was somehow not destroyed and henceforth did not go down in history as the catalyst for forging peace between Klingons and Humans. Picard decides to sacrifice himself, and the Enterprise that should have made history, in order for the proper timeline to be restored. *Voyager* also uses this plot device to tell its stories. In the two-part episode 'Year of Hell' (1997), Captain Janeway and her crew fight to survive the attacks of an alien race intent on destroying the ship because they want to change history. Each time the ship survives an attack the timeline is altered slightly, killing many of the main characters and destroying entire planets. At the end of the episode, the original timeline is repaired so that it is as if the crew experienced nothing.

Star Trek uses this method of storytelling because society requires a mode of expression that can accommodate different possibilities. People need a means through which they can exercise their complex and composite imagination; the multiform story provides that because it illustrates various alternative plots and outcomes. As Murray further states:

[The multiform narrative's] alternate versions of reality are now part of the way we think, part of the way we experience the world. To be alive in the twentieth century is to be aware of the alternative possible selves, of alternative possible worlds, and of the limitless intersecting stories of the actual world.[20]

With *Star Trek* the multiform story works because it has a narrative history which serves as a basis for many of its episodes; there is already a narrative framework in place for multiple plots to expand upon and characters to harmonise with. For fans, its 'alternate versions of reality' are part of the way they experience their own world and, as a result, part of how they identify themselves and want to imagine the future. As ever, science fiction succeeds in extrapolating ideas about the future by using contemporary methods of storytelling very much grounded in literary tradition. Rather than being a twenty-fourth-century tale about the future, *Star Trek* can, and may well always, be considered a story about contemporary society and how we deal with our own past and present.

3

CREATING AND COMPARING MYTH

STAR TREK
AND STAR WARS

One of the reasons for *Star Trek*'s popularity is that it does the work of myth ... By confronting through narrative those problems that are among the most unmanageable in ordinary life, myth opens a space for creativity within the irreconcilable polarities of our existence.[1]

According to Susan L. Schwartz, 'Star Trek is a vast modern mythos' that counteracts 'the fickleness of American culture and its search for the rational, factual, and real', even though 'it is not historically true.'[2] To an extent Schwartz is correct in her assertion, Star Trek does play the part of a modern-day myth; however, to say that it bears no resemblance to historical fact is imprecise. As I have already pointed out, Star Trek's cultural value with its own fans would be depreciated if it lacked grounding in historical fact. They watch the series because it is founded on an authentic representation of contemporary life inherently integrated with their history. Indeed, both Star Trek and Star Wars not only take historical facts and make compelling stories from them, they also use culturally inherited myths and symbols synonymous with the very roots of western civilisation.

In 1987, Lane Roth wrote the essay 'Death and Rebirth in Star Trek II: The Wrath of Khan', in which the mythic qualities of the death/rebirth cycle are ascribed to the plot of Star Trek's most popular feature film. The death and subsequent resurrection of Spock is given mythical significance thanks to the archetypal doubling motifs found in western literature. Both Kirk and Spock undergo transformations that subscribe to the myth and thus formulate them as a 'double hero', whereby Spock sacrifices his life to save his crew and Kirk's vision, or inner spirit, is modified to accept death as part of life and thereby understand what makes us human.[3] *Star Trek* uses myth intelligently; it adapts its stories to incorporate familiar mythical paradigms that figure centrally within our own society, history, and culture. These stories may be centuries old and have been resigned to the past, but *Star Trek* breathes life back into them by retelling them in a yet-to-be-decided utopian future.

Myth is an important mode through which histories can be written and told. Richard Slotkin describes myth as 'the primary language of historical memory: a body of traditional stories that have, over time, been used to summarize the course of our collective history'. Myths not only make up these stories they also 'assign ideological meanings to that history'.[4] If *Star Trek* is history then the mythical stories it uses to produce its episodes carry meaning. Myth also serves as a mode of national identity-making; a shared history common to those who have the power becomes myth when used to create a sense of collective cultural capital. Countries thrive on myths to create, substantiate, and preserve their national identity. Jeffrey Richards describes them as 'episodes from their history that are removed from their context, shorn of complications and qualifications, stripped down to their essentials and endlessly repeated as manifestations of the nation's character, worth and values'.[5] Therefore they are imbued with what Slotkin calls 'ideological meaning' because myths are created to represent nations and peoples who themselves have their own political and social agendas. For example, *Star Trek*'s 'exploration imperative' can be connected to the myth of the American frontier, but doing so endows *Star Trek* with numerous inherent culturally sanctioned meanings and ideological interpretations linked to westward expansion and Manifest Destiny. I examine such contradictions in the next chapter.

Although *Star Trek* uses the fantastic future in which to set its allegorical stories, I have stressed that it has looked to the past as a means of broadcasting its messages. The use of myth in this storytelling process further entrenches Star Trek as history; it is not a fictional view of a brighter future but rather an ideological view of a real past. Vivian Sobchack's earlier criticism of the series resonates through Robert Jewett and John Shelton Lawrence's examination of Star Trek's manipulation of myth taken from The American Monomyth:

> **Instead of a rigorously self-critical scientific outlook,** Star Trek
> **offers** pseudo-empiricism, **an empirical veneer of gadgetry,**
> **and crew talk applied to a mythical superstructure.**[6]

A myth common to the Star Trek narrative is the American monomyth, described by Jewett and Lawrence as 'a tale of redemption'.[7] The classical monomyth concerned the rite of passage and initiation of a lone hero who undertook great voyages and adventures: for example, the Greek heroes Hercules and Odysseus. The American version combines the lone-hero motif with an inherent urge to do good and be redeemed, to bring about the salvation of those less fortunate: the most obvious example of this would be the messianic figure of Jesus Christ. Both the 'initiation myth' and the 'salvation myth' form the unique American monomyth and at the root of them both is the underlying sense of freedom. In the cases of Hercules and Odysseus, freedom was personified by the pursuit to attain manhood through heroic acts of adventure; freedom for Jesus meant freedom from sin for those he had sacrificed his life to save. Jewett and Lawrence stress that the American monomyth 'secularizes the Judeo-Christian redemption dramas that have arisen on American soil'.[8] Link this with Orlando Patterson's statement that 'Christianity, alone among the religions of salvation, made freedom [its] doctrinal core,' and one can conclude that the desire for liberty, above all else, defines the monomyth and the heroes that follow it.[9] Yet protecting liberty and being redeemed does not save the hero from the obscurity of his isolation, he must leave those people he helps and go on his way to perhaps help others in distress. This idea is indicative of the archetypal Hollywood Westerns such as Shane (1953), The Searchers (1956) and The Magnificent Seven (1960), or the more modern comic-superhero movies such as Superman (1978) and Batman (1989).

For J. P. Telotte in *Science Fiction Film* (2001), one method of analysing myth in these sorts of films is the Jungian psychoanalytical approach. This approach 'treats film as a primary myth and thus a key reflection of cultural identity'. For Jung the individual was central, their personal journey on the path of individuation – 'an initiation into the demands of the human environment, combined with the gaining of a deep self-knowledge' – leads to a realisation and formation of the self.[10] In terms of *Star Trek*, the captain and the crew succeed in their mission by drawing together to defeat the enemy or save an alien society; in the process, the individual learns to survive and achieves maturity. Louis Woods and Gary Harmon have also identified Jung's concerns with opposites and the shadow in earlier episodes of the series 'as they interact in the formation of the nature, structure and functioning of the human psyche'.[11] Important episodes such as 'The Enemy Within' (1966) and 'Mirror, Mirror' exemplify *Star Trek*'s tendency to analyse human duality through the personification of the 'evil twin' or 'doppelgänger'.[12] For characters such as the cowboy or superhero, who act primarily on their own, there is a point in a film when the self is activated, perhaps triggered by scenes of personal disaster such as losing a loved one or assuming their superpowers for the first time, and they embark on their own personal mission to attain individuation. In *Star Wars*, Luke Skywalker decides to go with Ben Kenobi and become a Jedi after discovering that his aunt and uncle have been killed at the hands of the Empire.[13] Telotte points out that this method of analysis may not be as popular as the Freudian or Lacanian methodology but it 'remains attractive for the way it manages to explain the compelling and apparently mythic power of film'.[14]

The original series provides a wide range of texts that revolve around the spirit of the American monomyth. Kirk was the main protagonist (culprit) when it came to interfering with entire planetary societies and small village communities for the apparent greater good. By confronting the primary ideological core often represented by a central computer or omniscient machine, or a leader who has been misguided in his duties to practise democracy, Kirk would substantiate his desire to do good by defending his actions in the name of freedom for those people he thought were being oppressed. Kirk's moral vision 'partakes of the spirit and rhetoric of the *Pax*

Americana', whereby Kirk's zeal for the righteousness of the mission transcends any doubts over interfering with other civilisations.[15]

In 'Return of the Archons' (1967), for example, the crew of the Enterprise beam down to a planet where all of the inhabitants seem heavily tranquillised, then at six o'clock almost all go crazy and start looting and fighting. After an investigation, Kirk finds out that this behaviour is the will of Landru, the people's leader. At the end of the episode Kirk and Spock confront Landru, a highly sophisticated computer left by the real Landru to show the people a better way; Kirk argues that the highest good requires the people to have freedom to express their creativity. When Landru is convinced that it has been restricting the people's freedom and therefore detracting them from the better way, the computer short-circuits and the planet is set free. Another computer that controls the lives of an innocent society is seen in the episode 'A Taste of Armageddon' (1967), where a bizarre war between two planets is governed entirely by computers, but with real deaths. The machines calculate who has died, and then those individuals report to be killed in disintegration chambers. Kirk and Spock are unsurprisingly appalled at this situation and try to influence the leaders in stopping the bloody war, yet they are captured and as a last resort Kirk destroys the main computer. This action forces the peoples from the two planets to face the prospect of real war and, given the devastating results, they opt to talk with each other about peace. These two episodes juxtapose Kirk, with all the characteristics of a moral and just hero, against machines that are amoral and do not realise the power they have over people's lives. When faced with Kirk's logical and emotional outbursts they cannot retaliate and so Kirk assumes the mantle of saviour and sets the seemingly oppressed people free to determine their own destinies.

In episodes such as 'Errand of Mercy' (1967) and 'The Omega Glory', Kirk tries to reason with humanoids instead of machines to bring salvation to vulnerable and misguided people. However, the results are the same. Kirk manages to convince the Yang leader in 'The Omega Glory' that the holy words of scripture – bearing remarkable resemblance to the United States Constitution – are not only meant for the Yangs (Yankees) but also for their bitter enemy the Kohms (Communists). This not only proclaims Kirk as a redeeming heroic figure, showing the Yangs the error in their poor translation of the Constitution, but also as a saviour because he brings the long war to an end. Symbolically Kirk also brings an end to the cold war, which of course distinguished the contemporary political mindset in America, thereby certifying him as an American hero of the present as well as the future. His superiority is exercised through his ability to properly translate and interpret the Yang's Constitution by linking it to the original historic document which, within the Star Trek narrative, was over six hundred years old.

Kirk's monomythic role in 'Errand of Mercy' is turned against him as he tries to convince a community of simple farmers that they need his protection from the Klingons. Despite his attempts to show the Organians that the Klingons are going to subjugate them if they do not fight back, the colonists refuse to resort to violence. In desperation, Kirk storms the Klingon headquarters to prevent them from killing the Organians, unwittingly provoking them to use their telepathic powers to disarm both the Federation and Klingon troops. The Organians are revealed to be a superior peace-loving people who do not allow violence and thus offer an ultimatum to the warring commanders to stop fighting or their weapons will not function. Ironically, Kirk's role as monomythic hero is reversed and he is himself saved from annihilation, redemption this time coming on behalf of the Organians who have already created their own version of a utopian paradise. This episode, together with 'A Private Little War' (1968), 'A Piece of the Action' (1968), and 'The Apple' (1967), metaphorically comment on America's involvement in Vietnam. According to Mark Lagon's analysis of Star Trek of the 1960s, this treatment 'overtly examines the compulsion of American foreign policy-makers to feel that they owe it to other countries to interfere in their affairs'.[16] As result, America's belief in the monomyth comes under extreme pressure because Kirk represents both the aggressive version of American foreign policy and the more clandestine and socio-political versions synonymous with the cold war.

To see an illustration of the monomyth in later series, one need only look at the film Star Trek: Insurrection (1998) to get an impression of the mythic paradigms the series is employing to entertain its audience and fanbase. The crew of the Enterprise-E is called to investigate the erratic behaviour of the android Data on the planet

Ba'ku. After serious signs of foul play are discovered, Picard decides to remain on the planet against orders and tries to save the people of Ba'ku from a forced relocation reminiscent of the actions taken by the American government against Native Americans in the nineteenth century. The seven main characters – Picard, Riker, Data, Worf, LaForge, Crusher and Troi – act as redeeming heroes as they attempt to get the Ba'ku to safety and preserve their innocent tranquillity. In the process, they assume the mythical status of the American cowboy by fulfilling all the requirements of the American monomyth.

This plot strongly resembles that of *The Magnificent Seven* – and therefore its predecessor, Akira Kurosawa's *The Seven Samurai* (1954) – where seven skilled gunfighters are hired to protect a poor Mexican village, prepared to suffer the consequences and die in order to safeguard the innocent and protect their liberty. In *Insurrection*'s case, however, the crew is likely to be court-martialled rather than killed and their skills are not wholly reliant on handling a gun. Nevertheless, iconographically there is a little interplay between the two films in a scene where Picard, Data, Worf, Crusher and Troi have a Mexican stand-off with five robotic drones that have come to capture the Ba'ku. The five heroic crew members stare down the enemy with phasers in hand, music building up the tension reminiscent of the Elmer Bernstein piece, just like Chris, Vin and the rest of the Seven confront the vicious Calvera in a gun-slinging free-for-all last stand. This scene is representative of the mythical paradigms *Star Trek* uses to make a connection with its audience and also how it uses familiar cinematic images to add to the movie's overall entertainment level. However, with both elements combined, *Star Trek* is able to update an overused and out-of-date film genre by transporting its iconography to the final frontier. At the same time, it can also use the culturally sanctioned meanings attributed to the original to disseminate its own contemporary and socially aware messages to Americans already acquainted with the cowboy and Western genre. In effect *Star Trek* returns to a mythical history to tell its stories about the erstwhile determined mythical future.

The essence of the American monomyth can be seen in many *Star Trek* episodes because the crew, specifically Kirk and the Enterprise, explore space and help those in need of assistance – albeit breaking the rules of the Prime Directive (the prohibition against influencing other cultures) in the process. After they have achieved their goal they leave and continue their mission to 'seek out new life and new civilisations'. According to Jay Goulding, this constant cycle of heroism on behalf of the crew is a 'fundamental law of mythology – a never ending repetition'. For him, Star Trek promises much in the way of freedom, equality, and self-actualisation but instead delivers imperialistic flag waving whereby Kirk and his crew 'rarely come to rest ... fleeing or flying to the next planet, to the next battlefield, to the next conquest, struggling, denying themselves and sometimes dying but always holding the flag upright'.[17] Delivering its own brand of Federation democracy is what drives Star Trek's mission on the screen in the form of classic science fiction and, with its audience, in the mass consumption of common cultural myths. In the words of Jewett and Lawrence, the hero of the monomyth mirrors exactly what Star Trek's most renowned captain did in nearly every episode, except for 'recedes into obscurity' read 'continues his five year mission':

> A community in a harmonious paradise is threatened by evil: normal institutions fail to contend with this threat: a selfless superhero emerges to renounce temptations and carry out the redemptive task: aided by fate, his decisive victory restores the community to its paradisal condition: the superhero then recedes into obscurity.[18]

The monomyth may have first characterised the original series but it has also provided TNG and Voyager with endless stories in which the redemptive qualities of the two crews could be exercised in order to bring salvation to the aliens in trouble. To a great extent, Voyager signals a return to the simpler adventure format of the original series, yet the main theme seems to be based on Homer's Odyssey: the mythical struggle to return home is the most important objective. However, the latter two series indicate awareness that the original conception of the Prime Directive was inadequate; Kirk could not resist interfering with entire societies because he thought he knew better. As a result the newer captains try to employ a little restraint in their aid, even going as far as risking court martial to stop their superiors from interfering with innocent civilians – see, for example, Insurrection. The American monomyth lies at the root of why Star Trek keeps returning to these sorts of stories; it is a myth that carries great cultural significance for Americans, therefore Star Trek inevitably uses it to frame much of its historical narrative.

Star Trek is not alone in the manipulation of mythical science fiction; the Star Wars trilogy created by George Lucas was an attempt to bring back hope to a nation when it seemed in short supply in 1977. His vision was to resurrect the myths and legends that had once defined society, but had since been forgotten because people had more pressing social problems to deal with. The economy was at an all-time low, the Vietnam war had just finished with no clear victor, and Watergate caused scandal within a government that had already lost public confidence. America was in definite need of a cultural tonic that would inspire people and speak to their concerns and at the same time 'offer some timeless wisdom'.[19] Star Wars was to be George Lucas' prescription for America. This was in stark contrast with Lucas' previous science fiction film, THX 1138 (1971), which depicted a futuristic dystopian world where humans were reduced to bottom-line budgetary numbers and America was racked by racial, class and economic tensions indicative of late twentieth-century industrial society. However, as in Star Wars where 'a new hope' was literally reborn to save a way of life, the eponymous hero THX provided some optimism with his climb to freedom outside of his underground prison.

The two science fiction phenomena appear to have the same basic creative foundations – both were designed to speak to Americans in need of social and moral guidance. George Lucas and Gene Roddenberry were responding to their own social times and acted upon the contemporary issues that faced America in the 1960s and 1970s. Star Trek's serialised nature allowed it to keep up with contemporary social issues, as previously mentioned, and the individual spin-offs were able to adapt and change to suit American popular taste. Conversely, the Star Wars franchise – including the recent Episode I: The Phantom Menace (1999), Episode II: Attack of the Clones (2002) and Episode III: Revenge of the Sith (2005) – continues to rely upon the mediation of ancient myth to address American problems rather than being overtly influenced by newsworthy topics of the present day:

> Lucas devoured the great themes: epic struggles between
> good and evil, heroes and villains, magical princes and ogres,
> heroines and evil princesses, the transmission from fathers
> to sons of the powers of both good and evil. What the myths
> revealed to Lucas, among other things, was the capacity
> of the human imagination to conceive alternate realities to
> cope with reality: figures and places and events that were
> before now or beyond now but were rich with meaning to our
> present.[20]

Star Wars, and to some extent Star Trek, have taken history and myth
and transformed them into a new package, quite literally taking a
postmodern approach to looking back at the past to learn about
the present. This commodification of the past indicates a cultural
engagement with nostalgia so intimate and impervious that, as
Fredric Jameson has pointed out, 'we are unable today to focus on
our own present, as though we have become incapable of achieving
aesthetic representations of our current experience.'[21] Star Trek's
fixation with its own past in Enterprise is further evidence for its
postmodern entanglement with history and myth, only Star Trek
is romanticising about a history that has scientific and historical
grounding in reality. Jameson also explains that Star Wars' use
of nostalgia to convey the past metonymically is indicative of an
American yearning to return to more innocent times: the films
and Saturday afternoon TV serials such as Buck Rogers (1939, 1950)
and Flash Gordon (1936, 1959).[22] Adam Roberts links this yearning
in Star Wars to a particular period of science fiction literary history:
the Pulps of the Golden Age. As well as eulogising its SF heritage,
Star Wars 'translates it into something larger-scale, bigger-budget,
more sophisticated and glossy', acting as an 'intertextual force'
looking backwards 'over the history of the genre itself'.[23] Telotte
goes further and describes Star Wars as 'homage to a great number
of films and film types – the Western, war films, Japanese samurai
films – all of which have contributed to Lucas' vision'. This trend
is not unique to Star Wars but marks 'the stirrings of a postmodern
pastiche influence that has increasingly characterized our science

fiction films'.[24]

Where Star Trek has taken myth and 'clothed [it]', according to William B. Tyrrell, 'in the garb of science fiction' in order to present a possible and positive future, Star Wars has taken ancient myth and created an 'alternate reality', admittedly set in the past. Within this new – and at the same time ancient – reality, technological advancement and things of the future are set 'a long time ago in a galaxy far, far away'.[25] Steven Galipeau identifies it as a 'mythic time' created by the 'interweaving myths of technology and religion occurring in some other galaxy'.[26] For Star Trek, mythology is a narrative tool with which it can illustrate and correct historical indiscretions, frame many of its episodes and plotlines, and create hope for the future. At the same time, it makes fans believe wholeheartedly that Star Trek's reality has existed, still exists, and will continue to exist far beyond their lifetime. For Star Wars, mythology is a historically based series of symbols and characters which connect with human society and tell us how things were done in the past – perhaps this is why some fans of Star Wars say it is not science fiction but rather science fantasy.[27] For example:

'Most legends have their basis in facts.'
James T. Kirk, 'And The Children Shall Lead' (1968)

'… many of the truths we cling to depend greatly on our own point of view.'
Obi-Wan Kenobi to Luke Skywalker, Return of the Jedi (1983)

Both statements indicate how each series regards its method of mythic storytelling: Star Trek looks for a historical common ground with reality, 'legends' having 'their basis in facts'; Star Wars prefers to leave the storytelling to its audiences, allowing them to form their own opinions from the mythical framework Lucas created from a variety of sources, 'truths' depending 'on our own point of view'. Or, as Jay Goulding puts it more simply:

Star Trek as science fiction is overtly anti-mythic in its attempt to rationalize, systematize and package reality [à la Jewett and Lawrence's pseudo-empiricism], while Star Wars, as fantasy, is overtly myth-affirming, with its reliance on unseen magical forces which bring order to the personality and to the universe.[28]

To further argue this point, Jon Wagner and Jan Lundeen emphasise that 'while fantasy may bear a superficial resemblance to traditional myth in its rustic and magical character' – for example, *Star Wars'* battle between good and evil, young heroes and ancient sorcery – science fiction like *Star Trek* 'has a stronger functional parallel with older myths, because its futuristic setting entails a more serious kind of truth claim'.[29] Consequently, *Star Trek* begs questions such as 'what if?' and 'what might be?' that I have already identified are part of its compulsion to teach the audience how to 'learn from the mistakes of the past'. Nevertheless, both have acquired mythic status in the present and with that go the hearts and imaginations of millions of fans.

What is striking about *Star Trek* and *Star Wars* is the enormous amount they can tell us about society; how much they represent contemporary trends and tastes is just as significant as what histories and myths they use to create their own versions of an alternate reality. Both franchises have turned to their own historical narratives to resurrect new and exciting stories to keep their fans involved and interested: *Star Trek* has created a pre-Kirk series that charts its own journey through very detailed and catalogued history; George Lucas has concentrated on fleshing out and substantiating his original trilogy by investing millions in making three prequels that he hoped would recapture the imagination of cinemagoers. These acts of self-examination not only highlight science fiction's trend of looking to its forebears, but they also show how much American society has become disgruntled with its own time; to all intents and purposes the present is having a knock-on effect on what science fiction audiences want to see on their screens. As a result, the mythic and futuristic times offered by both series tender a way out of dealing with contemporary life; it is not because audiences want to live in a mythic past, but rather that history and myth offer a better template to fantasise about and create the future. Brooks Landon's claim that science fiction is not about 'what the future might hold, but the inevitable hold of the present over the future' makes clear that it is the present that determines what constitutes our science fiction.[30] Therefore, I would say that Star Trek and Star Wars both view myth as a means to counteract the turmoil and uncertainty of that present American, and perhaps global, society.

History is a representation of the past; it is information transformed into story, which, over time, becomes part of a shared mythology. These stories and myths are told by Star Trek as futuristic narratives; sometimes they are embedded in symbols and tropes or, as in the case of 'going back in time', in stories concerning the dilemma between right and wrong. The stories Star Trek recounts about the past in the future produce images that some Americans use to perceive themselves as individuals both separate from and within society and others use to recognise America as a community or nation. By telling the right stories, Star Trek can help America imagine itself acting as a community, pulling together to resolve its problems often tackled in weekly episodes, ultimately overcoming a national anxiety deeply rooted in the conception of its own history.

Having defined what sustains Star Trek's aptitude for telling good stories, and described the assortment of tropes and plot devices it uses to mediate its own historical narrative, the next chapter focuses on one specific mode of American narration: the Puritan Jeremiad. In this, I illustrate Star Trek's historical and cultural links to this peculiar and exceptional form of rhetoric. Therefore, the historical groundwork done thus far should help clarify some of the links I make in Chapter Four using the work of Sacvan Bercovitch and his seminal analysis, The American Jeremiad.

4

'FOR WE MUST CONSIDER THAT WE SHALL BE AS A CITY UPON A HILL, THE EYES OF ALL PEOPLE ARE UPON US'

THE AMERICAN JEREMIAD AND *STAR TREK*'S PURITAN LEGACY

'All your people must learn before you can reach for the stars.'
Kirk to Shahna, 'The Gamesters of Triskelion' (1968)

For Ziauddin Sardar, 'science fiction explores space,' but not the realms of outer space as one might think. Instead, he has observed that 'as a genre the space that science fiction most intimately explores is interior and human; to tell future stories it recycles the structure and tropes of ancient narrative tradition and to devise dramatic tension it deploys issues and angst that are immediately present.'[1] With such a definition in mind, I want to extrapolate what interior spaces *Star Trek* explores and what sort of ancient narrative structure it uses to tell the kind of future stories to which we have grown accustomed in its forty-year history. More specifically, this chapter concerns *Star Trek*'s links with the American foundational narrative: the American Jeremiad. It concentrates on how both the Jeremiad and *Star Trek* refer back to the past in order to prophesy a better future. The Puritan experience was based on the assumption that they were going somewhere better as God's chosen people; their exceptionalism would be proven to the rest of the world when America became home to the new Zion. *Star Trek* also promotes a form of human exceptionalism based on the American version that has permeated its history. Its look at the future revolves around the premise that spatial expansion can bring cultural and social improvement to humanity but more exploration of the human soul is required in order to fulfil our universal destiny.

The Jeremiad provided a link to the Puritans' ancestors by using their past sins as examples of how to continue and complete their divine mission in the future. *Star Trek* does the same by projecting America's historical and social transgressions, and its climate for change, onto the future universe in which it is set. The exceptionalist, progressive, expansive, prophetic, yet unfinished tones of the Puritan Jeremiad resonate throughout *Star Trek* because it bases its ethos on centuries-old themes and tropes first recognisable in the American continent when the Pilgrims set foot on Plymouth Rock in 1620. When John Winthrop spoke of a 'City upon a Hill' he was not only laying out terms for the foundation of a community in New England; he was also unwittingly producing a framework for the continuing progression of American exceptionalist tropes well into the twenty-first century and, as we see in *Star Trek*, into the twenty-fourth. It is this legacy which is at the heart of *Star Trek*'s message of a utopian future first mediated in the 1960s, and still being screened and written about after the turn of the century.

As we will begin to see in this chapter, notions of self-improvement and individual change become increasingly important to both the Puritan errand and *Star Trek*'s utopian message. The exceptionalism of the chosen community cannot be achieved unless the individual is prepared to change. This change must be for both the good of the community and the good of the individual and, as we see with regard to *Star Trek* and its fan letters, the individual has ultimate responsibility for their own actions and personal success. This is not a new development in the history of American culture; the archetype of the 'self-made man' has been an integral part of the American myth of success and self-improvement.[2] Since the publication of Benjamin Franklin's 'The Way to Wealth' (1757) and later his *Autobiography* (1868), originally written in four parts at different times in Franklin's career, the image of the self-made man has permeated American success literature.[3] Through concerted effort, a man of limited means could rise up and assume a higher position within the community, shine out as an example of how hard work could improve the nation.

John Cawelti has identified three main strands of thought on the meaning of the self-made man. These three different interpretations are responsible for the persistence of the self-made man figure as popular hero in American society; through their continued synthesis, the archetype survives. The first version of the self-made man emerges from the 'conservative tradition of the middle-class Protestant ethic which stressed the values of piety, frugality, and diligence' in one's life calling. According to Cawelti, this tradition achieved its highest popularity with the publication of the Horatio Alger stories for children.[4] The second version emphasised getting ahead, a largely economic definition of success. Cawelti describes it as having endorsed more secular qualities such as 'initiative, aggressiveness, competitiveness, and forcefulness'. These elements of the self-made man were most often found in the self-help literature of the nineteenth century, and are still present in today's money-driven society where 'getting rich quick' is of primary importance.[5] Finally, the third version of the self-made man is perhaps the most important in the context of this chapter and my overall argument: Cawelti defines its success as being 'tied to individual fulfilment and social progress rather than to wealth or status. This tradition also showed a greater concern for the social implications of individual mobility.'[6] So, rather than looking out for oneself, this version of the self-made man was concerned with his success in relation to the community as a whole; personal change being linked to community progress. It is this version, first identified in the works of Franklin and Thomas Jefferson and developed by Ralph Waldo Emerson in his concept of self-reliance, which Cawelti describes as being 'an increasingly important element of American thought', and one which I believe is integral to the formulation of *Star Trek*'s future utopia.

'THE SHIFTING SIGNS OF THE TIMES': THE JEREMIAD AND AMERICAN CULTURE

> Where there is no revelation, the people cast off restraint; but blessed is he who keeps the law.
> *Proverbs, 29:18, NIV*

If *Star Trek* represents a relationship with America's past, then it has to have some sort of connection with it, not only the history it takes as its subject base, but some sort of rhetorical and historical language which it can use to communicate and mediate. The Jeremiad, specifically the one that Sacvan Bercovitch writes about, is the glue that holds together the American past and the American future because it acts as a fluid typology that enables contemporary society to refer back for guidance. *Star Trek* acts as a marker for Americans, just as the Jeremiad did for the Pilgrim Fathers and their descendants so that they could stay informed of their mission status. Described as a 'litany of hope' for those who had lost faith in their mission, its usage and rhetoric of divine destiny need not be restricted to the Puritans. *Star Trek* inherited it from a distinct American tradition of lament and celebration, embodied by intellectual luminaries such as Emerson, Thoreau and Whitman and more recently exemplified by Martin Luther King's denouncement of segregation as a violation of 'America's errand to freedom' during the Civil Rights movement.[7] Edward Bellamy's famous utopian novel *Looking Backward* (1888) also celebrates the march toward America's future. Written at a time when the Progressive Movement aimed to reform urban American society by returning to community values of the small town, '*Looking Backward* anticipated the movement for reform not through the rousing rhetoric of revolution but by espousing rationalist principles.'[8] Much like the Puritan concern with the past and how it should influence the present, Bellamy stressed in his preface that the American utopia was achievable through faith and hard work: 'Nowhere can we find more solid ground for daring anticipation of human development during the next one thousand years, than by "Looking Backward" upon the progress of the last one hundred.'[9]

The American Jeremiad was the Puritans' method of understanding both their place in the New World and their destiny as a godly community on the frontier. It has been described by Sacvan Bercovitch as a 'ritual designed to join social criticism to spiritual renewal, public to private identity, the shifting "signs of the times" to certain traditional metaphors, themes, and symbols'.[10] *Star Trek* also behaves in this manner. In reliving moments of American history and mediating American cultural myths, it provides Americans with narratives with which they can form their own opinions about America's foundational experience and ultimately even their own personal identities. As already stated, it was created as a style of social commentary, intent on criticising America in the late 1960s during a period of extreme social and political turmoil, and today it still continues to mediate pictures of contemporary society on a futuristic background. For the purpose of this chapter, I specifically look at three feature films: *Star Trek IV: The Voyage Home* (1986); *Star Trek V: The Final Frontier* (1989); and *Star Trek VI: The Undiscovered Country* (1991). These three films form what I call a 'tri-part Jeremiad', referring specifically to the social and historical message they transmitted to an audience in the late 1980s and their response to a unique political climate influenced by the end of the cold war, the twilight years of Ronald Reagan's presidency, and America's transition to the status of the world's only remaining superpower.

The word 'Jeremiad' stems from the name of the Old Testament prophet Jeremiah, who was renowned for his emotional prophecies preaching God's word. The main theme of Jeremiah's writings was judgement; particularly the judgement on God's chosen people who had broken their covenant with the Lord since being brought out of Egypt, as recorded in the book of *Exodus*.[11] Jeremiah's method of denouncing and redressing his enemies and highlighting their failures in front of God formed the basis of an important style of European complaint as the established Church tried to hold back the tide of Reformation and the Protestant churches legitimised their claims of true sainthood. Although it was based on a European tradition of preaching hell and damnation, the American version of the Jeremiad developed to encompass a new-found zeal for hope in the future. The American Jeremiad was optimistic and promised success to those chosen to build a new Zion; most importantly it showed non-Puritans the infallibility of the Puritan cause and affirmed exultation. The American Jeremiad spoke to God's chosen people differently from those who were typically the object of the European sermon. It concentrated on the 'peculiar' people on a 'particular' mission to do God's will in the New World. Above all, the American Jeremiad characterised the Puritan 'errand into the wilderness', an errand that defined them as a people and as a community on the early American frontiers. Interestingly, Bercovitch sees the American Jeremiad as an evolving and progressive form of rhetoric, as apposed to Perry Miller who saw the Jeremiad as a means to tell the Puritan community that they had lost their way and the errand had failed.[12] This is where the Jeremiad's connection to Star Trek becomes significant as the message is ultimately positive rather than disapproving and pessimistic.

For Bercovitch, the American Jeremiad did look back on the past, this being what connected it to the previous form of rhetoric, but it looked back on the past in order to create a better future. More specifically, the American Jeremiad grew out of a sense of incompletion, because the Puritan errand had not failed, but rather stalled, and the Jeremiad was a means to remind the community that they had more work to do in order to fulfil their destiny and complete their divine mission. There was a dichotomy that looked backwards and forwards, using both images to instil angst and fear but also joy and hope at the entry into Zion. By 1668, preachers believed that the 'City upon a Hill' had been laid to waste, left desolate and forsaken, and the Puritan community had got lost in the 'wilderness'. Their generation had failed to continue what the original settlers had started and the 'City' had suffered as a result.[13] Cotton Mather stressed that the work and sacrifice of their fathers had fallen short of their goals, the American mission had failed.[14] He was well aware of how attitudes had changed and developed amongst Puritans so his Jeremiad was written 'not only ... to glorify the founders of New England', but 'also conceived with an awareness of the mission that New England had been assigned by Providence and with a concern for her apostasy from that calling'.[15] To counteract this fall from grace, Puritans had to redefine what they were about – they had to reshape their heritage. Through the Jeremiad, they substituted tribute for action, decrying failures by defining themselves as dedicated Puritans like their fathers. The Jeremiad became a mode of celebration, celebrating the work of their forefathers and redefining their work by celebrating its new successes.[16] By doing this, they made present the past, reclaiming the myth of the original Pilgrim Fathers in 1620 and, as a result, celebrating life became a religious act. In effect the Puritan errand shifted from one meaning to another, from them seeing themselves as an outpost for the Puritan Reformation in the New World to fulfilling their flagging venture with 'meaning by themselves and out of themselves'.[17] The latter development was to characterise American notions of the individual, offering American Puritans an identity as a citizen and as a warrior in the 'world-redeeming' vanguard of the Reformation.[18]

The visionary force of the Puritan Jeremiad lay in its use of such metaphors as garden and exodus, errand and trial, even a 'City upon a Hill'. The idea of how the Puritan migrants saw their errand is best exemplified in John Winthrop's 'Modell of Christian Charity' (1630), from which I have taken the title of this chapter, and where, aboard the Arbella, Winthrop outlined how he and his fellow migrants were performing an errand – a job – not just for God but for the whole world to see throughout history: 'For we must Consider that we shall be as a City upon a Hill, the eyes of all people are upon us.' If the errand had failed, then not only would they have failed God, but also history would see that original colony as a failure in the restoration of the Christian Church punishable by banishment from Heaven itself: 'If we shall deal falsely with our god in this work ... we shall be made a story and a by-word through the world.'[19] However, succeed in God's errand to sustain utopia in the New World and history would remember the colony as the first to do God's will, a community that would shine out as an example to the world. As the years passed, the Puritans became more 'American', giving rise to new themes of affirmation and exultation in their sermons. Yet the younger generations of native-born Puritans could not escape the original form of the Jeremiad they had inherited from their fathers since it was unmistakably optimistic in outlook, 'affirming to the world, and despite the world, the inviolability of the colonial cause'.[20]

Therefore, there was always a message of hope in the Jeremiad, for no matter if the pilgrims had failed to establish a paradise in the New World, they always saw the prospect of completing their mission in the future as long as they learnt from the mistakes of the past and steered their journey back on course.

A CHANGE IN THE CITY:
STAR TREK'S POLITICS OF THE COLD WAR

'People can be very frightened of change.'
Kirk to Azetbur, Star Trek VI: The Undiscovered Country

As mentioned in Chapter One, Vivian Sobchack states that 'despite all their "futuristic" gadgetry and special effects ... the *Star Trek* films are conservative and nostalgic, imaging the future by looking backward to the imagination of a textual past.'[21] The films referred to were the first three feature films to include the original crew – *The Motion Picture* (1979), *The Wrath of Khan* (1982) and *The Search for Spock* (1984) – and specifically how their 'futurism' entailed looking back on previous visions of the future in order to 're-enact the nostalgic drama of the television series' own death and resurrection'. Together, the three films represent a rebirth, death, resurrection cycle constituted by an 'intertextually grounded pseudo-history' and illustrated through their constant references to 'aging, regret, loss, and death' found at the heart of their narratives.[22] The next three films in the cycle provide a dramatic departure from nostalgic intertextuality and represent a much more complicated engagement with history and the future.

I

In *The Voyage Home*, Kirk and his crew are in exile on Vulcan after disobeying orders and returning to the forbidden planet of Genesis to rescue Spock's body in *The Search for Spock*. The Klingon ship they had commandeered was renamed HMS Bounty, indicating their mutinous journey. On their return home to face punishment, the crew intercepts a message from Starfleet Command telling all ships to stay away from Earth as it is under attack by an unknown probe targeting the planet's seas and disabling all technology and equipment. The probe itself emits loud and disruptive sounds that cannot be understood or countered. Spock translates these sounds as similar to whale song since they are aimed at the water and concludes that the probe's calls cannot be answered because the Humpback whales in question have been extinct on Earth for two hundred years. In an effort to stop the probe destroying Earth, the crew takes it upon itself to attempt time travel and go back in time to retrieve two whales so as to fulfil the probe's wishes for contact. At the same time as Kirk brings the whales back to the future to save Earth, he is also saving the whale from its inevitable extinction due to man's carelessness. Their self-appointed mission thus has two aims: save the Earth in their future by going back in history to find the answer; and save the whale in our present, accentuating the need for contemporary society to think about its impact on the environment and wildlife. According to Spock, 'to hunt a species to extinction is not logical.' But, however much the ecological example seems trite today, it is the Jeremiad-style message of learning from history that remains significant.

To save the chosen whales, George and Gracie, the film anthropomorphises them, thereby making them worthy of salvation and justifying eliciting their help in saving twenty-third-century Earth. As both a warning to his captain and a reminder to the audience, Spock says, 'if we were to assume those whales are ours to do with as we please we would be as guilty as those who caused their extinction.' So humans should become aware of the effects their actions cause both in their immediate present with the treatment of other indigenous species and in the future with regard to the long-term effects of over-whaling and the state of the Earth for future generations. Ultimately Kirk saves Earth from its own short-sightedness; the frailties and failures of our current generation are atoned for by his honourable mission to teach twenty-third-century Earth about the wrongs of history. When the whales reach the future, the probe finally receives an answer to its dangerous song; humans have made up for their past sins and learnt from the mistake. The probe relents, showing it to be an omnipotent god-like creature who has demanded proof of humanity's right to live and in so doing reaffirmed the message in *Star Trek*'s original ethos that we must learn from history.

On a narrative level, the television time-travelling series *Quantum Leap* (1989–1993) shared many of these qualities with *Star Trek*; both involved a determined sense of duty 'to put right what once went wrong' and 'change history for the better' as *Quantum Leap*'s opening credits stirringly eulogised. Nevertheless, its attempts at showing how history could be changed for the better were channelled through the very idealistic and strong-headed Sam Beckett who would stop at nothing to personally change history to facilitate his return to his own time. This is the exact opposite to what the characters *can* or *are supposedly allowed to* do in any of the *Star Trek* series or films, since they are governed by a strict policy of non-interference: the Temporal Prime Directive. This directive does not allow for history to be changed – what happened in the past is quite literally 'history'. Rather, it enables the narrative of the time-travelling storylines to posit questions such as 'what can be learned from the lessons of history?' and 'how can we not repeat the same mistakes?' In this sense, *Star Trek* acts as a moral guide to humanity's progress in life, making obvious what needs to be done but not providing its audience with all of the answers.

The fundamental philosophy in *The Final Frontier* is the human 'spiritual quest'. Whilst on shore leave, the crew of the Enterprise are asked to respond to a hostage situation on Nimbus III, the so-called 'planet of galactic peace', where a Vulcan religious zealot named Sybok is demanding a starship to take him and his followers beyond the great barrier to the centre of the galaxy. His intention is to find *Sha Ka Ree*, Eden, and meet with his maker. Unfortunately, on arrival at the planet at the centre of the galaxy, Sybok's god is revealed as a fraud whose only aim was to lure the starship into taking his presence outside of the barrier and spreading it throughout the galaxy. The meaning of Sybok's pilgrimage was misunderstood; he believed that God could be sought on a distant planet whereas Kirk at the end of the film emphasises by pounding his chest that, 'maybe he's not out there ... maybe he's right here – the human heart!' Sybok obtained loyalty from his followers by exploring their inner pain, drawing out the guilt that makes them who they are and releasing them from their torment. When trying to introduce Kirk to his pain and guilt he is unsuccessful because Kirk says that 'they're the things we carry with us – the things that make us who we are. If we lose them, we lose ourselves. I don't want my pain taken away. I need my pain.'

According to Ian Maher, within this film there is a distinct 'parallel between the outward voyage of the Enterprise and the inward human search to find meaning and purpose in a vast and sometimes frightening universe'.[23] This is nowhere more obvious than when the ship transcends the 'final frontier', only to find that God does not reside there 'but finds his home within the human heart' as a result of humanity's never-ending spiritual hunger to find out what awaits after death and in what form paradise will be offered to them.[24] For the Puritans, paradise was known to them; it was to be found in the New World and they had to make it work by using the Jeremiad as a method of encouragement. In The Final Frontier, Sybok realises too late that paradise does not come in the form he expected because his search was misguided and he lacked the proper means to find it. For Kirk, Spock, and McCoy, however, the opportunity to find the answers they seek has not passed, since they are willing to look within themselves and their friendship. This is reminiscent of the shift in the American Jeremiad's emphasis on fulfilling the Puritan venture with 'meaning by themselves and out of themselves', and at the same time reaffirming Star Trek's viewpoint that humans can shape their own destiny.

The next movie, The Undiscovered Country, deals with the possibility of peace between the Klingons and the Federation due to the fact the Klingons can no longer afford to maintain their huge defence budget. In establishing peace talks with the Klingon High Chancellor, the Federation seeks to help fund and encourage a treaty which will reduce both parties' military force. However, the Klingon Chancellor is assassinated and Kirk and McCoy are arrested as scapegoats to cover up the secret plot between certain Klingon and Federation factions to stall the peace process. These factions did not believe in change and could not foresee peace between the two once sworn enemies so they used Kirk's hatred of the Klingons as a motive for the assassination. Thanks to Spock, the real perpetrators of the crime are revealed and the Enterprise is able to save the peace conference. However, Kirk was not ashamed of his feelings toward the Klingons, a fact recognised by the Chancellor when they met for dinner on board the Enterprise: 'You don't trust me, do you. I don't blame you. If there is to be a "brave new world", our generation is going to have the hardest time living it.' Change is the biggest obstacle for Kirk and his crew as they try to enact peace. To get to the 'undiscovered country' (a metaphorical Promised Land of peace in the future) takes courage and the ability to change history by looking within the human soul. This film unites familiar themes from the previous two movies with the need for faith in the goal of the mission, and uses them to obtain what is in simple terms entry into 'a brave new world' of peace. Released in 1991, The Undiscovered Country can be seen as a Jeremiad for post-cold war America.

As in Hamlet, the 'undiscovered country' represents the unknown, and as Hamlet is fearful of taking his own life because he does not know what form death will take, so is Kirk fearful of what peace between the Klingons and the Federation might do to him. Both he and Spock discuss how they have grown old and that change has come at a high price: their retirement from Starfleet. Yet Kirk is aware of the important steps he has taken to enable peace 'to stand a chance' and cognisant of the next generation, who have the chance to live in a more peaceful future, a reality uncovered in Star Trek: The Next Generation, where a Klingon serves aboard the Enterprise-D. The motivation for peace in The Undiscovered Country satisfies two dilemmas: firstly, it brings a close to the narrative cold war between Klingons and humans which by the time of TNG's universe Gene Roddenberry wanted eradicated; secondly, it parallels contemporary society's attempts at terminating an ideological conflict that was becoming irrelevant as the world turned to a global economy. Having faith in the fact 'that the universe will unfold as it should' is what underlines the message of the film and is a considerable feature of the American Jeremiad's original message to the Puritan settlers who themselves doubted the durability of their own divine mission.

In the three movies I have analysed there is a clear historical message being communicated through what I have termed a tri-part Jeremiad, the three parts being the message, the means and the motive. This arrangement mirrors Perry Miller's understanding of the Jeremiad as a form of triptych but in this case no segment outweighs another; thus condemnation does not prevail over the prophetic vision of a better future.[25] Firstly, in The Voyage Home, the plot centres on the crew travelling back in time to rescue two

Humpback whales in order to save the Earth of the future from being destroyed and in the process repopulate the species after its eventual extinction in the early twenty-first century. This plot clearly stresses the *message* that humanity can learn from the mistakes of the past by literally 'saving the whale' today and as a result change the future for the better. Secondly, in *The Final Frontier*, the crew travels to the centre of the galaxy to seek God. However, when the only god turns out to be a false idol they realise that what they were searching for resided in their own hearts all along. In other words, in the search for an answer to the question of life the journey will not take us beyond the boundaries of our own physical existence, it will make us turn inward to examine our humanity. Once we understand ourselves then our mission of self-edification will be complete: the *means* to redeem the human journey lies within ourselves. Lastly, in *The Undiscovered Country*, whilst the Federation attempts peace with the Klingons, the crew battles to save their captain who was accused of the assassination of the Klingon leader. The story not only reflected the then current political climate of America at the end of the cold war, it also spoke of an ideology of faith in the ongoing efforts to maintain peace and bring an end to ideological conflict. Ultimately, it suggested that the *motive* behind the eventual peace between the two superpowers was an ongoing mission toward a metaphorical Promised Land – an undiscovered country – which would require the ability to not only accept change but also live with it.

II

As *Star Trek* was addressing humanity's rejuvenated mission in the latter part of the 1980s, America's fortieth President, Ronald W. Reagan, was attempting to make America great again. To do this he would inspire the people with mythic tales from the country's once-celebrated past, hoping to finally forget such traumatic events as the assassination of JFK, defeat in Vietnam and Watergate so that the country could look to a brighter future. As Jon Roper described, 'if the past was a problem, it could be fixed through reinvention and revisionism,' and that was exactly what Reagan tried to do in his presidency: 'Reagan reached into America's mythological past to try to recall the driving optimism of the American dream.'[26] Just as Kennedy had used the image of the frontier made famous by

Frederick Jackson Turner, Reagan re-established America's mission 'in language redolent of John Winthrop and the Puritan "errand"', hoping to overturn years of sorrow and regret after Vietnam and America's failure to bring democracy to Southeast Asia:[27]

> **With all the creative energy at our command, let us begin an era of national renewal ... We have every right to dream heroic dreams ... And as we renew ourselves here in our own land, we will be seen as having greater strength throughout the world. We will again be the exemplar of freedom and a beacon of hope for those who do not now have freedom.[28]**

As this excerpt from Reagan's 1981 Inaugural Address exemplifies, the celebratory and optimistic tones of the Jeremiad had re-emerged to provide America with a renewed vision of how the future should and could be for Americans. At home, Winthrop's 'City upon a Hill' would be re-imagined to provide Americans with the life they desired; and abroad it would again shine out as an example, 'a beacon of hope' to those nations who had scoffed at America's failure to deliver its promises. Once more, American exceptionalist rhetoric was employed to reaffirm America's self-appointed task to make things right, only this time there was an uneasy sense of nationalistic patriotism permeating through Reagan's idealistic orations – America and the Western World had a common enemy: the Soviet Union. To defeat the 'evil empire' and win the cold war would mean forgetting the immediate past and instead putting faith in something more pure. As Roper described it: 'The restoration of faith in the nation's imperialist mission, involved a sense of being unencumbered by historical embarrassment rather than of remaining haunted by the past.'[29] The Puritan form of the Jeremiad, based on an unerring religious belief in the New Israel, was adopted by Reagan to turn embarrassment into pride and transformed into what Frances Fitzgerald calls a 'secularized, or, rather, a deicized version of nineteenth century Protestant beliefs about spiritual rebirth, reform and evangelism'.[30] Reagan was not the first to employ such rhetorical tactics in American political history; many presidents, politicians and journalists before had heralded

America's mission using very celebratory language describing the nation's duty to promote freedom, first to the Native Americans, then to the Americas and finally to the rest of the world.[31]

It was not enough to speak of America's exceptional position, however. Reagan wanted more from the American voters and, in his many official speeches throughout the 1980s, he continually used the imagery of the Puritans setting sail for America in the Arbella to reinforce his message of 'a glorious tomorrow'. He equated the challenges facing modern Americans with Winthrop's sermon about building the 'City upon a Hill' and demanded that '[America] once again be full of leaders dedicated to building shining cities on hills, until our nation's future is bright again with their collective glow. You have it within you to make it happen.'[32] Paul D. Erickson recognised Reagan's intelligent use of the American Jeremiad in his book *Reagan Speaks* (1985) and connected it to Bercovitch's then-recent assertions about the optimistic nature of the Jeremiad. He noted that Reagan applied 'the tropes and strategies of his ultimate optimism to nearly every issue', thereby 'translating Christian regeneration into patriotism and civic duty'.[33] To put it simply, the ability to change the world for the better lay within Americans themselves and his patriotic words of encouragement kept reminding them of that fact. As I have already mentioned, this was also a fact literally brought home to American audiences in 1986 and 1989 when *The Voyage Home* and *The Final Frontier* disseminated the same message of self-improvement through self-examination.

On the eve of his final week in office, Reagan gave his Farewell Address to the Nation and, as on many previous occasions, looked back on America's Puritan roots. He described how he had imagined America as 'a tall, proud city built on rocks stronger than oceans'.[34] Having used the Puritan analogy in no less than seven separate public speeches and engagements, Reagan was not unfamiliar with the concept of imagining America as a city. Nevertheless, in this specific address he intimated that anybody could become a citizen of that city, not just Americans: 'If there had to be city walls, the walls had doors and the doors were open to anyone with the will and the heart to get there.' Just as Kirk asked for those he encountered to look into the human heart for strength, Reagan emphasised that it was the power of those faithful who believed in America that helped the once-defeated nation regain its position as an exemplar of world democracy: 'We've done our part ... My friends: We did it ... We made a difference. We made the city stronger, we made the city freer, and we left her in good hands.' However, this euphoria was not in keeping with Puritan or even *Star Trek* tradition, since the President believed his goal had been achieved at the end of his term of office. The American Jeremiad never suggested that the Puritan mission had been completed and certainly did not congratulate them on making the 'City' stronger. Likewise, *Star Trek*'s version of the Jeremiad never confirmed whether the Promised Land had been reached or whether humanity had succeeded in making the future better than the past. Rather, it transmitted the message and the means through which people could do it, but showed humanity was forever on a journey to completion. The American Jeremiad provides a typological link between real life and *Star Trek* in the 1980s, but such subtle differences as whether or not America had accomplished its lofty design keep *Star Trek* detached from Ronald Reagan's enveloping patriotic and entirely exclusive envisioning of what the future might bring. Instead, *Star Trek*'s 'tri-part Jeremiad' stands out as an inclusive example that the abilities of one nation and the imagination of one president is not enough to fulfil mankind's utopian destiny.

III

In a positive sense, the Jeremiad works for *Star Trek* since its main message from the original series until now is that the future will be a better place than today: no hunger, poverty, racism or war. In order to achieve this state, humans as a society must learn from the past so as not to recreate those same problems in the future. The main focus of the Jeremiad, as I have said, was that it was used as a guide to achieve the Puritan's utopia in America. Transfer this onto the films discussed and we see that, through Kirk's example, *Star Trek* is promoting a similar message as a guide to contemporary society that the imaginary future might be possible if we start to get things right now. Even coupled with the political developments of the 1980s, which saw Reagan turn to America's exceptionalist Puritan roots, *Star Trek*'s message still exemplifies a common goal of examining ourselves which resonates throughout the franchise and throughout its global fanbase. Nicholas Meyer, co-writer of *The Voyage Home* and director of *The Undiscovered Country*, reflecting on his involvement with the movie franchise in a recent interview, insists that the movies worked because *Star Trek* is made of more than just a 'good story' or 'vivid characters':

> **It seems to me *Star Trek* works best as a pop allegory or a contemplation of problems with which we are familiar here and now ... [*Star Trek*] *IV* was about the environment. *VI* was about Western-Soviet politics and fear of the future.**[35]

Perhaps its longevity, and the reason why it remained popular even when it was not on television, can be ascribed to the fact that it uses the Jeremiad form as a means to communicate with its audience about those very problems that Meyer indicates are 'familiar here and now'. As I have tried to stress, the Jeremiad was a very powerful way of telling early Americans what they had to do.

In an undeniable sense, the Jeremiad was used by people who believed themselves to be exceptional – better than the rest of humanity. The Jeremiad excluded everyone else. This fact was illustrated by the Puritan view that the Indians they encountered were savage warriors of Satan who had to be assimilated or eradicated so that America could fulfil its divine destiny.[36] This sort of ideological background can therefore harm *Star Trek*'s aim, which is to ultimately show the future as better than today, with everyone as an equal member of society, not excluded from it. By examining Reagan's use of the Jeremiad and the symbolism of John Winthrop, I have tried to locate *Star Trek*'s contemporary use of the Jeremiad, but I have also tried to emphasise that there are differences between the exclusive politics of the 'cowboy' President and the inclusive politics of utopian science fiction drama. The Jeremiad used to preach to America during the late 1980s was very patriotic and relied on the ideal of America still being the exceptional country. Reagan himself mistakenly thought that America had succeeded in creating the fabled 'City upon a Hill' thus proving its exceptionalism. Yet Reagan was falling into the same trap as his political predecessors who believed they had achieved national glory through freedom. What had actually occurred over time was the destruction of the American

Frontier, the subjugation and extermination of Native Americans, the aggressive expansion into neighbouring territories in the name of manifest destiny and the continual involvement with ideological military operations overseas. The Jeremiad in the three films analysed did not proclaim that the Federation was the pinnacle of exceptionalism, or that the journey had been completed; much more effort was required from humanity in order to prove its worthiness.

In connecting a literary theme such as the Jeremiad with the film and television phenomenon of *Star Trek*, this chapter has addressed the developing interface between literature and media studies, particularly the convergence of methods used to analyse literature, film and popular culture. Consequently, I have found that such an analysis has shed new light onto what some might say is an 'overdone' area of science fiction research. Ultimately, I want to stress that what connects *Star Trek* with America's Puritan heritage is not an exceptional and exclusive view of the future but rather a determination and belief in the potential for humans to progress peacefully and make our future better than it could be. For Bercovitch, 'the Puritan legacy to subsequent American culture lies not in the theology or logic or social institutions, but in the realm of the imagination.'[37] *Star Trek* is part of that legacy and, as we will see in the following three chapters, it has continued to fuel the same kind of hope about the future in its fans as did the American Jeremiad for the Puritan's desire to find salvation in the Promised Land.

II

A NETWORK OF SUPPORT

IDENTIFICATION AND EMOTION IN *STAR TREK* FAN LETTERS

> Americans of all ages, all stations in life, and all types
> of disposition, are forever forming associations ...
> Nothing, in my view, deserves more attention than the
> intellectual and moral associations in America.
> *Alexis de Tocqueville,* Democracy in America *(1835)*

> Sarjenka: Is anybody out there?
> Data: Yes.
> *A Child initiates first contact with a passing space
> traveller, 'Pen Pals' (1989)*

Henry Jenkins uses Michel de Certeau's term 'textual poaching' to describe how fans rewrite *Star Trek* TV shows and movies in order to produce their own narratives which they then share amongst each other in the form of novels and music.[1] Likewise, studies by Constance Penley and Heather Joseph-Witham have analysed the prodigious output of the more active and creative fans mentioned in Chapter One. These studies have brought critical attention to what might have seemed an overdone and outdated subject and have highlighted how important *Star Trek* fan culture is to the fields of media and reception studies. Yet, their work is limited by its exclusive focus on those more marginal fans who are producers of new texts rather than more 'typical' fans who consume the original text but do not write stories or 'filk music', dress up, or manipulate video material.[2] The *Star Trek* movies and TV shows play an important role in the emotional and affective lives of American fans; therefore I want to investigate in the following three chapters the ways in which fans actually talk about the show and their engagement with it. Similar work has been done, using models of cultural reception, by Helen Taylor on women's responses to *Gone with the Wind* (1939) and in Ien Ang's analysis of *Dallas* (1978–1991).[3]

As I have shown in Part One, the *Star Trek* text revolves around traditional American themes of utopia, community, and self-improvement. In Part Two, I want to show how these three themes are replicated in published letters exchanged by fans. The letters I analyse recount *Star Trek*'s impact on fans' daily lives. In Chapter Five, for example, *Star Trek*'s vision of a future utopia is consistently referred to in letters as the fans' ideal future, a model for how

America can be changed for the better. Alternatively, in Chapter Six, some fans appear to draw on their communal love of Star Trek in making sense of traumatic and significant life events, while, in Chapter Seven, fans talk about how the text helps them improve their social lives and makes them stronger, more confident, people. In sum, these letters highlight the ways in which fans use and adapt notions of utopia, community and self-improvement to help express their personal stories and feelings. In the process of the textual analysis of the aforementioned sources, I want to establish the precise role Star Trek plays in fans' daily lives. As well as eliciting themes from the letters such as when fans watch, and to what extent particular moods determine the episodes they choose to watch, I want to understand and conceptualise how this form of relationship with the series emotionally affects those fans. I intend to follow on from Part One's assertion that 'Star Trek acts as a canonical reference to what makes America American,' by analysing how much watching the show has reportedly helped its fans in daily life. Such an analysis of how fans identify with the series will also provide an understanding of Geoff King and Tanya Krzywinska's statement in their comprehensive study of science fiction cinema: '[Science fiction] offers the pleasures of excitement, fantasy and escape, while also grappling with some of the oldest questions about what it is to be human.'[4]

Finally, it is my intention to extrapolate how far one might regard the Star Trek fanbase as a collective 'network of support'. I believe that those fans who communicate through writing letters to fan magazines and publications are doing so in an attempt to contact fellow enthusiasts and share their own personal experiences, whether they are positive or emotionally traumatic.[5] By doing so, the fans are able to reveal private and delicate information and at the same time realise that others may have had similar experiences. For instance, all the fans who are distressed at the loss of a friend or family member describe Star Trek as being integral to the recovery process, which suggests that they see its multiple texts as a form of encouragement. When talking about this in letters read by other fans, their affection is passed on through a cohesive fibrous network that allows for intimate but positive exchanges. Star Trek fan culture is a collective network, multilayered and interwoven with numerous channels of communication – all of which offer communal support on many personal levels. It should of course be stressed that I will be putting forward evidence for the existence of this 'network of support', as seen in the function of the letters and the communal arena in which they are published. Therefore, I am not proposing that this network actually 'helps' fans overcome emotional distress or that Star Trek solves all of the world's problems. However, fans do recount how they believe that Star Trek has helped them and so it is legitimate to assume that, because they do believe in its capacity for support, this very belief may be a factor in their self-improvement and improved lifestyle.

5

'A REASON TO LIVE'

STAR TREK'S UTOPIA AND SOCIAL CHANGE

'If you can explain everything, what's left to believe in?'
Old Man #2 to Janeway, 'Sacred Ground' (1996)

Star Trek's goal is to promote the multicultural future of America, however impossible it may seem. Gene Roddenberry's ideological foundation for the series was to show that there was such a thing as 'Infinite Diversity in Infinite Combinations' (IDIC). That through a constant 'didactic project to engage the experiences and politics of the 1960s', Star Trek could address real problems America was facing when it came to race and the politics of pluralism.[1] Unfortunately, according to Daniel Bernardi, this premise was 'inconsistent and contradictory', and as a result Star Trek only succeeded in participating in the subordination of minorities on the screen and embedding them in the 'white-history' narrative that Roddenberry had originally set out to attack.[2] However, Star Trek's utopian message of diversity and peace continues to be one with which millions of its fans engage. Their letters indicate just how important Star Trek's conception of utopia is to their daily life and how their vision of life should progress. In effect, the fan letters I look at in this chapter show an enduring faith in the future that Roddenberry created on-screen; going against current public and political discourses that emphasise our future will not be better than our present and that society will continue to decay rather than progress.

In political terms, Russell Jacoby describes an 'era of acquiescence, in which we build our lives, families and careers with little expectation the future will diverge from the present'. For him, on the eve of the new millennium, America's 'utopian spirit – a sense that the future could transcend the present – [had] vanished'.[3] The main reason for this apathetical turn, according to Jacoby, is that America has abandoned its utopian ideals, which had sustained dissent and the inspiration for social change. Furthermore, the critics, writers, and intellectuals that once strove to attain these ideals have apparently given up their fight; Americans are losing the will to reclaim their vision of utopia. If this does not seem discouraging enough, Rick Altman believes America is losing its ability to even imagine a utopia, let alone achieve one. The science fiction genre once offered viewers the chance to imagine their own worlds, films of the 1950s allowed audiences to talk about the possibilities of science and the images of science fiction. Today, Altman argues that movies like *Star Wars* and series like *Star Trek* have spoken to the masses and offered them a unified, commercialised vision of the world because producers are interested in creating larger, more homogenous audiences. Whereas science fiction 'once served as a monument to real world configurations and concerns', it has since 'increasingly taken on what we might call a pseudo-memorial function. That is, they count on spectator memory to work their magic ... Their minds filled with prepackaged memories provided by generic memory-masters.'[4] Therefore, if this is the case, the fans who write letters about *Star Trek*'s future and its impact on their struggle to achieve a utopia are being brainwashed; they are not imagining their own worlds but are replicating a homogenised world separated from contemporary society and detached from the contexts of their own lives.

I do not believe this is the case with the fan letters I look at in this chapter. As Anthony Easthope points out, 'Someone will only invent a science fiction utopia if they are dissatisfied with the real world they live in.'[5] Consequently, *Star Trek* fans not only take inspiration from the utopian framework that Roddenberry created; they also want to imagine a better world because they do not believe that this world is good enough. Not only are the fans concerned for their own personal situation, but they are also concerned for society as a whole and they want to stress how using *Star Trek* as a guide might help to steer people in the right direction. Social change, as well as utopia, is an important objective for the fans in these letters. Jacoby's and Altman's arguments that Americans are losing interest in changing society appear not to apply to these fans who hold fast to the idea that Roddenberry's vision and the Star Trek text can be catalysts for social change. In fact, their attempts to imagine and write about a future utopia follows Fredric Jameson's point of view that '"to imagine utopia" constitutes an important political act because it challenges and criticises the alienation of late capitalist society.'[6] If they are not hardened political activists, Star Trek letter writers can be at least described as interested participants in social change.

Richard Dyer states that the two 'taken-for-granted descriptions of entertainment, as "escape" and as "wish-fulfilment", point to its central thrust, namely, utopianism'. Utopia, the manifestation of 'something better', is imagined in entertainment through the desire to have something we cannot get in our own daily life. For Dyer, the particular form of entertainment he describes is the movie musical – a genre that can provide images of escapism and fulfilment. Like Star Trek, the musical provides audiences with a positive representation of reality, where life is significantly different from the more humdrum daily grind that most people endure. However, Dyer sees limitations in entertainment's depiction of utopia. It does not present an accurate model of what a utopia should be like, 'as in the classic utopias of Sir Thomas More, William Morris, et al. Rather the utopianism is contained in the feelings it embodies'.[7] This is true for the musicals that Dyer has analysed but for Star Trek it cannot apply since, as I made clear in Part One, the series portrays a future utopian reality that works and acts as a model for its fans. Star Trek possesses both the utopian world and the feelings it embodies; it is the feeling of utopia that fans talk about in their letters in connection with the conception of its reality. Indeed, the coupling of an authentic model for utopia and the relevant sensibilities that go with it persuades fans to believe that Star Trek gives them 'a reason to live'.[8]

As an American utopia, originally imagined by one person and loved by millions more, Star Trek shares similar ground with the utopian world imagined by L. Frank Baum in The Wonderful Wizard of Oz (1900) and its thirteen sequels.[9] Baum created what has been described as a 'socialist' utopia' which saw Dorothy and Toto transported from a barren Kansas to Oz, a world of plenty and magical characters.[10] In Oz everyone is equal, there is no poverty or hunger and (almost) everyone lives in peace and harmony – if there is trouble, such as the Wicked Witch of the West, then by the end of the story Dorothy and her friends easily triumph. Jack Zipes sees Oz as 'a specific American utopia ... a place and space in the American imagination' and, because Dorothy Gale and her family eventually come to live in Oz rather than continue farming in Kansas, 'it embodies that which is missing, lacking, absent in America.'[11] America, at the time Baum wrote his first book, was going through a national crisis: farmers were struggling to make a living, depression and strikes characterised the 1890s, and war with Spain was testing the country's mettle.[12] To his readers, children in particular, Baum's utopia offered something different. Oz's popularity in the early part of the century continues to this day; according to Zipes, it 'stems from deep social and personal desires that many Americans feel are not being met in this rich and powerful country'.[13]

Like *Star Trek*, then, Oz is an American utopia that many find attractive. Its vision of the simple life allows for escapism and wish fulfilment. There is also an element of American self-help which characterises Dorothy, Scarecrow, Tin Man and Cowardly Lion's quest. As they search for a way home to Kansas, brains, a heart and courage, it soon becomes apparent that they had the ability to acquire those things all along: Dorothy could have used her magic slippers to go home at any time; the Scarecrow was always smart but never applied his wisdom; the Tin Man was always compassionate but confused this with his desire to love; and the Cowardly Lion was always brave but he never before had people he cared about to defend. They lacked the faith in themselves to change. As the story progresses, they find their faith to change and as a result all get their wish. Alison Lurie believes this to be particularly true of the 1939 adaptation; as a Hollywood allegory of the 'rags to riches' story, *The Wizard of Oz* depicts Dorothy and her friends fulfilling their wishes through music, whereas at the same time millions of Americans were still struggling in the Depression.[14] However, as Dyer stipulates about the musical, Oz only gives the feeling of utopia – it is not an accurate model for it. Unlike *Star Trek*, *The Wonderful Wizard of*

Oz and its sequels were 'designed solely to entertain the young' and were not didactic moralising stories that offered readers answers to the social problems of the day and possible ways of implementing them.[15] One reason for this could be because the Land of Oz 'has no overriding law or principle except variety' – Dorothy roams the country and meets extraordinary people and animals, getting into seemingly impossible dangers with them, and then moves quickly on to the next adventure with hardly any explanation or detail.[16] Star Trek's universe is the exact opposite, it is firmly rooted in the real and regimented, and its history is based on actual events that have happened in our history. The enormous amount of scientific technology and techno-babble that characterises its future is painstakingly based on the science of today; its accuracy assures a convincing utopia. What is more, because the fans immerse themselves in this history, Star Trek's American utopia seems more plausible as the boundaries between reality and fiction keep on merging.

Although Dyer's understanding of entertainment and utopia does not include a suitable model, he does suggest ways in which entertainment can achieve utopia, even if it is unclear how that utopia will function. 'Dyer categorises the experience offered by entertainment into five "utopian solutions",' suggesting that they are related to specific inadequacies, or problems, in society.[17] These utopian solutions do appear in the letters because fans identify them in the Star Trek text; the fans have an idea of the utopia they are aiming for – they see it on the television-screen every week. The five problems with their corresponding utopian solutions are as follows:[18]

Social Problem	Utopian Solution
1. Scarcity and the unequal distribution of wealth; poverty in society	Abundance and material equality
2. Exhaustion; work as a grind; pressures of life	Expressions of energy; work and play united
3. Dreariness and monotony	Intensity; excitement and drama
4. Manipulation; the feeling of being controlled: sex roles, advertising etc.	Transparency: open, spontaneous, honest communications and relationships

5. Fragmentation: job mobility, rehousing, legislation against community	Belonging to a community; communal interests, community activities

The first problem is touched upon in a letter by Danielle Ruddy, particularly the ideas of poverty and inequality. She acknowledges the contemporary social problems of today such as war, hunger and racism and hopes that 'one day *Star Trek* – a work of fiction – will become a reality.' Roddenberry's vision is very important to that reality; she says that he provided the world with 'a glimpse of the future', implying that it will happen, and that future utopia will be 'one where mankind didn't fight over land and money, where there was no hunger, and it didn't matter what color, race, or gender you were'.[19] Gerald Gurian goes one step further and writes about how *Star Trek* made a form of social contract with its audience as it played out its adventures of space travel in the future: 'By the 24th century, we were assured that Earth would have solved the devastating problems of mass poverty, hunger, and disease.' Not only was Gurian convinced by *Star Trek*'s 'promise', he believed that this 'overwhelmingly positive portrait of humanity' was a 'major factor in the global appeal' of the franchise.[20]

Expressions of work and play united in fan letters often describe how the *Star Trek* text directly contributes to the person's work day, how their affection for a particular character or series influences their attitude to work and how much enjoyment they get from it. In a letter I also examine in Chapter Nine with regard to *Star Trek*'s pedagogical applications, Mark Emanuel Mendoza describes his career as being very closely tied to *Star Trek: The Next Generation*. He studied to be 'exactly what *Star Trek* indeed is: a teacher'. In fact, he describes himself becoming a primary school teacher at the same time TNG 'was born'.[21] Mendoza relates how the lessons he learnt from the show helped him in the classroom as he transferred those lessons to the children. It appears work for Mendoza is a combination of his passion for the show and his passion for teaching kids. Shamira, a bellydancer from New York, writes about her first initiations into the *Star Trek* universe – watching the Orion slave girl dance in the pilot episode, 'The Cage' (1964). This inspired her to become a bellydancer and now she can live the dream of being part of *Star*

Trek by doing her job every day. She describes the series as 'a cosmic dance' painting a 'romantic and exciting design in the universe, in human thought, in [her] mind', and she says she was drawn to both Star Trek and bellydancing because they 'are fascinating, glamorous, and mysterious'.[22] Shamira's private life as a fan and her public life as a bellydancer feed off the energy she sees in the utopian future the series portrays. The character she first admired was the role model for a child wanting to become a professional dancer.

In the letter by Gerald Gurian previously discussed, issues over the 'dreariness' of life, as described in Richard Dyer's list of social problems, are addressed alongside his opinions on Star Trek's utopian future. Gurian believes that the series 'played a pivotal role in shaping and influencing' his 'character and basic understanding of right and wrong'. It was important to him that the original series was fun and provided 'exciting action entertainment'. This is key to Dyer's analysis of entertainment and utopia – that it was intense and exciting drama which could help take the viewers away from their ordinary lives and transport them to a place that was exciting and promising. Gurian believes this to be true of the series, and it was an important part of his viewing experience: 'Star Trek provided a bona fide cast of larger-than-life heroes espousing core values such as honesty, integrity, loyalty, bravery, compassion, self-sacrifice, and perseverance despite seemingly insurmountable obstacles.'[23] Gurian's statement about what the characters espoused also alludes to the fourth problem and solution proposed by Dyer: manipulation and transparency. Utopia is possible because the main Star Trek characters are seen as honest and compassionate, amongst other things, therefore helping to cure social problems such as racism, sexual discrimination, and prejudice: 'Mankind would no longer be divided by petty politics or racial prejudice.'

For Douglas Mayo, Star Trek's depiction of utopia gives him a place where he feels accepted and wanted. Being disabled has excluded him from some important social relationships in his life, how he relates to his family being the most significant. He sees Star Trek's future as a template for how he can build relationships today and a place where he will be able to have those important relationships tomorrow:

> Because of my [Cerebral Palsy], neither my parents nor my
> brothers knew to interact with me in any meaningful way,
> nor did they try ... [At school] one month ... I spotted a *Star
> Trek* book ... Here was a world through a story in a book that
> challenged humankind to rise above physical appearances,
> to work together as a team for a greater good, something
> I had wanted on a personal level all of my life ... Through
> repeats I watched every episode of *Star Trek*. I understood
> *Star Trek*'s vision for humankind to take hold, a place where
> I would be accepted regardless of my disabilities, and
> I desperately wanted it in my own life. *Star Trek* for me
> became more than television, it became my hope of a better
> life...[24]

Problems relating to his disability – acceptance, inclusion, work, daily life – are, in Mayo's words, addressed by the possibilities *Star Trek*'s utopian future offers; society will be more open and transparent, therefore utopia is assured.

The fifth pairing in Dyer's definition of utopia in entertainment will be addressed in the next chapter regarding community and communal interests. However, it is important to state here that most fan letters I have studied described the notion of community in a variety of ways: from very simplistic terms such as watching the series with the family to meeting fellow enthusiasts at college and remaining friends for life. Underscoring these communal relationships is the idea that *Star Trek* as a television show gave fans the opportunity to meet people and have fun that would not ordinarily have been open to them. Dan Harris says in his letter that he is 'grateful to *Star Trek*; besides being a great series, it is because of the show that I met my closest friend'. Some thirty-five years later, Harris and his friend still reminisce about how they met at college, measuring their time as friends by how many *Star Trek* movies have come out since 1968.[25]

Returning to a theme I touched upon earlier, the notion of *Star Trek*'s promise of utopia is a recurring component of fan letters. Jason Lighthall, like others, believes that *Star Trek* aims 'to teach morals and values' and it does this by having 'thousands of different species from different worlds who come together to try to better themselves as a civilisation, while trying to deal with social conflicts in the right way'.[26] For Lighthall, the fans have a big part to play in that mandate. For example, he actively sought to join a fan group, thus learning 'better communication skills' and 'to treat people with the utmost respect', and he believes them to be 'intelligent and sophisticated people who love to dream about what our future could be'.[27] As we have already seen, Gerald Gurian believes that *Star Trek* 'assured' its audience that social problems will be solved by the twenty-fourth century, which is a step beyond Lighthall's belief in the possibilities of human achievement. However, both Lighthall and Gurian's opinions differ from those of another fan, whose belief in the future remains firmly rooted within the fictional text of the series. Marco Di Lalla 'embraces' Roddenberry's 'ideas and visions', confessing that 'not a single day goes by without [him] wondering if, eventually, humanity will conquer all of its problems and difficulties', just like on *Star Trek*.[28] Di Lalla writes that he thinks of *Star Trek* 'as actually being the real fate reserved for our species', intimating that not only will society change and utopia be achieved, but that screen events will become reality.[29] A fair leap one might think, but with the series' attempts at basing the future on actual events and current technological developments, could some fans conclude anything different?

Throughout the fan letters there is an identifiable narrative progression which talks about *Star Trek* moving utopia from a burgeoning ideal to a realised reality. Some fans believe in the possibility of achieving utopia but recognise that there is a lot of work to be done if society is to be changed; other fans see that this change will occur, sooner rather than later, and that *Star Trek* has a part to play in initiating that change. Finally, there are some letters that talk of *Star Trek*'s utopia as if that were the ultimate goal, that somehow Roddenberry's vision is an accurate depiction of what the future will be like. This last form of narrative would seem to be heavily based on ideas that I looked at in Part One, namely how *Star Trek*'s future history is taken by some fans as being part of America's real future; the merging of the two in the text somehow influencing the audience's take on reality. However, it is important to bear in mind when examining the content of the letters that the overall trend corresponds to a particular narrative of 'changing for the better' I also identified within the *Star Trek* film texts. Fans recognise that work needs to be done to achieve utopia, just as the Puritans recognised that they had to change in order to establish Zion in the New World. Accounts of how personal change leads to a better life replicate many of the narrative tropes identified in self-help literature and self-improvement narratives and will therefore be discussed in Chapter Seven, yet I should reiterate here that *Star Trek*'s version of a utopia remains the fans' ultimate goal. It appears that achieving that goal can be made easier by trying to implement one of two things: personal change or social change.

The following letter highlights the delicate position *Star Trek* occupied in the late 1960s with regard to war in Vietnam and concepts of social change. Gregory Newman describes *Star Trek* as recognising 'our world of war, racial prejudice, and poverty' giving 'us hope of a future glorious world'.[30] Scholars such as H. Bruce Franklin have understood that it also tried to comment on a war that was rarely given coverage on television except for patriotic news reports. For Franklin, *Star Trek* 'parabolically displaced the Vietnam War in time and space', showing just how much America was being transformed by conflict.[31] These sorts of contemporary messages built into the original series are not lost on fans today; therefore they would not have been lost on those fans who watched the series for the first time, especially those fans who were directly affected by the war either through serving, getting wounded or losing loved ones. DeForest Kelly, Dr McCoy from the original series, when asked about the impact of *Star Trek* in the 1960s, identified the Vietnam veteran as someone who was especially open to the show's ethos: 'We struck a note, a chord, with the youth of this country and particularly those who came back from Vietnam.'[32]

Franklin has identified a shift in *Star Trek*'s attitude to the war similar to a shift seen in Newman's letter. Two episodes, 'The City on the Edge of Forever' (1967) and 'A Private Little War' (1968)[33] represent *Star Trek*'s belief that Vietnam 'was merely an unpleasant necessity on the way to the future'. Two later episodes, 'The Omega Glory' (1968) and 'Let That Be Your Last Battlefield' (1969),[34] 'openly call for a radical change of historic course, including an end to the Vietnam War and to the war at home'; both signify a change due to the 'desperation of the period'.[35] Newman's letter also recognises that war might have been needed, yet, instead of being found in a shift illustrated by Franklin's analysis, these two theories exist simultaneously because Newman does not see them as being different from one another but as a result of *Star Trek*'s faith in the future. The letter endorses Franklin in that the series was interested in both showing how the world could be different after war had ended and also how important the war was in American society at the time – perhaps war was the only way such a utopian future could be secured. When Newman says that while he and others 'were fighting and dying in Vietnam while prejudice, poverty, and drug wars raged around us, *Star Trek* kept alive a dream of a better world', it implies that *Star Trek*'s future was going to be the result of such extreme sacrifice; something worth fighting for. However, he also writes how *Star Trek* 'gives us hope of a future glorious world, a world of benevolent human beings of all races who work together with beings from other worlds to peacefully explore the vast universe with awe, courage, hope, love, and curiosity', implying that war solves nothing and the only way *Star Trek*'s future will become a reality is through a unification of peoples, regardless of race and cultural differences. After and despite the war, Newman writes that '*Star Trek* kept Vietnam veterans focused' on the possibility of peace, it helped them find the strength to continue applying its doctrine of universal peace even when they had returned home. This suggests that not only did his experience of the war return home with him – to be identified by the term 'veteran' – but also that the war on racism, drugs and poverty had become personal to him and universal to those veterans who shared his love of *Star Trek*.

Newman's opening statement – 'The year was 1966 and I was a black soldier in the U.S. Army' – reveals the highly volatile situation in which he was involved. In 1966, the US Secretary of Defense, Robert McNamara, drew up 'Project 100,000' which aimed at increasing manpower for the war by conscripting large numbers of the poor; this would also serve to help rebuild 'the fabric of black society' by 'curing' them of 'idleness, ignorance, and apathy'. Such a policy caused immeasurable distrust within the African-American community and they received little comfort from the fact that blacks were disproportionately represented in the officer corps and were more likely to serve and die in combat than their white comrades.[36] The war, it seemed, was not about fighting the enemy, but rather continuing to fight the kinds of overt racism that had confronted African Americans before they left for Southeast Asia. According to Tom Engelhardt, it was not only aspects of white racism that made their way to Vietnam but also the ideas that grew out of the Civil Rights and Black Power Movements. Furthermore, those ideas which found sympathetic ears in Vietnam returned home with black soldiers who joined militant organisations such as the Black Panthers because they felt that they still had fight left in them – that they would be the ones to lead an armed revolution in the streets.[37] However, Newman's letter emphasises that he saw a different outcome from his time in Vietnam. Rather than bringing home the 'revolution' with the gun, he saw that *Star Trek*'s view of the future could be achieved through adherence to the 'dream of a better world'; a sentiment that, according to him, many Vietnam veterans followed and 'focused on'. It would seem that Newman believes that direct action is not as important as the philosophy of unity and peace in which many fans – especially the veterans – should believe when there is 'trouble' and times are hard. A sentiment shared by fans in my next chapter.

6

HELP WHEN TIMES ARE HARD

COPING WITH TRAUMA THROUGH THE *STAR TREK* COMMUNITY

> 'How we deal with death is at least as important as
> how we deal with life, wouldn't you say?'
> *Kirk to Saavik,* Star Trek II: The Wrath of Khan

Community, according to Zygmunt Bauman, 'is a "warm" place, a cosy and comfortable place'.[1] Within a community, we are safe from the dangers of the outside world and are able to find common comfort with the people that share in it. 'In short, "community" stands for the kind of world which is not, regrettably, available to us,' even though it is the one thing we are always trying to achieve. One might say that *Star Trek*'s vision of utopia is equally as unavailable to its fans as is the notion of community. However, the letters in the previous chapter indicate that fans do put faith in the future and are prepared to work for it. Likewise, in this chapter, the concept of a *Star Trek* fan community is achievable. In their discussions of certain forms of trauma, fans are beginning to create a community through correspondence that in the short term they believe contributes to their individual rehabilitation. Sharing stories of trauma satisfies the most attractive tenant of community, what Bauman describes as counting on 'each other's good will'. In moments of sadness, he sees the possibility of relying on other people's good will as intrinsic to the fluid working of an established community: 'When we fall on hard times and we are genuinely in need, people won't ask us for collateral before deciding to bail us out of trouble.'[2] Indeed, the letters in this chapter indicate not only that some fans find comfort from telling their story or reading stories about other people's experiences, but also that *Star Trek* is seen as a supportive text that does not ask for anything in return. In effect, the 'community' is achievable so long as *Star Trek* continues to offer something to its fans.

Bauman's assertions over the implausibility of community are resoundingly supported by the political scientist Robert Putnam. In his monumental work *Bowling Alone: The Collapse and Revival of American Community* (2000), Putnam sees America as having become less community orientated and Americans more disconnected and isolated from society.[3] Where once Americans went bowling in organised leagues, part of a structured local community, within the last decade more and more Americans have been 'bowling alone' – symbolising the fragmentation of community life and lack of social connectedness.[4] Securing a democracy means having a 'strong and active civil society' where members of that society contribute to their local community; consequently, the creation of sound social networks is crucial to getting on in daily life.[5] Today, Putnam sees decline in almost every area of American community life: local politics, clubs, organisation membership, church groups, sport and social societies, parent-teacher associations. The number of people willing to get involved with these kinds of groups and actively participate in local affairs has grown significantly smaller. However, Putnam has recorded an increase in mass membership of national organisations, where 'the only act of membership consists of writing a check for dues.' This means that they may 'root for the same team' and 'share some of the same interests' but ultimately they are 'unaware of each other's existence'.[6] These new forms of grouping embody elements of the social connectedness that Putnam laments, but they cannot provide real community because the members do not interact or care for each other – unlike *Star Trek*, they do not get people talking.

If it is possible to describe the *Star Trek* fan letters as evidence for the existence of a community then the act of writing them and sending them to be published can equate to what Putnam calls 'writing a check for dues'. However, he believes that modern-day organisations cannot stand as communities because members do not care for each other. This is obviously not the case for *Star Trek* fans. We have already seen that they routinely stress how much they care for society and the future, and, as we will see in this chapter, they also show signs of sympathy and compassion toward fellow trauma sufferers. Instead, this characteristic would appear to follow what Robert Wuthnow describes as the rapid expansion of 'support groups' in American culture. The support group 'meets regularly and provides support or caring for those who participate in it'. The most familiar kind of group would be of the 'self-help' variety such as 'Alcoholics Anonymous' or 'Anger Management'.[7] The current trend for this new form of community searching is often criticised and lampooned in the media – one just has to watch an episode of *The Simpsons* or the film *Anger Management* (2003) to get an idea of its place in the national psyche – but, as a form of social capital, Putnam sees it as a positive development. However, Wuthnow does not believe the support group is effective in rebuilding communities: 'Some small groups merely provide occasions for individuals to focus on themselves in the presence of others ... We can imagine that [they] really substitute for families, neighbourhoods, and broader community attachments that may demand lifelong commitments, when, in fact, they do not.'[8] As with all new forms of social organisations, support groups do not 'play the same role as traditional civic associations'; hence, America continues to become a fragmented society.[9] The fan letters that talk about personal trauma share similar attributes with Wuthnow's description of support groups and can therefore be considered as evidence for a particular kind of community – one that emphasises individual, shared experience but without any civic association. However, fans that underline *Star Trek*'s influences on their renewed outlook for the future appear to be moving beyond self-interest and into the area of civic duty – to achieve personal happiness or a better future we have to work together to achieve it.[10]

One of the most prevalent forms of communal fan letter that can be found is what I call the 'Help When Times Are Hard' letter, one in which the sender has written about how much *Star Trek* helped them overcome very difficult social, emotional, and even physical obstacles in life. This type of letter communicates how fans use *Star Trek*'s message of peace and harmony as a source of communal hope and strength. What I intend to show is that *Star Trek* has always been seen as a form of support and counsel. Whether this development is part of wider social trends seen in American society, reflecting the increasing fragmentation and lack of any sense of community, is something that has already been considered in this chapter. That some fans see *Star Trek* as an important part of their lives is not in doubt; however, that fans should turn to it to seek comfort rather than their families, friends, or traditional forms of medical and psychological counselling is an important aspect of fandom that needs to be assessed. Ultimately, I suggest that all the letters I have collected and analysed are connected by a sense of mutual self-improvement and shared life experience. These facets of letter writing are representative of a fan community very much part of contemporary American culture.

When studying fans through their personal correspondence, it is perhaps too easy to attribute their confessions of being comforted by *Star Trek* to the connections between social and psychological conditions. Joli Jenson, in her work on fandom as pathology, describes how excessive fandom has been seen 'as a form of psychological compensation, an attempt to make up for all that modern life lacks'.[11] Fans are a potentially dangerous group of ostracised individuals who have nothing better to do than fantasise about their favourite TV show or star. Of course, this is a very narrow-minded view of cult fandom, and Jenson points that out. At the very least, fandom is a form of community discourse that not only offers support to individuals through interaction with each other and the focal text but also helps to maintain people's own personal relationships with family, friends, and individuals. Fandom does not make up for things that are lacking in our lives, because that would seem to imply that we are all lacking important social skills, making us all some form of cultural hermits. Instead, as I want to build upon in this chapter, fandom offers a sense of personal empowerment where investment in *Star Trek* provides the necessary tools to help cope with events in daily life. As Lawrence Grossberg states, being a fan of a particular text allows people 'to gain a certain amount of control over their affective life, which further enables them to invest in new forms of meaning, pleasure and identity in order to cope with new forms of pain, pessimism, frustration, alienation, terror and boredom'.[12] People have to deal with stressful events throughout their lives – whether they describe themselves as fans of something or not – and they all deal with them in their own different ways. Sharing their individual experiences through the letter format opens up their discourse to a community that does have one commonality: an acknowledgement of *Star Trek*'s supportive qualities.

It is interesting that Grossberg does not specifically mention death as something which fans learn to cope with by investing in the text – perhaps coping with pain and pessimism might include coping with bereavement. However, pain is a topic that Camille Bacon-Smith has looked at in connection with the *Star Trek* female fan audience in her seminal work *Enterprising Women: Television Fandom and the Creation of Popular Myth* (1992). In her research of fan writing, Bacon-Smith paid close attention to a form of literature known as 'hurt-comfort' fiction. This term describes stories where one hero suffers – most often physical pain but sometimes illness – and the other hero comforts them. According to Bacon-Smith, these stories 'say that one way of dealing with personal pain is to recognize the suffering of those we care about and return their attention and comfort'.[13] Even though these stories specifically refer to physical pain experienced by fictional characters, in some senses I would propose that Bacon-Smith's statement could also apply to letters regarding the pain of bereavement. Fans seem to recognise that pain and respond to it by consulting the *Star Trek* text and writing their feelings down on paper. This act in itself shares the pain; other fans read the letters, respond, and thereby reply by comforting the person who is suffering. Furthermore, Bacon-Smith goes on to describe how writing these kinds of stories was not primarily for fun but rather it 'fulfilled some of the deepest needs of community life'.[14]

Fans who were experiencing turmoil in their lives responded by writing stories which put their favourite characters (usually Kirk and Spock) into a situation where one of them suffered and the other comforted.[15] The literature was merely a symbol for the specific discourse of support that the fans were sharing. Often the fans would contact each other about the story just to talk about it before they wrote anything: 'Isolation continues to break down as new readers discuss [the] work. The writer even finds satisfaction in helping others when fans tell [them] that [their] story has affected them and offer stories of their own in turn.'[16] With regard to the letters I have gathered, Bacon-Smith's theories about 'hurt-comfort' fiction might possibly help us to understand why and how Star Trek fans turn to the text when they suffer a loss; how writing about that experience in the form of a letter will offer them some form of comfort. However, it is important to keep in mind that Bacon-Smith was examining a specific form of fan literature that had a specific readership and was almost entirely produced by women. The letters I examine have been written by all types of fans, all ages, both male and female, from those who never watched Star Trek before their trauma to those who dress up and take part in organised Star Trek fan activities. Therefore, I want to stress that Star Trek fan letter writing can be considered part of a larger social movement that not only acknowledges the series as an important factor in fans' affective lives but also recognises certain intrinsic cultural elements that all people share when dealing with bereavement.

Trauma is 'an enabling fiction, an explanatory tool for managing unquiet minds in an overwhelming world'. Kirby Farrell believes that trauma has this explanatory power because in some form or another 'people feel, or are prepared to feel ... as if they have been traumatized.'[17] Whether it is a clinical syndrome or a literary trope, trauma functions as a 'strategic fiction' that allows us to account for 'a world that seems threateningly out of control'.[18] In coping with death, injury or psychological damage, utilising a traumatic narrative helps to overcome the senselessness of the traumatising event and helps manage and motivate how we get on with our lives in a stressful modern society.[19] For Farrell, the act of talking about trauma and recounting its occurrence has some heroic meaning and as such it inspires the sufferer and their audience to make positive changes in their lives.[20] Both in this chapter and in Chapter Seven, sharing traumatic stories about how Star Trek helped people overcome stressful periods empowers the individual through a pattern of self-help narrative common in American society. As the American Jeremiad inspired the Puritan community to change and recreate utopia in the New World, Farrell sees their 'vision of traumatic violation' as having 'aroused in them a rage to start anew, with an astonishing indifference to hardship and death'.[21] In all the letters analysed, trauma, and its shared recollection, is a channel for self-improvement and community-building.

The following letter from Kenneth Westfall, a Vietnam veteran, continues to underscore the 'dream' of a Star Trek future analysed in Chapter Five, but his experience of Star Trek came after he had returned home from war. In this particular case, Star Trek was part of a rehabilitative process to recover from his wounds, both physical and mental:

> After serving nine months in Vietnam, I was wounded and sent back to the States. As a result of this wound, a plate now replaces a small area of my forehead, which led to a disability retirement from the service in May, 1968 ... Four more years went by, during which my opinion of mankind's future was, to say the least, very grim ... [When Star Trek and I finally met] it was as if an egotistical door of ignorance, tightly closed in my mind, was slowly pushed open and the onrush of thousands of dreams, possibilities, probabilities and theories, all mixed with hope, knocked it right off its hinges.[22]

Kenneth Westfall's letter deals with the more personally harrowing aspects of Vietnam, such as the injury and psychological trauma that affected thousands of veterans on their immediate return and many years following. Soldiers who fought and civilians who watched it unfold on television felt deeply traumatised in confronting their own mortality for the first time – conceding that America's self-image was not invincible. Vietnam, more than any other war, 'had demonstrated that the body politic could be dismembered'.[23] According to Fred Turner, the war had taught Americans that 'the ties that held them together as a nation, ties that many Americans had long taken for granted as permanent and strong, could be cut.'[24] Physical injuries such as those suffered by Kenneth Westfall epitomised and symbolised the pain America felt as a nation; however, Star Trek was his way of relieving and overcoming that pain:

'It was as if an egotistical door of ignorance, tightly closed in my mind, was slowly pushed open.' This letter is a result of Westfall's desire to finally exorcise the emotional trauma and feelings of guilt that had made him believe 'mankind's future was ... very grim'. Marita Sturken sees national and personal recollections of the war as being part of America's cultural memory and as such they serve 'important needs for catharsis and healing'.[25] His wish to recollect and retell such events is also one characteristic of a 'central dialectic of psychological trauma', which sits in opposition to the other, exemplified by the desire to forget or deny that those events had ever happened.[26] The fact that the second characteristic is overcome through Westfall's efforts to communicate his story to Gene Roddenberry (the letter was originally sent to Lincoln Enterprises)[27] validates fans' beliefs – and the argument I will be pursuing in the next chapter – that writing to *Star Trek* and communicating with fellow fans motivates them to achieve their goals in life through a particular form of self-help discourse.

The act of telling a personal story to help recover from physical and emotional trauma, making it 'part of a fully felt narrative',[28] is something which many *Star Trek* fans have attempted to do by either writing letters to their favourite actors or to fan magazines. This inclination to share their life experiences with others and relate how *Star Trek* has helped them is not limited to the war story I have discussed but also applies to letters that deal more personally with death, disability and illness. Families and individuals use *Star Trek* as a means to release their feelings and share in its recuperative qualities.

According to social psychologist Colleen Murray, 'death may be the last taboo issue in family science and family therapy,' and many individuals seem to deny the fact that death is an inevitable part of family life and all families will encounter the varied stresses that it can bring upon them.[29] However, *Star Trek*'s related ability to provide emotional relief to those who have recently experienced bereavement seems not only to help individuals to cope with the loss, but also appears to teach them a life lesson.[30] Virginia Walker's letter exemplifies a dual property which *Star Trek* possesses: After a sustained period of familial loss, where three close people unexpectedly died, the author recounts how she 'came back to life' when introduced to *Star Trek*. Once the period of mourning had ended, Star Trek taught her that life was too precious to waste on thinking about the past, and that 'the only thing we ever really have is the future.'[31] Such an epiphany is a common characteristic of letters sent by fans who have suffered traumatic events such as death and illness, yet often those fans had never watched Star Trek before they suffered their loss. Death and emotional distress, in the case of Virginia Walker, was a catalyst for her eventual introduction to the world of Star Trek; after watching several early episodes, the author went on to write about how her involvement with organising a fan club and many national conventions offered her a new perspective on life: 'Before I wore blinders ... maybe I've grown up.'[32] This intimates that Star Trek replicates, even replaces, the supportive role of the church, which has been commonly recognised as one of the 'positive factors' in emerging from mourning.[33] Creativity, the second recognised factor, appears also to be part of Star Trek's ability to help fans convalesce as the author describes how her 'field of interest is now virtually unlimited'.[34]

Spiritual development is a significant aspect of fan letters and many fans attribute their rehabilitation and conversion to Star Trek's 'baptism by television'. Susan Sackett likens their need to share such experiences with others to those newly converted to a religion who become 'its most fervent proselytes';[35] again, this helps them recover from their emotional and physical loss. Finding comparisons between Star Trek fandom and religion is not a new scholarly pursuit but such investigations do provide an interesting insight into the letters in this chapter. For William B. Tyrrell, Star Trek not only 'offers the comfort of religion' but for its fans it also represents a world where they belong, just as Virginia Walker found that she 'came back to life' when she was introduced to Star Trek.[36] For Michael Jindra, Star Trek 'does not have the thoroughgoing seriousness of established religions, but it is also not mere entertainment'. The combination and interplay of the two facets is a sign of its unique 'vitality'.[37]

It is this sort of 'vitality', linked with a supposed ability to aid in the memorialisation of deceased loved ones, which characterises fan letters and is exemplified in the letters written by both American and British audiences. Star Trek's effectiveness in the mourning process is perhaps not restricted to an American audience but rather emphasises the universality of its message. The following letters share similar themes, the most noticeable being the fact that those who were grieving watched episodes of Star Trek to help overcome their grief and to try to come to terms with their loss. Individually, the authors indicate that specific types of episodes helped with their own specific situations. Sandra Bunner, who lost her husband and son 'in a tragic accident', watches 'certain episodes', thereby 'bringing back special memories' of when they all watched them together.[38] The *Voyager* episode 'Imperfection' (2000) reminded Andrea Dearden of her father's long-term illness and death.[39] In another letter, 'heart-warming and emotional episodes of Star Trek: *Voyager*' helped Philip Arkinstall come to terms with the deaths of four close friends.[40] These examples express that if some fans need an emotional pick-me-up, they might perhaps turn to a more dramatic and 'heart-warming' episode, or if they need to be reminded or comforted then they might rewatch one or more episodes to recreate a special memory. These varied uses of Star Trek episodes can be attributed to the fact that Star Trek is such an open text, something I have explored in Chapter One, and that to a large extent it has become reality for some people who want to believe that it is true, or, as David Gerrold puts it, 'it represents a future we would like to make real.'[41] In fact, all of the letters I have discussed seem to question Daniel Bernardi's theory that Star Trek is a constrictive and absolute mega-text because the fans take different personal meanings from episodes, and often the emotions they feel when watching a specific episode change when they watch it a second or third time under less stressful circumstances.[42] The mega-text is therefore not fixed and authoritarian but rather flexible and receptive.

For Mark Bird, the episode 'Pen Pals' spoke to him at a particular time in his life. Being bullied at school and feeling isolated because his family kept moving meant that he could not settle into a stable environment during his teen years. Bird, who had not watched Star Trek before, recounts how he tuned in and watched, saying 'it captured my feelings at the time perfectly: a lone voice crying out into the void, desperate for someone to listen to it.' Not only did the episode appear to reflect how he was feeling, but it also inspired him to feel better: 'Then, out of the darkness, comes the sound of a single voice crying back ... When I found Star Trek I discovered there were many people who watched it and enjoyed it as much as I did.'[43] Star Trek represented an epiphany for Bird; he realised he was not alone and he could have friends, originally lacking in his life, by joining the Star Trek community and sharing how he felt with people who experienced similar emotions when watching the same episodes. In his letter, he describes how the physical act of looking for company in 'Pen Pals' inspired him to search out others; finally finding them at conventions and fan clubs who welcomed newcomers. His sense of belonging to a community is affirmed at the end of the letter when he, like many other writers of letters previously analysed, starts to imagine a possible future. In this future, 'humankind will evolve to the point where differences can be overcome and where society can rebuild itself, working collectively,' with the Star Trek community as a guide, 'to advance beyond the constraints of this world and expand to others'.[44]

The final letter written by Avril Storm Bourbon[45] indicates a strong bond shared between certain Star Trek fans, a bond characterised by playing Klingon at conventions and social gatherings:

> I have known and loved many friends I've met at conventions who also play Klingon, but the most Klingon of them all was my friend and 'Captain', Chuck. The man lived, breathed, and ate Klingdom; he knew *every* word to *every* [author's emphasis] Klingon song ever sung on *Trek*, and was totally devoted to Klingon fandom. Sadly, he was killed in a car accident in February '98, in a fierce El Niño rainstorm ... To honor him as a Klingon we would gather around [his coffin] and send him out with a Klingon Death Howl ... When our breaths were spent, our shoulders sagged with relief, like a weight had been lifted. We would always miss him, and remember him, but with joy ... When people make fun of Trekkers, especially those of us who run around cons dressed as Klingons, and call us geeks and nerds, I shrug it off. Because I know better. Everyone needs something to believe in, to carry on. Everyone needs somewhere to belong.[46]

Her grief felt over the death of a close friend who 'lived, breathed, and ate Klingdom' just as she does suggests a special sense of community that reacts in similar ways to death as would a family. Robert Habenstein has noted that 'death initiates significant responses from those survivors who in some way have personally or vicariously related to the deceased. Inevitably, the collectivities in which the dead person held membership also react.'[47] Therefore, the *Star Trek* collective that role-played with the deceased suffered just as much as his family; they chose to stay in character and mourn his death in a different way by performing the Klingon Death Howl first seen on a *Star Trek: The Next Generation* episode, 'Heart of Glory' (1988).[48]

Such use of *Star Trek* ritual can only be understood if we refer back to those critics who see it as a form of secular religion. Bourbon says that she did not care what people thought of her dressing up as a Klingon because it allowed her freedom within a community: 'everyone needs somewhere to belong,' and that place would be with others who lived Klingon. William Tyrrell sees such a declaration of devotion as a 'ritual cry to a world where [one] belongs, where [one] has it all together'.[49] If Bourbon and her friends then wish to live as Klingons – by the code laid out for them in certain episodes and fleshed out in licensed *Star Trek* literature – then she would also want to mourn death as a Klingon. The act of role-playing becomes less of a game but rather a way of life (or death).[50] Such a development raises some interesting questions: Does this renunciation of traditional religious belief and ritual indicate a breakdown in American society? Has the notion of a traditional spiritual community, often desired when death affects a group, given way to a reliance on fictional methods of emotional security that can be construed as superficial? Perhaps in a sense one might agree that *Star Trek* does pose a threat to traditional forms of communal bereavement and therefore endanger established methods of caring such as therapy and attending church because it ultimately relies on a select few writers and producers to decide what should be included in the *Star Trek* universe. Therefore, the desire to make entertaining television programmes dictates the ritual content exemplified by the Klingon Death Howl. Perhaps Robert Putnam in *Bowling Alone* would disagree with this 'alien' approach to remembering the dead, as it circumvents traditional customs by using television and mass media as the basis for collective mourning.[51] However, Robert Bellah's concept of a 'civil religion' would counteract those suppositions. He sees 'civil religion' as 'an understanding of the American experience in the light of ultimate and universal reality',[52] which is how Bourbon, Walker and all those who write about the death of a loved one see *Star Trek*'s vision of a better future (a future where the world lives in harmony) helping in their rehabilitation.

Star Trek, then, has taught those fans who turn to it in grief to cope with death not to be frightened or suspicious of it – even when death comes unexpectedly as in a car accident – but to use it as a form of personal strength. The community of fans to which Bird, Bourbon and Walker belong acts as a network of support where those lessons offered by *Star Trek*'s vision, and expressed by Klingon Death Howls, can be shared. Writing about their experiences allows those who are reading the letters access into the community, making it even larger. Scholars and social critics who lament America's demise as a nation of close communities would do well to consider how *Star Trek* fans cope with death through the examination and repeated watching of human and 'heart-warming' stories shown on television. If 'bereavement is complex, for it reaches to the heart of what it means to be human and what it means to have a relationship,'[53] then *Star Trek* fans would appear to have a sound understanding of the emotional and traumatic effects death has on the living, and the series would appear to have a humanising effect on its fans, teaching Americans the value of relationships and what will make them more human.

There is a sense that those fans who have written about their bereavement do so to find a voice. It is this voice that articulates the level of grief they are experiencing, which ordinarily they might find hard to share in public with their friends. With so many similar stories to share, the people who write these letters do so in an attempt to become part of a special community, one that offers support through a common dialogue based on the *Star Trek* fan experience. In the next chapter, we can see further development of a *Star Trek* fan community through letters pertaining to disability and illness. The discourse that these letters share is not only based on a need to communicate traumatic events, but also a common desire to 'get better' and improve.

7

THE PLEASURE OF THE TREK

CONFESSIONS OF SELF-IMPROVEMENT AND INDIVIDUALISM

> 'Like many of our people, they need something to believe in ... just like I did ... something larger than themselves ... something that will give their lives meaning.'
>
> *Worf to Gowron, 'Rightful Heir' (1993)*

In the previous two chapters we have seen how fans write about *Star Trek*'s utopian future and the possible communal effects it has on their daily lives. Notions of trauma and fan affection are bound up in a positive network of support where fans feed off both the series and the correspondence of other fans. In this chapter, I examine fan letters that share similarities with those previously discussed but also contain individual accounts of personal self-improvement. These letters recount how *Star Trek*, and even individual characters, provided inspiration for a personal change for the better. Such confessional narratives of self-improvement correspond to those narratives of self-help and success discussed in connection with the American Jeremiad and *Star Trek* in Part One.[1] With regard to the letters in this chapter, stories of self-made success, not necessarily financial, are retold as a form of personal healing. Improving one's character or way of life is seen as a real possibility thanks to the positive individualism of the series and is also an important step that has to be taken in order to achieve the utopia so celebrated in Chapter Five.

Before I continue with an analysis of the letters, I want to try and theorise why Star Trek is seen to be able to offer its fans such inspiration and guidance. Returning to a point I made earlier, Star Trek is an open text and can therefore accommodate multiple personal and distinctive beliefs and opinions. Fans read into the series what they desire based on a framework of utopian futurism and collective improvement. Beyond the actual confirmed text of the series, fans are able to live out their own personal fantasies, as we have seen in slash fiction, and therefore bring to the text multiple readings that help inspire their own daily lives. In a sense, Star Trek follows Roland Barthes' analysis of narrative in The Pleasure of the Text (1975). Barthes describes two kinds of text: the Text of Pleasure and the Text of Bliss. The first text is closed to the reader, an ideological text that is easily consumed where the pleasure comes from the 'comfortable practice of reading'.[2] The second text, the text of bliss, is open and does not resolve the ideological contradictions encountered in the first. It forces the reader to critically and 'actively engage with the text in the production of its meaning'.[3] Separately, these two definitions of a text contradict each other, and they are often used to differentiate between popular, mainstream culture and the radical avant-garde.[4] However, in this particular case, Star Trek combines the two by its definition as a product of popular culture and its categorisation as a radical text created in the 1960s in opposition to contemporary political, social and cultural trends. As we have seen, its fans view it both as a pleasurable text, one in which they can immerse themselves without conflict, and also one with which they can actively engage and use to improve their own lives and the lives of people in their own community. The 'pleasure of the Trek' appears to be twofold – fans both love to watch it and critically engage with it. Personal stories that confess such pleasure and bliss conform to a particular narrative of self-help.

Throughout the 1980s and 1990s, the television talk show became America's public voice; its audience members and guests are prepared to engage in often heated debate to reveal personal and private information that they believe will help them overcome particular problems in their lives – whether they be physical, emotional, or social. Like the fan letters I have examined, the forum provided by the talk show encourages the audience – at home or in the studio – to 'tell its own stories, to agree or disagree, confirm or contradict, confront or support the speaker, generating a polyphony or 'cacophony of narratives' on and beyond the small screen.[5] This 'cacophony of narratives' is a collection of confessions and personal revelations that both encourage and support fellow audience members; multiple self-help narratives contributing to the overall self-improvement ethos. Talk shows can provide an emotionally safe environment where people can divulge very delicate information, and gain support for doing so; in many cases this can be dangerous, as the physical set-up of the studio often leads to violent conflict and emotional distress.[6] Fan letters negate such obvious safety problems while still offering readers and writers the chance to read and share what fellow fans have gone through. However, the benefits of the talk show appear to continually outweigh the disadvantages of public violence and ridicule. The talk show and fan letter can offer the capacity to gain personal power over one's problems, what Joshua Gamson describes as breaking the 'monopoly on truth'. In writing about the process of 'coming out', Gamson talks about how personal testimony allows homosexuals to find self-empowerment. They reclaim truths taken from them in popular discourse and reiterate their own position within the contexts of their own sexuality.[7]

Disclosing is a form of power-play that characterises not only the process of coming out but also talk shows and the narrative form of the fan letter. 'The ability to confess publicly has become a sign of power and control'[8] that defines the letters I discuss in both this chapter and those preceding; in this case, the belief in helping oneself and changing for the better is inexorably linked to *Star Trek*'s inbuilt narrative of self-improvement. Where once confession or therapy was an enclosed and private process, akin to the Catholic act of confessing one's sins or consulting a qualified psychiatrist, confessing in the public sphere is now the American cultural norm, a reference to the therapy groups discussed in Chapter Six. According to Jon Dovey, openly discussing personal stories through intimate speaking, or in this case letter writing, 'is validated as part of the quest for psychic health, as part of our 'right' to selfhood'.[9] *Star*

Trek's text can be seen as the fans' map on this quest for selfhood since they often describe in their letters how characters and events inspire them to be better people and achieve personal happiness. Of course, it is dangerous to assume that the series really acts in this way – as we will see in some letters, fans do point out that Star Trek only pushes them to change, nothing more – therefore we must remember that as individuals these fans, like all people, have the potential to improve or change, whether they believe Star Trek is to be congratulated or not.

According to Fred Pelka, 'we live in a health chauvinist culture – a culture that often regards the disabled and ill as morally inferior to those who are able-bodied and healthy.'[10] For Hanley Kanar, this sentiment stands not only for America but also for the seemingly utopian future of Star Trek which, she maintains, 'still cannot envision a way to comfortably include individuals who have disabilities'.[11] Even some of those who have suffered immense physical pain and suffering, either through an accident or disability, fail to realise the damage they do to the disabled community by speaking out and saying they will 'find a cure!' Stereotypes of disabled people who cannot cope in the able-bodied world are further enforced thanks to 'celebrity cripples' such as Christopher Reeve who constantly pledged that he would fight his disability; such feelings, according to Kanar, make the disabled body into a prison from which people should escape rather than something of which they should be proud.[12] However, as we have seen with Douglas Mayo in Chapter Five, Star Trek did offer a vision of the future where his disability would be seen as normal: 'a place where I would be accepted regardless of my disabilities.' How can two such conflicting ideas about the same series exist, and is there a compromise? It may lie in the concept of a Star Trek community which offers forms of emotional support to those who feel ostracised or isolated from American society for some of the same reasons Kanar accurately describes in her article.

Star Trek has almost completely ignored the disabled community in its vision of the future and Kanar has convincingly analysed DS9's treatment of disability in the episode 'Melora' (1993). Leah Van de Berg has also examined how disability was encoded and stereotyped in the TNG episode 'Ethics' (1992).[13] What these analyses show is that Star Trek's vision is flawed due to its reliance on contemporary cultural stereotypes; I have offered my own analysis of how the series is tarnished by its use of American history and myth as a basis for its future. However, for Douglas Mayo to say that 'it became my hope of a better life,' the series must offer something that remains separate from such critical readings of its text. That something may well be the sense of community which I have previously discussed.

Mayo indicates that he might never have recovered from the effect his childhood had on his self-esteem, but after seeing a glimpse of a better future in a *Star Trek* novel he wanted to make a difference:

> In 1959, I was born prematurely with Cerebral Palsy (CP) affecting my entire right side. I was the second of eventually four boys, all close in age. As I grew older, I incorporated *Star Trek*'s hope and vision of what mankind can achieve as my own ... When I rose to become the president of my local union I had the opportunity to put a number of *Star Trek* life lessons to use: how to be a good leader, make a tough decision, make a difference, look for other options. These are all valuable lessons that can be found through a variety of sources, but for me *Star Trek* is where I looked for affirmation.[14]

Throughout his letter, Mayo describes how his life was changed by watching *Star Trek* and using Captain Kirk as an example of what he could achieve. On account of his own hard work, Mayo even recovered from a car accident that temporarily confined him to a chair, intense physical rehabilitation spurred on by the fact that James T. Kirk 'did not accept defeat'.[15] *Star Trek* did not dominate his life; one could suggest that his life was dominated by the desire to even the score with his brothers who did not try to relate to him as a child coping with CP. *Star Trek* was where he 'looked for affirmation' and, even though it might not have depicted disability in the future, it taught 'valuable lessons' in which Douglas Mayo truly believed. Despite neglecting a minority that feels outcast in American society, *Star Trek* still represents a positive mindset, which many of the minority use to help themselves. Importantly, people like Mayo are not wishing to be cured, thereby harming the image of disability as stipulated by Kanar; they are trying to integrate into society despite the pain and prejudice. *Star Trek* is not their blueprint but their inspiration. The following letter from a British fan conveys similar attitudes to the series:

> When my doctors and I found out that I had anorexia, I didn't really take it in – until I ended up in hospital and was given only a few days to live. During those few days I went into the television room and happened to see *Star Trek: Voyager*. After that, I never missed an episode for the whole year I was there. I like *ST:VOY* because Captain Janeway is such a strong character. She would do anything to get her crew and herself safely home. In a way, it was like that with me, I had to do anything to eat and stay alive. The battle against my illness wasn't easy. It was the hardest thing I've ever done. I have to thank Kate Mulgrew for being such an inspiring actress. *ST:VOY* showed me that I shouldn't just lie there and let myself die, and that I had to stop thinking people like me for the way I look instead of the person I am. I'm not saying that *ST:VOY* cured me straight away; that took a lot of work, and sometimes my illness still causes me stress. And I'm not saying that *Star Trek* rules my life, because I have a career as a hairstylist and make-up artist. It's just something I enjoy watching. People with anorexia need to find something which sends them in the right direction – and *Star Trek* did it for me![16]

For Nicola Corbett, watching Star Trek was not a guarantee for success, in fact she had never watched an episode before being in hospital had given her the opportunity to sit down and experience one. It is important to remember that watching Star Trek did not cure her anorexia, 'that took a lot of work', and all three letters I have looked at in this section point out that it was not a magic cure. What Star Trek did do for Nicola Corbett was to offer a sense of not being alone in suffering with her illness, that her anorexia was not going to beat her and that she 'shouldn't just lie there'. Captain Janeway was not only a role model, a figure of strong will and determination, but she was also like a friend who inspired confidence in the way Nicola Corbett felt about herself and persuaded her that she had to stop worrying about physical appearances. *Voyager* seems to have provided a form of aftercare that proved indispensable following a long period in hospital.

As she coped with such extreme illness, *Voyager* provided support and guidance just as a close friend or a form of counselling would: 'People with anorexia need to find something which sends them in the right direction – and *Star Trek* did it for me!' This intimates that, for those fans who feel isolated due to illness, recent bereavement, or disability, *Star Trek* provides social connectedness integral to the healing process, whether it be mental, physical, or a combination of the two. Robert Putnam states that, 'social connectedness is one of the most powerful determinants of our well-being.'[17] Since he believes that America has lost its sense of social connectedness, perhaps living within a fan community or even having a simple affiliation with a programme like *Star Trek* could help in the prevention of, or recovery from, illness. Nicola Corbett's letter comes from a British fan magazine; the following letter was written by an American and shares similar sentiments. Both Mayo's and the anonymous woman's next letter exemplify a national affinity with wellbeing that Putnam has researched in *Bowling Alone* and is something to which I will now turn:

> In March 1970, my husband died. Until July 1971, I was as a zombie (almost). In July 1971, I became ill and had to be hospitalized for three weeks. Of course, my doctor effected the physical recovery, but it was not until I started getting *involved* in *Star Trek*, that my mental outlook vastly improved. All my family will say I am crazy for making the statement, but *I* believe it to be true. When I started identifying with *Star Trek*, I started again to believe in the future of mankind … [author's emphasis][18]

Putnam sees 'bowling alone' as one of America's 'most serious public health challenges' because as more and more Americans become isolated and detached from local communities their health will deteriorate.[19] Such concern is corroborated by a substantial amount of statistical data that is printed in his book, all of which indicates a connection between poor health and lack of social capital or good health and strong social ties with families, friends, and clubs. One statistic, resulting from a survey taken over the past twenty years in America, reports that a lack of social capital can be dangerous: 'People who are socially disconnected are between two and five times more likely to die from all causes compared with matched individuals who have close ties with family, friends, and the community.'[20] With this statistic in mind, it is no wonder that those fans who see themselves as part of a *Star Trek* community, whether they organise conventions or only contribute letters to magazines, attribute such a large part of their improved health and mental outlook to the positive sensations they get from watching the show.

Jason Lighthall's letter, discussed in Chapter Five, describes how the characters on the series 'are able to deal with ... conflicts in a peaceful and diplomatic way' and by copying them he has 'begun to learn new ways of dealing with people and respecting them in a more mature and social manner'.[21] Far from taking an individual character such as Kirk or Janeway as his role model, Lighthall sees every character as contributing to his personal improvement. What is more, all fans appear to share similar learning experiences because they share one purpose: to help make Roddenberry's utopia a reality. Lighthall goes on to say 'most people who are *Star Trek* fans are also highly motivated, and are more likely to succeed in life because of that,' implying that being a fan sets himself and fellow enthusiasts apart from other people. This form of exceptionalism is a familiar trope in American culture, identified in the Puritan literature of the seventeenth century, and Lighthall's reference to a select group shows that he believes *Star Trek* fans are one of the few in America that can succeed in their mission. However, this mission of bringing about utopia is not a selfish one, as Lighthall verifies that 'we want to change our future so that we can improve our life and the lives of others'; like the American Jeremiad, Lighthall's letter confirms a message, a means, and a motive for personal change.

It is interesting to note that the letter stresses individual change within a supportive community: 'Being part of the *Star Trek* community has changed me.' Marco Di Lalla's letter also points to individual progress within the fan community. After surfing the Internet and finding fellow gaming enthusiasts, Di Lalla joined a *Star Trek* club that played role-playing games; as a result he has had 'the opportunity to write great stories and share them with other people across the world'.[22] By sending ideas back and forth, Di Lalla was able to get supportive feedback from other fans which he believes contributes to the pleasure he gets when watching and writing Star Trek stories. In his group, he can 'talk freely and openly about [Star Trek] without being teased, laughed at, or called a freak'. These are strong words, but it is obvious that Di Lalla feels threatened if he talks about his passion in public. The group to which he belongs gives him that safe place offered by the format of the talk show to express his individuality. This in turn has given him what he calls 'confidence, strength, and imagination'.[23]

These three qualities are replicated in other letters that depict personal achievement. Jeanna F. Gallo recounts how she started to write 'fanfic for the old paper "zines"' and then began to write scripts in an attempt to get them made into real episodes. Eventually one of her stories was made into the TNG episode 'Sub Rosa' (1994) and another inspired the *Voyager* episode 'Distant Origin' (1997). She found that, as well as getting support from the show, the producers helped her enormously in trying to write and submit ideas to the studio: 'They gave a lot of self-confidence and allowed a lifelong sci-fi fan and Trekker to make her tiny mark on *Trek* history'.[24]

Other fans talk about how particular actors have inspired them to be creative, not just in writing scripts, but also by helping to promote products. After buying and listening to Brent Spiner's album, *Ol' Yellow Eyes Is Back*, Kathy Warren writes in her letter how she felt so indebted to Spiner for bringing his character Data to life that she wanted to give something back to him. She decided to try and get the album played on local radio (without Spiner knowing) and promoted it to radio stations around the country so that listeners could hear the music she enjoyed. Taking time out of her own life, she strove to get the album played everywhere she could think of in an effort to boost sales. Warren believed her personal efforts were justifiable because Spiner, and *Star Trek*, gave her so much to enjoy in her life. Furthermore, as an entertaining text it encourages the sort of self-confidence and imagination she gained and used when promoting the album: 'It extols the highest virtues of humanity and shows us, in a very entertaining fashion, where we can use some serious improvement'.[25]

In comparison to the Vietnam veterans discussed in the previous two chapters, another veteran recounted a very different experience about the war and how *Star Trek* helped him in an interview discussed in Star Trek *Lives!* (1975). In this particular case, Captain Pierre D. Kirk recounted that he had survived countless Vietcong ambushes by using *Star Trek* dialogue to confuse the enemy and get his company to safety.[26] As the real Captain Kirk compared his situation with his fictional namesake, he discussed how the army had used aspects of command and leadership exemplified in *Star Trek* to train new cadets at Officer Training School. As well as recognising Kirk's shrewdness as a 'soldier' and 'diplomat', Pierre Kirk defended instances in the original series when the captain had to use force by stating that 'in a real military situation a leader cannot say, "You guys go and do that." He says, instead, "Follow me".'[27] Such was Pierre Kirk's passion for *Star Trek*, and particularly the character of Captain Kirk, he not only continued to believe in the series during combat in Vietnam but also used certain messages that he found useful and pertinent to him in order to survive quite dangerous and life-threatening scenarios. This example of popular culture intruding into real life was not uncommon in Vietnam and indicates how much the war had become intertwined with the American psyche. Perhaps the most renowned example of this is what doctors termed the 'John Wayne Syndrome'. Just as Pierre Kirk assimilated fictional media elements into his Vietnam experience, young soldiers diagnosed with 'John Wayne Syndrome' internalised the mythical ideals of 'superhuman military bravery, skill, and invulnerability to guilt and grief' personified by the iconic roles played by Wayne in Westerns and war films.[28] The image that he portrayed on-screen was taken by the soldiers as a model of how they should fight the war. Since John Wayne always came home a hero, they believed the same could happen to them. The brutal and traumatic experiences of Vietnam proved that war was not like the movies, however, and Wayne's heroic image was entirely fallible. Even the popular American children's toy, the Slinky, found its way into the combat zone; soldiers threw them into trees to 'act as makeshift radio antennas'.[29] What these cultural amalgamations intimate is that, under extreme pressure, people chose to put their faith in something they felt familiar with, something from their childhoods or personal to them, in order to cope.

The example of Pierre Kirk is also interesting as it relates to a phenomenon discussed in Richard Drinnon's book *Facing West: The*

Metaphysics of Indian-Hating and Empire-Building (1997); specifically how, as on the American frontier with the demonisation of Indians, the demonisation of the Vietcong in Vietnam made it easier for Americans to kill them.[30] The atrocity performed at My Lai in 1968, where over 200 civilians, including women and children, were murdered by an American company, exemplifies how American soldiers began to imagine Vietnam as 'Indian Country' where 'savages' lurked behind every tree.[31] For their part, the soldiers were like the European settlers who had landed in America to tame the wilderness; the Vietnamese were like the savages who had to be converted in order to be redeemed. Pierre Kirk did not necessarily act out a version of 'cowboys and Indians' with his company, but the use of *Star Trek* language and dialogue to interact with his comrades and presumably discuss the enemy suggests that combat had become for him some form of role play where he interacted in a manner akin to the fictional series.[32] Such role playing could be seen to have had a relatively positive effect on Kirk, who relieved the pressures of combat and command by connecting with his role model, Captain Kirk. However, Kirk's war-zone metamorphosis into the 'real' Captain Kirk from the Enterprise has a detrimental effect on the popular conviction that *Star Trek* had an anti-war subtext to its stories – something that H. Bruce Franklin has already assessed with regard to early episodes as seen in Chapter Five. The appropriation of *Star Trek* language and Kirk's strong character does indeed highlight how much fans report that they integrate the series into their lives, especially when they are experiencing a particularly stressful or daunting period. Pierre Kirk's vision of self-hood, in that particular situation, merged with the fictional universe of *Star Trek* resulting in a feeling of personal strength.

Perhaps we could assume that, without the support of the *Star Trek* episodes and the notions of community and familiarity they bring to individuals, those people who have written letters might not have recovered so quickly and gained new belief 'in the future of mankind'. William Shatner and Chip Walter have observed similar trends in their investigation of people who are working on the science of tomorrow; fans who have been inspired by *Star Trek*'s vision of the future to become scientists and engineers. Through interviews, the authors identified how some fans went to college to learn about the science they saw on the programme:

> NASA engineers, artificial intelligence gurus, particle
> physicists, biochemists. They probably all had the
> wonderment disease before they saw a single *Star Trek*
> episode or read a page of science fiction, but seeing it must
> have acted like a reverse inoculation, a booster shot, that
> made the disease worse.[33]

I want to underline here that part of the reason fans look to *Star Trek* when they feel the need for emotional or mental support, and therefore transform the series into a collaborative medium, can be ascribed to the developments I analysed in the first half of this book. *Star Trek* provides a sense of an ideal world amplified by the fictional history of the future; in order to escape from such traumatic life events described in this section or to change their lives for the better, fans seek to assimilate all that they believe *Star Trek* stands for. It is such a belief in the deeply rooted American trope of self-improvement that characterises *Star Trek* fandom and, as I have already examined in Part One, can also be found in its Puritan form in the American Jeremiad and the *Star Trek* feature films.

Of course, making out *Star Trek* to be a modern day (futuristic) version of the Ben Franklin/Horatio Alger myth of America is a damaging construct. A point alluded to by Hanley Kanar's argument that those wishing to find a cure for disability help to perpetuate stereotypes of disabled Americans and the disability pride movement. Therefore, I want to finally stress the important role fans play in their own forms of self-improvement, not forgetting the gratitude felt for doctors, friends, and family; they are not inhibited by their affection for the series. Sharing their experiences in letters emphasises how much they want to communicate their feelings to other fans and is characteristic of a distinctive form of fan discourse.

III

FANS
ON FILM

EXPLORATIONS OF
FUTURE HISTORY
AND *STAR TREK* FAN CULTURE

'She has an illusion and you have reality. May you find
your way as pleasant.'
The Keeper to Pike, on Vina's choice to stay with the
Talosians, 'The Cage' (1964)

'Surely you realise that *Star Trek* is just a TV show?'
'So was *Brideshead Revisited!*'
'You're angry so I'm going to ignore that!'
Frasier to Noel, 'Star Mitzvah', Frasier (2002)

In this last section of case studies, I look at how fans interact
with the Star Trek series through a concern for the fictional text
and what steps they take to help legitimise it for themselves as an
alternative way of life. In Chapter Eight, I examine fan letters that
address the latest series, Enterprise, and how it represents a return
to traditional American and Star Trek notions of exploration and
utopia. Chapter Nine is devoted to an analysis of the science fiction
fan film Galaxy Quest and the positive portrayal of Star Trek fans
realising their individual potential within a supportive community.
Together, these chapters define the Star Trek fan as both a provider of
analytical comment (able to contribute to a specific debate centred
on the Enterprise series) and subject of critical analysis (through the
representation of the fan on the movie screen).

Fan audiences have been, and will always be, able to offer their
own opinions on the object of their affection and, of course, the Star
Trek audience is no different. Henry Jenkins describes audiences as
'active, critically aware and discriminating' and for the purposes of
this final section I want to look in closer detail at those fans of Star
Trek who could be described as 'critically aware and discriminating'.[1]
By this I mean that Star Trek fans are able to recognise certain flaws
and characteristics of a particular series that perhaps work against or
counter the original ethos that Gene Roddenberry wanted to achieve
when creating Star Trek. In the case of Enterprise, many fans are aware
of how awkwardly the overtly American opening title sequence
sits in relation to Star Trek's vision of global equality and humanity
working together without national prejudice. Fans' reactions to this
new development will thus be the focus of Chapter Eight. The Star
Trek franchise is well known for its history of fan/text interaction;

its survival was supposedly guaranteed by an enthusiastic letter campaign targeted at the studio, even though it was organised by Roddenberry himself.[2] As Jenkins has observed, 'Star Trek fans were, from the start, an activist audience, lobbying to keep the series on the air and later advocating specific changes in the programme content, the better to reflect its own agendas.'[3] Therefore, Star Trek has a tradition of fan/text interaction that goes beyond simple expressions of affection to include interpretation, debate and, at times, conflict. What is more, these modes of interaction between the fans and the text are largely based on a detailed awareness of how the series has developed, evolved and, most importantly, how the fictional future history of the show inter-links with real history. The series' visions of the future became the talking point between fans who immersed themselves in the minutiae of Star Trek's taxonomic narrative history described in Chapter One. Nancy Baym's analysis of soap fandom can help us to understand the reciprocity between Star Trek fans and the detailed narrative. She maintains that 'fans share knowledge of the show's history [through online debates and correspondence], in part, because the genre demands it. Any soap has broadcast more material than any single fan can remember.'[4] In the case of Star Trek, remembering the thousands of characters, plot points, and historical entries gives fans a certain level of esteem within the community.[5] This intertextuality becomes significant when a new episode, or indeed a new series like Enterprise, contests specified historical events within the fictional timeline. As we will see in Chapter Eight, sometimes fans contest the relationship between reality and Star Trek's conception of the future. At other times, as we will see in Chapter Nine, the fans' capacity to remember and have faith in the fictional narrative helps them to achieve new levels of self-improvement that were perhaps not open to them within mainstream society.

Issues over the validity of the Star Trek canon, expressed through fan letters published in specialist magazines and on the Internet, are not a new occurrence. What I want to stress is that fans are interested in making sure that their canon is not damaged or affected by the actions of the producers and writers of new episodes, or perhaps even by the opinions of some cultural critics who openly dislike Enterprise. The kinds of issues and debates surrounding Enterprise's opening titles are ones that have been thrashed out and discussed by fans of other popular media products. For example, Star Wars fans are no strangers to intense debate as they try and defend their appropriation of George Lucas' strictly rigid fictional narrative canon. Often friendly in nature, these debates revolve around notions of story accuracy and characterisation.[6] However, in one particular case, regarding the new character Jar Jar Binks, conflict arose over whether Lucas was right to include such a 'childish' and childlike main character. The fans' hatred of the new addition to the canon was a 'tactic aimed at preserving the fans' "good" object of Star Wars as "serious" and "culturally significant".'[7] For fans of Star Trek, this type of concern for seriousness and cultural significance is an important part of their correspondence relating to Enterprise and their depiction as an audience in the movie Galaxy Quest.

8

POLES
APART

FUTURE TIME, *DEEP SPACE NINE* AND *ENTERPRISE*'S 'FAITH OF THE HEART'

'The game wouldn't be worth playing if we knew what
was going to happen.'
Sisko to wormhole alien, 'Emissary' (1993)

'It's been a long road / Getting from there to here.'
Enterprise *theme, 'Where My Heart Will Take Me' (2001)*

In this chapter, I examine further Star Trek's faith in the future by
comparing two of its most dissimilar series: Deep Space Nine (DS9)
and Enterprise.[1] DS9 is set in the twenty-fourth century; Enterprise
takes the year 2151 as its starting point. Both series have distinctive
views of how humanity deals with conflict, life in space, diplomacy,
exploration and our faith in the future. All of these qualities are
represented in opposite ways. DS9 shows a more flawed and
uncertain approach to our future progress in space; as if the future
is undetermined and the human journey is far from complete. On
the other hand, Enterprise's optimistic and, I would say, innocent
prediction of humanity's first steps beyond the solar system arises
because the history of the future is already 'set in stone'. Specifically,
much of Star Trek's future history previously recorded in past series
prevents Enterprise from covering new ground and expanding
upon the voyage; it cannot deviate or change a narrative past that

has literally happened already. Through an analysis of episodes in both series and *Enterprise*'s contentious opening title sequence, this case study reveals how they deal with history and humanity's future in space; how they have understood *Star Trek*'s central utopian principle whilst also trying to examine how we interact with each other in the present. I must stress that both series embody *Star Trek*'s paradoxical view of a bright future based on a history that does not exist in the present. However, since much of *Star Trek*'s popularity is based on its catalogued historical narrative through which its fans live out their own fantasies, the dangers of reflecting back on time are obviated through a process of self-selection. Fans realise that much of this history is distorted so they can either choose to ignore it or assimilate it into their own imagination of the future.

I

The universe in which *Deep Space Nine* is set is an ambiguous one in comparison with the universes of previous *Star Trek* series. The writers and producers stressed that the characters were to be fallible, have obvious faults and, most important of all, would face complex situations in space that no longer have easy answers.[2] Its premise was suggested by Paramount executives as being: 'Rather than a "Wagon Train to the Stars", a "Rifleman" in space'.[3] The look and feel of the show would prove to be far darker and more serious than its contemporary *The Next Generation*. For example, being set on a space station meant that if any exploring was to be done then the unknown would have to come to them. This confined setting implied that there would be more chance for character development. They would be allowed to grow as the stories they were involved in became more complicated and less resolvable in a single weekly episode. Chris Gregory argues that 'DS9 concentrates more on the growth the characters experience as a result of the unfolding narratives of the series itself' rather than their individual actions in separate and varied storylines.[4] For Gregory, DS9 bears a striking resemblance to a soap opera since it incorporates narrative structures very similar to those used in soap television such as complicated and involved character back-stories and interwoven story arcs, plus the highly developed historical narrative I discussed in Chapters One and Two:

The stories are linked by continuing 'soap opera'-type
subplots such as Bashir's ineffectual attempts to romance
Jadzia, Sisko's difficulties with his adolescent son, Jake, and
Odo's continual pursuit of Quark. It is emphasised that *DS9*
is a multicultural community in which there will be less focus
on the 'military' life of Starfleet as seen on *TNG*'s Enterprise,
and in which relationships between characters will be less
bound by their rank and position.[5]

In Karin Blair's article 'Star Trek Old and New: From the Alien
Embodied to the Alien Imagined' (1997), she distinguishes between
the older, better-known series and DS9 in order to evaluate the shift
that has taken place from Star Trek's outward exploration of society
to a more inward-looking approach. DS9, in her opinion, tends to
examine individual identities and personal relationships more than
past series, which were concerned with an expansion of humanity
on the final frontier. Blair recognised that Star Trek returned to the
enclosed space of the individual and how that individual interacts
with others, rather than continuing with outward exploration;
American society as a whole needed to look inwards to examine the
state of the nation as it drew near the end of the millennium and the
dawn of a new global community:

Having reached a certain limit in outward exploration, we
must come to know ourselves as collaborators in the making
of our own networks and identities, which requires closure
as well as openness, moral feeling and human decency as
well as pragmatism, expansiveness and intelligent curiosity.
Above all perhaps an acceptance of ambiguity is needed;
values can give warmth as well as clarity.[6]

From these examinations of DS9, one can identify that the theme of
ambiguity was an important part of the series' ongoing narrative;
as this chapter's introductory quotation from the 1993 series pilot
episode states. Therefore, all that was previously assumed from
other Star Trek series would be irrelevant. Even the ever-present
optimism of Star Trek was not guaranteed, since humanity was going
to be tested on the frontier space station and some of the main
characters were going to be found wanting. In terms of closure, the

series finished without giving the audience all the answers; the crew did not stay together, so fans were uncertain if they would see these characters again in a movie like the four which followed the end of *The Next Generation*.

In the final episode, 'What You Leave Behind' (1999), long-standing relationships come to an end and new beginnings form. Characters who have been friends for seven years such as Bashir and O'Brien have to say farewell as their careers and partners take precedence. Bashir finally becomes involved with the conjoined host Dax after several years of failed attempts at seduction. Chief O'Brien decides to leave the station and return to Earth with his family so that he can teach at Starfleet Academy. Colonel Kira, who originally despised the presence of the Federation and wanted more autonomy for her planet Bajor, becomes commander of the station after Captain Sisko departs. Her partner, the shape-shifting Odo, decides to return and live with his people, once at war with the Federation, to teach them that humans do not pose a threat to their freedom or territory. Worf leaves the station to be Federation Ambassador to the Klingon Empire. The Ferengi bartender Quark remains on board the station to continue his clandestine money-making schemes. Most significant of all, Jake Sisko and Kasidy Yates are left behind as Benjamin Sisko begins a journey of self-discovery as the Emissary for the celestial Prophets of Bajor. These non-corporeal beings act as protectors for the Bajorans, and Sisko is their representative. After the war with the Dominion finished, Sisko believed his job was done, yet, the Prophets told him that his mission had only just begun. For the first time in a *Star Trek* series, the main character, the captain, leaves his crew and family to fulfil another destiny. His whereabouts are unknown and it is unclear whether he will return. At the end of the episode, Jake and Kira look out into space unsure of what Ben Sisko is doing or if he will ever return. This ambiguous ending illustrates the nature of DS9's entire series and is indicative of its manipulation of the *Star Trek* mythos. Besides Worf, who continues to appear in TNG movies, every DS9 character has an open-ended future within the *Trek* universe.

Such uncertainty gives fans a chance to make it up for themselves, so that they can experience more – there are no plans for any follow-up movies, so fans have to develop their favourite characters in their own ways. One example of this is in the new series of novels that has been published following the season finale. These imagine how the station survived after the war and how Jake, Kasidy and the rest of the crew have coped with the loss of Captain Sisko.[7] However, the stories are not part of the *Star Trek* canon, therefore the events that take place in them are not legitimate within the future history. As I pointed out in Chapter One, everything that appears in the television series or on the movie screen is deemed as official within the fictional *Star Trek* universe. Literature such as the technical manuals and fact files produced under license to Paramount are also seen as canonical because they expand upon material aired on-screen and are used as points of reference for further episodes and movies. However, the novels and fan literature are not seen as canonical because the stories they tell have not 'happened', they have not taken place on-screen and are therefore unofficial. Some are produced as officially licensed books by Paramount 'who has decreed that anything that's televised as *Star Trek* is "Star Trek fact", whereas anything that's printed is "Star Trek fiction".'[8] This means the future of DS9 is still as undefined as it was after the final episode.

The overall ethos of DS9's final episode focuses on *having faith in the future* even though the characters have no idea what is going to happen to them. Sisko tells his wife Kasidy that they may not be together for a long time but when he returns it might seem as if he were only gone a day. That is the nature of the Prophets who do not live in human linear time but rather live outside of time and can therefore deliver Sisko back to Kasidy before he had even left. Without the concept of linear time, the Prophets do not understand history and do not understand humanity's preoccupation with memory, remembering and eulogising the past. When Sisko says to the Prophet Sarah (his mother) that his time as Emissary is nearly at an end she responds, 'Your journey's end lies not before you but behind you,' and he finally realises his position as religious messenger for the Prophets: his time on the station was only the beginning. This lack of a concluding narrative for the Sisko character is representative of the series' failure to bring adequate closure to many of its ongoing stories. For many fans, this offers an opportunity to imagine what might be next. However, for those who are aware of the detailed yet fictional history of the Federation,

Enterprise does not provide this opportunity because it is playing out the history of the Federation as it should have happened – as it is meant to happen in order to reach the time of TNG, DS9, and *Voyager*. Star Trek's historical confinement is something which needs explaining so that we can comprehend *Enterprise*'s turn to the past.

II

Star Trek is recall performed as prediction. It disguises the past, repackaging it in the future. In other words, future prognostication literally becomes a thing of the past. We have already seen the future. We have seen the future prescribed, inscribed, and etched into our memory on *Star Trek*. We know how it will all turn out.[9]

The defining premise of *Enterprise* is the pioneer spirit, space exploration at its most rudimentary level, not much advanced from today. It charts the history of Roddenberry's future, where fan favourites such as the transporter and warp drive are in their infancy. *Enterprise* provides definitive fan interaction and appreciation because it caters to their fascination with Star Trek continuity and the franchise's penchant for describing the history of the future. The first few episodes exemplify this development by concentrating on key events in Star Trek lore. The pilot episode 'Broken Bow' (2001), for example, reveals new secrets behind the birth of Starfleet and recounts how the Vulcans opposed humanity's first steps toward the final frontier. 'The Andorian Incident' (2001) expands upon this trend by concentrating on the Andorian species first seen in the original series, but not regularly used in more recent episodes, and builds up a whole new social and cultural history around their characters. What these stories are actually doing is called 'retconning', an 'abbreviated term for the act of retroactively adjusting continuity', and 'is a long-established staple in the world of comics, where characters' origins are forever being raked over, fleshed out and sometimes adjusted for perceived "newer" audiences'.[10] In other words, *Enterprise* is using retcons (an insertion into the fictional narrative chronology) as a means to construct the future history that both fascinates and compels the more serious fans. For those less concerned with the intricacies of Star Trek history, the message exhibited in DVD and video advertising signals the franchise's retrospective narrative agenda: over a picture of the new ship's Captain, Jonathan Archer, reads the tagline, 'MEET KIRK'S CHILDHOOD HERO'. It seems that the future is far closer than we think.

This pull towards the past has increased exponentially since the terrorist atrocities in New York, so much so that film-makers are reportedly having to go further back in time to rediscover the 'youth of mankind' in the classical world of Greek and Arthurian legend.[11] *Smallville: Superman the Early Years* (2001–), an American teen action drama about Superman's life at high school, highlights this trend episodically by creating a totally new Superman for the new millennium. Instead of seeing him in his familiar costume taking on super-criminals in Metropolis, the audience gets to see how he developed his powers and learnt to cope with girlfriends, school and teen angst before leaving the familial innocence of farm life in Kansas. The regression from the city back to the countryside attests to the major impact September 11 had on the American psyche; nothing could have prevented those planes crashing into the World Trade Center and therefore the future looks more terrifying and insecure than ever before. Perhaps returning to the innocence of the past, seeing Clark Kent grow up to become Superman, reassures people that there may yet be hope to come from this 'post-millennial confusion'. What is more, being set in the present affirms that this Superman is not just a comic-book hero from the 1940s or a camp crusader from the 1970s, but a living presence who shares in America's current cultural and social dilemma.

According to Donna Minkowitz, '*Enterprise* was birthed before September 11, but it seems tailor-made for this time of alien-hating and macho heroism.' Her main reason is that it gives *Star Trek* 'a convenient excuse for turning back the galactic clock on race and gender', which Minkowitz sees as the two main failures of the new series.[12] With regard to race, *Enterprise* supposedly champions white supremacism with its harsh depiction of the Vulcans as dominators who stand in the way of human creativity. In terms of gender, *Enterprise*'s world is chauvinistic because only two of the main crew are female: T'Pol's only role is to stand in the background and warn the captain about his actions; Hoshi resembles Lt Uhura – she steps in to hail Starfleet and be mollycoddled by her male crewmates on away-missions. These criticisms of *Star Trek*'s treatment of race and gender are not new; they were often aimed at Gene Roddenberry and the original series and are the subject of many academic works. However, Minkowitz believes that following the progress seen in TNG, DS9 and especially *Voyager*, these developments are a step backward in science fiction broadcasting. Consequently, *Enterprise* not only returns to the narrative history of the Federation, it also replicates the inconsistent history of the original series, where Roddenberry's liberal humanist ethos was continually offset by conservative representations of race and his own stereotypical views on how women should dress in the future.

The opening titles on *Enterprise* were a departure for a *Star Trek* series, as they were the first to be accompanied by a song: Diane Warren's 'Where My Heart Will Take Me', sung by Russell Watson. For Minkowitz, this new addition to *Star Trek* convention is just as regressive as previous incarnations with its 'boasts about resisting alien domination'.[13] To some extent, this observation is correct; however, I believe that the opening titles embody more than just a xenophobic reaction to the international community. The scenes from human history depicting the evolution of spaceflight and humanity's passion for exploration locate *Enterprise*, and therefore *Star Trek*, within a very specific tradition of American exceptionalism:

Enterprise **Title Sequence Visuals:**[14]

A Kon-Tiki crossing the Pacific Ocean;
HMS Enterprise and nameplate;
Auguste and Jean Piccard, High Altitude Balloonists;
Charles Lindbergh and The Spirit of St Louis, 1927;
Space Shuttle Enterprise, unveiled by the *Star Trek* cast in 1976;
Amelia Earhart;
The Wright Brothers at Kitty Hawk, NC, 1903;
NASA Explorer Submarine;
The Bell X-1 and Chuck Yeager, 1947;
Alan Shepard and Apollo 14, 1971;
John Glenn aboard Space Shuttle Discovery, 1998;
Dr. Robert H. Goddard, Rocket Pioneer;
Apollo 11 Moon Landing, 1969;

Sojourner, the robotic Mars rover, 1997;
International Space Station;
Lunar Orbiter, 2039;
The Phoenix's first test run, 2063;
NX 01 Enterprise, 2151.

It is this tradition that perhaps accounts for Enterprise's turn to the past at a time of American uncertainty. When the nation feels threatened, deprived, or isolated, American society requires an affirmation of its role within the larger global community. This role is depicted in the title sequence as being a leader in the development of spaceflight and a pioneer in the technological advancement of human civilisation, but it is not restricted to the fictional history of Star Trek. America saw its mission to land on the Moon and beat the Soviets in the space race as an extension of its mission to bring freedom to the world. The rhetoric of exceptionalism is part of America's self-appointed mission and has its roots in the exploration and settling of the American continent first initiated by the God-fearing Pilgrim Fathers.

Star Trek's appropriation of what appears to be an overtly American version of history seen in the opening title sequence indicates that it is trying to ground its vision of the future in a mythic retelling of the past. Celebrating American achievements at sea, in the air and in space appears to be part of a process of 'reinterpretation' or 'revisioning' of history which Sarah Neely describes as a 'retrovision'. A 'retrovision is a "vision into or of the past" and implies an act of possessing the ability to read the past, in the way that one would possess a prophetic vision'.[15] For Deborah Cartmell and I. Q. Hunter, retrovisions are 'makeovers of history', and I apply the term to Enterprise here since it is trying to refashion Star Trek's universal history by making it part of a very specific American mythic history.[16] Overall, the retrovisioning of Star Trek history is an appealing component of America's return to its exceptional past. Deborah L. Madsen believes 'exceptionalism has always offered a mythological refuge from the chaos of history and the uncertainty of life ... it was the legacy of the Old World for the New.' Enterprise offers an American society unsure of the future the very same refuge through a revisioning of a celebratory past. Furthermore, as Madsen believes that 'exceptionalism is now the legacy of the United States for us all,'[17] *Enterprise*'s future also appears to be the only one that we as a global community can achieve because it has eliminated all vestiges of humanity's international achievements and replaced them with images of America's attempts at exploring space.

The ethos of both the title sequence and the pilot episode, 'Broken Bow', is to *have faith in the past* because the past is reassuringly comforting compared to the political and social upheavals at the beginning of the twenty-first century. *Enterprise*'s 'faith of the heart' as described in the title song persuades the audience that *Star Trek*'s future is going to be a reality; the exceptionalism personified by America's aviation achievements in the credits proves that the future will be a bright one. Such optimism, however, can only come if you have faith in the past, celebrate American success and ultimately rely on America 'getting' you 'from there to here'. The optimism of *Star Trek*'s utopian future is still present but in a rather conservative and backward-looking form. DS9's faith in the future is clearly focused on what is unknown, unseen and uncontrollable. *Enterprise* seems to be saying that, at the turn of the century, just three years after DS9 ended, such uncertainty will not bring us any closer to *Star Trek*'s future; rather a predestined confidence will help us achieve utopia. As a result, the vast future history of the *Star Trek* universe diminishes as all of humanity's accomplishments and desires are confined within the exceptional rhetoric of a mythical American history. *Enterprise*'s narrative can go no further than its forebears and likewise its prognosis for the future is foreshortened.

III

From my analysis of fan letters relating to *Enterprise*, I would suggest that the constrictiveness of *Star Trek*'s exceptional future history is offset through the fans' engagement with the televisual text. Fans, particularly British fans, are well aware of the potentially isolating and offensive effects of the overtly American *Enterprise* opening titles. In a letter printed in the *Radio Times* one British viewer writes:

> **The montage of historical film in the opening credits of *Enterprise* presents a narrow view of the development of space travel, with no sign of the first space travellers**

– male, female or canine – who are presumably of the wrong
nationality to be celebrated. I seem to remember that Ensign
Chekov used to have something to say about such matters.[18]

The viewer is clearly trying to point out that the Star Trek canon
is at risk of overlooking its international elements – the famous
Russian ensign to name just one – and that its historical source is
beginning to be restricted to an American version of future history.
The viewer appears not to agree with Star Trek's isolationist U-turn
and points out that Enterprise is looking back on a very nationalistic
and masculine version of events.

In this next letter, entitled 'Yanks for the Memory' and sent to the
UK Star Trek Magazine, one fan tries to express his concerns about the
Enterprise credits in an openly comedic fashion by pretending to be
Vladimir Putin, yet it still shows just how much fans pay attention
to their favourite show:

Have you noticed that the opening credits show lovely
images of Mankind's achievements, or should I say American
achievements? It seems that they are the only ones that
do anything according to Enterprise. I think we should have
seen maybe the first man in space (Yuri Gagarin), the first
man-made object in space (Sputnik), the first space station
(Mir) and let's not forget also that we Russians did heaps of
other cool things in space way before Mr. Armstrong went on
his little trip! What would Chekov say about the above being
missed out?[19]

This letter shows signs of sarcasm that hides a deeper concern over
Enterprise's lack of international history. The fan actually tries to list
his own version of images to counteract those used in the credits,
also assuming a Russian identity in which to do it. Positioning
himself alongside Chekov in Star Trek's mythos draws attention to
the imbalance whilst also legitimising his own argument by using
official canon. Ironically, the fan's faith in Star Trek's future history,
signified through his use of Chekov's nationality and status as
original cast member, overcomes the retrovisioning of the space
race and Enterprise's faith in the American past. Fan criticism of the

titles is not restricted to an international arena. Americans too have written to point out the nationalist overtones of the spaceflight imagery. In a letter taken from an *Enterprise* forum on the Internet, one US fan indicates an appreciation of the musical accompaniment but again calls attention to the lack of Russian input:

> lov [sic] the theme. Have been almost moved to tears by the eimagery [sic] until...

> Only American space-craft are used in the titles. Oh I know there is the British Frigate (no USA at that time) and the International Space Station (mostly US), but what about Sputnik, Gargarin? [sic] Especially if you consider how repetitive and hackneyed some of those NASA shots are (that Apollo stage burning up in Earth's atmosphere, puleaze! [sic] Is that an invitation to litter or what?).[20]

In reality, *Star Trek*'s shift to the right in its latest series is not as significant as the fans' (both American and British) desire to critically engage with the important issues that pervade society in the early part of a new century. They are very aware of *Star Trek*'s pluralist tradition and important standing in American popular culture; they are determined not to let it become the product of a narrow-minded return to the past, but rather the symbol of a refreshingly open-ended future.

For those who decide what actually goes into the canon by means of the episodes and official literature, the future history and the realities of the universe around it offer an exciting way of telling important stories. Such stories have captured imaginations and taught several generations the valuable life-lessons from past, present, and future society. As seen in Part Two, the official *Star Trek* canon has become the fans' template for life, a blueprint for how society should and could be. In *Enterprise*, future history acts as an emblematic and implicit marker for past and present American cultural values; far removed from the more ambiguous characteristics of DS9's vision of the future. Because of this limitation, Daniel Bernardi has theorised that the fans' canon is vulnerable to contamination from the same social issues that tarnish America's own literary and historical canon.[21]

Nevertheless, perhaps the fact that there is a divide between the fans' own interpretation of the text and what appears on-screen allows *Star Trek* to escape being totally affected by the same ideological problems America suffers. Furthermore, as my analysis of DS9 has shown, not all *Star Trek* series celebrate American history as does *Enterprise*. DS9 is itself a serious attempt at criticising the human reliance on history as an outline for the future. Fans can and do criticise the fictional reality provided by *Star Trek*, thereby creating strong individual identities and negating the dangers of a naturalising and ultimately over-powering historical narrative.

9

'OH MY GOD, IT'S REAL!'

CROSSING THE FRONTIERS OF *STAR TREK* FANDOM IN *GALAXY QUEST*

'Can you talk to people in space on those?'
Jason Nesmith questions the usefulness of his prop communicator, Galaxy Quest *(1999)*

'And you people ... you're all astronauts on some kind of ... star trek?'
Zefram Cochrane to Commander Riker, Star Trek: First Contact *(1996)*

Star Trek is one of the world's most popular television series and its audience's affective investment, in terms of depth and duration, has arguably surpassed that of any other US show. Through a case study of the science fiction comedy 'spoof' *Galaxy Quest* (inspired by the Star Trek phenomenon), I argue in this chapter that Star Trek fans are revealed as part of a supportive community within the American cultural mainstream.[1] Crossing between narrative reality and the fictional reality in which the fans engross themselves, the renowned SF series is a major subject of the film. Its fans are portrayed as functional agents who both watch and enjoy the show and are rewarded for their devotion by being incorporated into the very narrative that feeds their passion for the series. Indeed, I want to emphasise that *Galaxy Quest* achieves two objectives as a science fiction movie. Firstly, it replicates images of space as the final frontier, affirming concepts of the American Western and the ideology of American exceptionalism through popular culture (as of course does the Star Trek series). Secondly, and more importantly, it portrays fans of such popular culture as strong and competent individuals who are part of a supportive and culturally integrated group. This is in contrast to some media stereotypes which portray fans as members of an insular community of 'geeks' and 'nerds' who avoid contact with a perceived normal society. By way of joining these two objectives, I focus on the film's exploration of the frontier concept through the transgression of personal boundaries. For example, in many instances the figure of the fan (both alien and human) is motivated and empowered through an act of individual achievement reinforced by a devotion to their object of affection – the Galaxy Quest TV show. This demonstration of cult fan behaviour is a refreshingly original presentation of Star Trek fans since it underlines just how important notions of self improvement are to the science fiction community and the Star Trek narrative.

Initially, I want to draw attention to the visual and narrative connections between Galaxy Quest and Star Trek. From these comedic references, we can identify the film's attempts at creating a frontier narrative where space and space travel are seen as redeeming features. The main characters are initially tested on this final frontier and are found wanting because they do not believe in its reality. The heroic figure of the ship's commander is representative of the fictional figure of the cowboy, familiar to the Western genre, and he plays an active role in convincing his crew that space travel and extraterrestrial life are a reality. Following on from this examination of the film's narrative, I highlight how Galaxy Quest directly portrays Star Trek fandom as a positive social pursuit.[2] Using the show as a template for life, Star Trek fans (and Galaxy Quest fans) feel that they are able to improve themselves. However, it is only after accepting the frontier of space as a reality, the next step toward the future of humanity, that the crew in the film are able to complete their mission and achieve a level of self-confidence that had been previously unavailable to them. Galaxy Quest, and therefore Star Trek, appears to only acknowledge the American vision of the frontier – a place of individual achievement – meaning the characters are being assimilated into what we already know to be an exclusive and overpowering ideology. Nevertheless, through an examination of *Star Trek* fan letters, I show how both American and international fans avoid such cultural assimilation and instead tend to concentrate on the series' humanist and universal philosophical messages as their means of self-improvement.

I

Twenty years after the original *Galaxy Quest* TV series was cancelled, its stars continue to make convention appearances and earn a living by opening shopping malls and signing autographs. Just as *Star Trek*'s original series was cancelled after three years, the cast of *Galaxy Quest* have found themselves unemployed and typecast, unable to break away from the characters they played and hated. Jason Nesmith, who played the hero Commander Peter Quincy Taggert, is reviled by his fellow actors because he has proven to be the most popular with fans and has not missed a chance to make his own publicity deals without them. It was often rumoured that *Star Trek*'s William Shatner did not get on with his fellow actors because of professional differences and opinions regarding scripts, screen time and personal attitude. Rather light-heartedly, Shatner responded to Taggert's character by saying: 'Certainly I don't know what Tim Allen was doing. He seemed to be the head of a group of actors and for the life of me I was trying to understand who he was imitating!'[3] In his and many of the original cast's autobiographies, this issue is discussed and their feelings have been made public. Shatner has long ago apologised for his behaviour during the production of *Star Trek*; however, Nichelle Nichols admits in her autobiography that: 'Even now, I'm not so sure he is convinced or really understands how we felt or what we suffered.'[4] *Galaxy Quest* creates this same dynamic to acknowledge the original series but also to create tension that can be resolved as the actors are forced to assume their roles for real and work with each other to save the day. It is while Nesmith is trying to broker a deal for himself, excluding the rest of the cast, that he is enlisted by the real aliens called Thermians to assume command of his old ship and help them defeat their enemy Saris. As the story develops, Nesmith begins to realise that this is a 'real' situation and that the Thermians have copied everything from the *Galaxy Quest* TV show in order to defend themselves from Saris and his army. After returning to recruit his crew – Gwen Demarco as Lieutenant Tawny Madison and Alexander Dane as Dr Lazarus to name just two – the once-fictional ship NSEA Protector is literally brought to life to defend Thermia and recreate the action-adventure series called *Galaxy Quest*.

The actors who play the main characters Nesmith, Demarco and Dane – Tim Allen, Sigourney Weaver, Alan Rickman – bring certain filmic intertexts to the roles they play. In *Galaxy Quest*, Dane is supposed to be an out-of-work Shakespearean actor who prefers the stage to routine convention appearances. Rickman plays the role with a knowing arrogance balanced with a stereotypical British accent to emphasise the character's attitude to the job. His theatrical Englishness also alludes to the English actor Patrick Stewart who plays Captain Picard. Weaver of course is predominately known for her role as Ellen Ripley in *Alien* (1979) and its sequels. In *Galaxy Quest*, her character purposely appears to be the antithesis of Ripley, therefore increasing the role's comedic value: Demarco is vain, air-headed and overtly sexualised; Ripley is tough, independent, and smart. Tim Allen's star persona is partly linked to his 'bluff machismo' from the sitcom *Home Improvement* (1991–1999) but more importantly it is positioned alongside notions of the frontier and space thanks to him voicing the character of Buzz Lightyear in *Toy Story* (1995) and *Toy Story 2* (1999). The tension between Buzz the astronaut and Tom Hanks's Woody the cowboy represents what Paul Wells calls a recognition 'that the frontier is no longer about an implied communality or consensuality in pursuit of the way west, or the conquering of the universe, but the management of identity and purpose' in a fragmented world. In terms of *Galaxy Quest* then, Allen as Hollywood star, Nesmith as TV star and Taggert as fictional hero are roles inherently tied up with Allen's previous role of Buzz, which in itself was a role characterised by the fictional space ranger toy and real-life astronaut dichotomy.[5]

The Thermians refer to the episodes as 'historical documents' and believe that all of the characters, situations and technology aired on-screen are real; they live by the teachings of *Galaxy Quest*. This mirrors the situation with *Star Trek*, where many fans try to recreate costumes, props and even mannerisms so as to be exactly like their favourite character. In many cases, those who dress as Klingons have even tried to adapt their social lives to the rituals and customs Klingon characters perform on-screen. Peter Chvany has examined the activities of the Klingon fan community on the Internet and asserts that they have become 'American ethnics'; a community of people whose investment in convention performances and the fictional history of the Klingon culture 'gives way to belief in their reality, to conviction, to "identity"'.[6]

The similarities between *Star Trek* and *Galaxy Quest* do not end there. Many of the props, gadgets, technology, aliens, and language used in the film pay homage to the original series. For example, the 'NSEA' designation of the Protector is a homophone of the prefix 'NC' used in ship numbering in *Star Trek*. The desert planet scene where Nesmith has to fight a giant CGI rock monster is a tribute to William Shatner's idea for the finale to *Star Trek V: The Final Frontier* (1989). Shatner wanted rock monsters to attack Captain Kirk whilst he was stranded on a planet and trying to get back to his ship. However, after one experimental monster suit and a hefty sum of money, it was considered too expensive and unrealistic so Shatner had to make do without the monsters.[7] One *Galaxy Quest* fan website even creates a franchise back-story for the film; borrowing the front covers of some famous *Star Trek* publications and inserting characters and images from the movie, the website imagines a world where *Galaxy Quest* is *Star Trek*.[8] These few examples show how the writers and director of *Galaxy Quest* managed to weave textual and extra-textual references into the narrative that catered for fans of *Star Trek* who have the inside knowledge to recognise them. The movie appears to be aiming at two target audiences: the comedy film audience and the *Star Trek* fanbase.

As a frontier narrative, *Galaxy Quest* recycles the myth of the American hero, the captain of the ship being the one that the Thermians call upon to help them. Just as Robert Jewett and John Shelton Lawrence have analysed this phenomenon in *The American Monomyth* (1977), Michael Coyne notes that the American Western as a film genre revolved around 'either a community, essentially a social construct, or an odyssey'.[9] Most Westerns actually combined these two tropes, having a lone cowboy figure enter a community to save it from ruthless cattle herders or gangs of thugs, then continue on his own lonely quest never to be seen again. The comedy ¡Three Amigos! (1986) parodies this tendency in Westerns by having three out-of-work actors revive their cowboy movie roles to help save a Mexican village. Believing that they only have to show up and perform a few tricks, the actors suddenly realise, as do the crew in Galaxy Quest, that this performance is actually for real and that their lives are as much at stake as those of the vulnerable villagers.[10] Richard Slotkin has recognised science fiction's, and indeed Star Trek's, debt to the Western and stated that the series projects 'a myth of historical progress similar to that in the progressive Westerns and "empire" movies of the 30s and 40s'. In Galaxy Quest, Nesmith as Commander Taggert is the Thermians' only hope – through the combination of individual action and cast teamwork he can save them from Saris. For Slotkin, 'the tale of individual action [by the cowboy] is presented as the key to a world-historical (or cosmic-historical) struggle between darkness and light,'[11] therefore Nesmith's role as Taggert is crucial for the Thermians' survival and his own redemption as a failing TV star. However, instead of returning to a life of solitude like the eponymous hero in Shane (1953), continuing to attend conventions and scratch a living for himself, Nesmith and the whole crew get a new series on television.

It is clear that Taggert is modelled on the character of Captain Kirk and Nesmith on the real-life persona of William Shatner, therefore his position as catalyst is very important. Taggert enables both the aliens and the fans to have faith in their own actions and in so doing allows them to become intrinsic 'actors' in the 'plot' to save Thermia. When pioneers were on the American frontier, all they had to live by was their ability to adapt to the terrain. Indian techniques were most often used because they were their only means of survival – they had to adapt. Often this would turn the pioneer into what Frederick Jackson Turner termed 'a new product', because he had dropped the old ways of the Europe he had left behind and become like the Indian.[12] This 'new man' would go on to expand across the western frontier, bringing with him the civilisation he knew back home. Galaxy Quest is repeating this transformation on the frontier of space and like Star Trek it is emphasising that the celestial frontier is a positive medium for the evolution of humanity. The belief that the future of humanity lies in the stars is not new; it is central to the aesthetic, scientific, and political movement referred to as Astrofuturism. According to De Witt Douglas Kilgore, Astrofuturism 'posits the space frontier as a site of renewal, a place where we can resolve the domestic and global battles that have paralyzed our progress on earth. It thus mirrors and codifies the tensions that characterize America's dream of its future.'[13] Such was America's fascination with space being the next frontier to be colonised, NASA spokesmen continually campaigned for more money by using American pioneers and explorers such as Lewis and Clark as examples of American creativity and ingenuity.[14] The ideology that drove the exploration of the American frontier was to be the model with which Astrofuturists could plan their next assault on space.

As well as acting like the cowboy hero and saving the Thermians, Nesmith plays an essential part in trying to convince his fellow actors that *Galaxy Quest* is real and that all of the narrative elements that made up the original scripts have been recreated by the Thermians. Nesmith asks his crew if they would like to see the ship, as they are still not convinced that their trip into orbit was real. As the crew enters a lift onboard the Thermians' spaceport they are unaware that they are about to see the Protector in full view. The glass lift travels down the length of the spaceport giving the whole crew a chance to see the ship, which gleams white in the darkness of space as floodlights and work crews bounce off its hull. Just as in *Star Trek: The Motion Picture* (1979) where the Enterprise is being prepared for departure in dry-dock, the Protector awaits its famous command crew and the Thermians watch in awe as the launch time approaches. Alexander Dane, who played Dr Lazarus in the original TV show, stares at the ship and gasps, 'Oh my God, it's real!' and in so doing confirms to himself, the crew, and the audience that *Galaxy Quest* has become reality. It is as if the seriousness and validity of the situation is not confirmed until the ship is visually identified. Compare this to the aforementioned scene in *The Motion Picture* and we get an idea of how important the visual identification of the ship is to these two movies. Both the Protector and the Enterprise confirm to the characters that things are real, in one case that the Thermians are telling the truth and in the other that the Enterprise has returned after being absent from our screens since 1969.

Vivian Sobchack has described the Star Trek movies as a nostalgic and historical series. The scene where Kirk sees his old ship for the first time is particularly exemplary of the film's nostalgic turn to the past:

> The 'futurism' of the *Star Trek* films is nostalgically backward-looking to earlier versions of the future – perhaps best dramatized in *Star Trek: The Motion Picture* when Kirk (and the film) nostalgically gazes at the refitted but still familiar (and now technologically old-fashioned) starship *Enterprise* for what seemed to some less nostalgic spectators an interminable length of overreverent screen time.[15]

Galaxy Quest's version of this does call attention to the nostalgia felt for the original TV show and the intimation in Dane's voice as he expresses his disbelief does suggest that he is as reverent as perhaps Kirk might have been in Star Trek. However, this scene in *Galaxy Quest* does not have the same meaning as it does in The Motion Picture. The crew are made up of actors and have no experience with the reality of space flight; conversely, Kirk's life was the starship Enterprise and so his reverence for its form and rebirth in the dry-dock alludes to something rather more emotional and deeply felt. Daniel Bernardi has described how sensually this scene is played out, with soft music and glowing lights, Kirk's face reveals his affection for his old ship rather like that shown toward a woman. Both he and Scotty admire the ship for so long that it becomes voyeuristic in nature: 'Like the representations of women in Hollywood cinema, the Enterprise is a feminized figure eliciting scopic desire.'[16] In quite a crucial way, the ship in Star Trek belies its reality since it becomes an object of male obsession and female eroticism; something that perhaps Kirk and Scott cannot obtain. Christine Wertheim has similarly argued that a scene in Star Trek: First Contact also reflects an overtly sexual veneration of spaceflight. She sees Commander Riker's and Lt. Commander LaForge's fascination for the Phoenix (the first vessel to fly at warp speed) as a primal sexual encounter: 'Cooing over this artefact, touching in it awe like two little boys wanking a giant collective member'.[17] Perhaps in this case actually touching the ship gives them a sense of reality. In Galaxy Quest, a similar scene only serves to prove to the crew that they are living out reality and that ideas of fantasy are irrelevant; there are no sexual overtones.

No matter how these scenes have been analysed – the psychoanalytical approach to *First Contact* totally misinterprets what the actual scene was trying to promote – I feel that they all have similar effects on the fan audience. Both the *Star Trek* and *Galaxy Quest* scenes visually confirm the reality of the ships, therefore providing proof that the narrative has some basis in fact. For the Thermians, this fictional narrative has always been real to them, yet, for Nesmith and his crew, it is only a recent revelation. For the fan audience, the *Star Trek* scene was a cinematic reality that confirmed their affection for the series. Such a concentration on the visualisation of *Star Trek*'s fictional reality contributes to the fans' personal investment in the narrative and the overall 'mega-text' of the franchise. As maintained by Piers Britton and Simon Barker, 'realism prevails in the design' of series such as *Star Trek* because it is 'essentially escapist; suspension of disbelief is crucial'.[18] Therefore, the visual fascination for the details of the Enterprise and Protector enables the audience and Nesmith's crew to achieve that crucial suspension of disbelief making the narrative all the more real. In 1976, before the new Enterprise was unveiled by its captain to movie audiences, fans' personal investment in the franchise was at an all-time high as they managed to convince NASA to name the first space shuttle after the famous starship. An intense letter campaign, supported by George Takei (Sulu from the original series), convinced officials that its new space programme should follow the futuristic example set by *Star Trek*.[19] In this instance of fan devotion, reality was directly affected by fiction, the 'mega-text' would from then on always include the test vehicle Enterprise as the first space-faring vessel to bear the name.[20] This moment in America's history of space exploration has become entwined with *Star Trek*'s vision of the future – fiction influencing fact influencing fiction.

II

Using the *Galaxy Quest* episodes to rebuild their society, the Thermians copy everything to the last detail, even down to the favourite meals of the main characters. Such enthusiasm for the series came about because Thermia was almost destroyed by Saris. In order to survive, they used the messages and examples seen in *Galaxy Quest*. They literally became new people, changed, through desire for survival, into individuals that live by the teachings of Taggert and his crew. The Thermian leader, Mathesar, recounts when asked about the historical documents:

> Yes, for the past hundred years our society had fallen into disarray. Our goals, our values had become scattered, but since the transmission we have modelled every aspect of our society from your example, and it has saved us ... your courage, and teamwork, and friendship through adversity. In fact all you see around you has been taken from the lessons garnered from the historical documents.

The harshness of the final frontier of space forced the Thermians into changing the structure of their society so that they could survive; in effect, they crossed the frontier of their own personal boundaries as well as the frontier of space. The documents were seen as the best examples of how to survive on this new and violent border. Being fans of the series, their need for a stable reality called for the assimilation of a fictional narrative with which they were already familiar. Life on Thermia was enriched by their passion for a series which emphasised individual achievement and social betterment through helping alien life across the galaxy, and Taggert was a hero they could rely upon; his ethos was fundamental to the rebuilding of a stable, organised, and productive society. As I have previously suggested, the archetype of the 'self-made man' has been an integral part of the American myth of success and self-improvement. Indeed, some fan letters closely mirror self-help literature as they describe *Star Trek*'s role as catalyst for their own personal progress. In the film, this idea runs concurrently with the astrofuturist premise that the frontier is a place of renewal; both notions of improvement and rebirth characterise the Thermian and fan attitude to the *Galaxy Quest* TV show and its main characters. As an aside, the film's use and the Thermians' mastery of technology also imply 'individual power and toughness', something which Rupert Wilkinson describes as 'servo-assisted virility', meaning the individual's mastery over the machine.[21] Cult fans are being positively portrayed by the aforementioned dichotomy which contrasts profoundly with images of the *Star Trek* fan so routinely mocked on shows such as *Saturday Night Live* and caricatured by the 'Comic Book Guy' in *The Simpsons*.

Human fans of *Galaxy Quest* are also vindicated in the belief that it is real. As Taggert and Madison are trying to stop the self-destruct system set off by Saris, they contact Brandon, a convention attendee and committed fan, using the hand-held communicator. Taggert had accidentally swapped his with Brandon's at a convention but did not notice because he had lost his temper and told Brandon to stop believing *Galaxy Quest* was real. When they reach him he is sitting making a model of the Protector in his bedroom, surrounded by posters, figures, books and drawings from the *Galaxy Quest* series, yet he is seemingly unperturbed that his toy communicator is flashing and calling out to him from space. Taggert asks Brandon to help them find the self-destruct room, knowing that he would be the best-equipped person to ask, but Brandon reminds him that *Galaxy Quest* is not real because he had said so at the convention. Taggert desperately shouts, 'It's real!' Brandon ecstatically replies, 'I knew, I knew it!' His whole belief system is seemingly affirmed in one short moment. Just as the crew confronted the ship and realised *Galaxy Quest* was a reality, Brandon's epiphany is equally significant to the film. Both he and his friends had always maintained that the show was real, so their hobby was to collect and learn all that could be learnt about the ship and its technology. Taggert's plea for help was their reward for such devotion. Working online, along with three friends, Brandon is able to guide Taggert and Madison to the right room and help them stop the ship from exploding. As they do this, Brandon also tells Taggert about the secret 'Omega 13' weapon; something which many fans believe to be a mechanism for going back in time. This is only Internet speculation, however, because *Galaxy Quest* was cancelled before the secret of 'Omega 13' could be revealed. This information will become invaluable at the end of the film as Taggert has to activate the 'Omega 13' to go back thirteen seconds in time and stop Saris from shooting him and his crew.

The actions of Brandon and his friends are crucial to the resolution of the film and to the success of Taggert's mission to save the Thermians. Without their 'nerdy' pursuit, Taggert would not have been able to stop the ship from exploding. In the scenes described above, Brandon's world is quickly legitimised as he helps Taggert. His parents are seen to be worried that he spends too much time locked in his room making models and not playing outside with his friends. It is his (and his friends') inside knowledge gained by spending so many hours locked away that saves the Thermians; their hobby is proven to be worthwhile. Even more importantly, it is when Taggert calls on him and confirms that Brandon's 'world' – his room – is real that Brandon takes on a new active persona. He becomes useful in ways that his parents would not have thought possible. He crosses between the lines of fiction and reality and at the same time changes from being an introverted boy to an energetic doer – a new man – who puts his acquired knowledge to good practical use.[22] The fictional frontier of Galaxy Quest has positively changed Brandon's character into someone who is valuable to the community, an individual who can help the community with their problems. Mathesar had said that Thermia had copied the crew's 'courage, and teamwork, and friendship through adversity' in order to survive extermination; somewhat differently, Brandon had achieved the same things in order to help the Thermians.

The theory of social representations might help illustrate the significance of the 'historical documents' to the Thermians and fans in Galaxy Quest and, likewise perhaps, certain episodes to fans of Star Trek.[23] 'Social representations,' according to Martha Augoustinos and Iain Walker, 'refer to the stock of common knowledge and information which people share ... they are comprised of both conceptual and pictorial elements. Through these, members of a society are able to construct social reality.'[24] The original episodes of Galaxy Quest formed both an ideological and visual template for how the Thermians could rebuild their society and how Brandon could become 'a new man'. For Serge Moscovici, social representations 'are cognitive systems with a logic and language of their own' and, like the documents the Thermians and fans employed, 'they do not represent simply "opinions about", "images of" or "attitudes towards" but "theories" or "branches of knowledge" in their own right, for the discovery and organisation of reality.'[25] Therefore, on a purely cognitive level, the Galaxy Quest TV show represents a reality for the social construction of their world. Social psychology in this respect suggests that fans of media texts, as portrayed in the movie, take the episodes as signifiers of reality. Their reality becomes the fictional narrative depicted on-screen and in return that futuristic text becomes the world in which they live. For some fans of *Star Trek*, the line between fiction and reality is often blurred when they act, dress and live as their favourite character. This is not to say that they believe *Star Trek* is real, as the Thermians do of *Galaxy Quest*, but using the theory of social representations does draw attention to the fans who articulate through writing letters that the series plays an important role in their lives.

I want now to return to these letters written by *Star Trek* fans because, even though *Galaxy Quest* does portray media fans as positive contributors to society, it is only when that society conforms to a certain American ideal that they become empowered. Historically, attitudes toward self-improvement and the frontier have consistently been focused on a very exclusive part of American society. They have excluded groups that do not agree with the way that a white, Anglo, male society has viewed American progress. For example, Native Americans were excluded from America's vision of the new frontier because they were obstacles to the supposed advancement of civilisation. In letters that express *Star Trek* fans' appreciation for the series, the frontier of space and ideas of self-improvement are discussed but the focus remains on a very international and diverse vision that maintains space is there for everyone to explore and anyone can change their life for the better. Both American and British fans voice similar opinions about *Star Trek*, as do the Thermians and fans about *Galaxy Quest*, but these opinions are devoid of the so-called 'mega-text' that looms large over the fictional narrative of both TV series. It is actually those fans who try to live the narrative – the people who dress and act Klingon examined by Heather Joseph-Witham or Peter Chvany – who have become the image of *Star Trek* fandom and are therefore stereotyped as introverted people isolated from society. The letters here indicate that fans of cult media texts are able to separate fiction from reality, unlike those in the film, and can focus on the philosophical message of *Star Trek* rather than its obvious narrative.

In a letter published in the edited collection entitled *Trekkers*,[26] Mark Emanuel Mendoza articulates how watching *Star Trek* inspired him to become a teacher. Not only does he thank Gene Roddenberry for this motivating nudge along his career path, he also states how he tries to use the characters and episodes as moral guidelines when he teaches young people. He believes that the positive and moral messages that Roddenberry encoded into the stories are helpful in teaching children about life and its many pitfalls:

> *Star Trek* is not really science fiction. It takes place in space and there are Klingons and Gorn to deal with, but I fervently believe that *Star Trek* is *LIFE*. The virtues and skills taught by this landmark piece of Americana are ones that helped develop leadership and humanity and continue to do so.[27]

Mendoza goes on to hypothesise that the only way that a bright future can be assured, where Roddenberry's dream of utopia can become a reality, is to follow his example. The key factor is knowledge and *Star Trek*, for him, inspires the pursuit of knowledge because it is a series based on both physical and personal discovery:

> The Key to the future is knowledge. But much more than knowledge, a person should have insight and enlightenment. I believe that the characters we have all come to know personally and to love are so important to us because they are all part of every one of us. My job is to teach my students to be Data and to start them on a mission of discovery.[28]

Mendoza appears not to be the only one that believes *Star Trek* can be useful in the classroom. Two teachers from a North Hollywood high school have been using examples from *Star Trek* episodes to help teach subjects such as maths and science to children who would have previously found these subjects hard going. Indeed, utilising jargon and illustrations from the series in the classroom has helped 'kids get involved in spite of themselves' according to the school's headmistress.[29] The two teachers, who are fans, dress up to make the classes seem more fun and use the futuristic lexicon to make maths and science more accessible. It is not the fact they are teaching *Trek* as if it is a possible reality (warp drives and transporters) which is important, but the fact that they recognise its huge impact as popular culture icon, as does Mendoza.

As well as *Star Trek*'s instructive merits, Mendoza also points out its ability to help develop interpersonal skills such as working with people in a group and taking charge. For him, *Star Trek* taught tolerance and acceptance of different individuals and their talents: 'I learned about the advantages of having a diverse command crew, each with his or her own talents and limitations.'[30] Having the ability to work with people from all walks of life has helped him achieve a respected position within his local school district. Even coming from an ethnically diverse home town like El Paso and being of Hispanic descent, Mendoza still sees *Star Trek* as a positive influence on children of all races. Its vision of an exceptional American future, based on the conquest of the final frontier, incorporating all that once excluded people of a non-WASP background is seemingly overlooked by Mendoza because he believes its utopian philosophy and moralising advice are more important. For the fans of *Galaxy Quest*, believing in the reality of the technology was just as vital as believing in its supportive narrative, if not more so. On the contrary, in Mendoza's letter and through the Hollywood teachers' example, it is noticeable that believing in the technological structure of the future is not as essential as the Roddenberry 'utopian dream', which drives many *Star Trek* fans to write about how they feel.

International fans are also aware of the utopian message that Roddenberry's *Star Trek* was trying to communicate and thus contradict its faith in the exclusive and over-powering dogma of the American frontier as seen in *Galaxy Quest*. In the following letters, British and Australian fans respond to the concept of self-improvement and the frontier being the catalyst for personal growth but they do not see it as a national ideology. Instead, trying to improve oneself is the key to a future where nations and boundaries do not exist. One Australian fan writes:

> There are many futuristic movies where the Earth has been blown to pieces, or all the races in the universe apart from ourselves turn out to be brutal savages, waiting to tear us limb from limb. *Star Trek* shows that we will pull through, and humans will care for Earth, and take pride in it, in the 24th century. Action, adventure, good humour and good morals as well.[31]

It is clear from this letter that the writer believes that humans will put all other differences aside and concentrate on making Earth the utopian paradise that Star Trek so often depicts. Implicit within the fan's opinion is the notion that we will start to realise that the best way to create Roddenberry's future is to concentrate on the environment rather than personal gain and national supremacy. Earth as a world of many nations, pulling in many directions with different agendas, should work as a unit so the future can be bright. No one nation – or one nation's method – should oversee this transformation. Fans appear to be emphasising in their letters to other fans that national identity is not what distinguishes them as people; rather, one could say they are identifiable as global Astrofuturists without the links to 'America's dream' as described by De Witt Douglas Kilgore.[32]

The last letter, written by a British female fan, also ignores national ideology as a defining factor in the reality of Star Trek's narrative. In this instance, Samantha Hattingh feels that a particular character (Captain Janeway) has made Star Trek all the more real as she has influenced her life in many different ways:

> This year I celebrate my 30th birthday ... [and] I look back and reflect on the people who've had a profound influence on my life ... at the top of my list would be the formidable *Captain Kathryn Janeway*. No one will report on what I've said and convey it back to the remarkable creators of and writers for the character of Captain Janeway. Likewise, Kate Mulgrew will never hear how her masterful portrayal of a powerful, fictional, futuristic character helped to shape my ordinary life.[33]

Acting as both an inspiration and a role model, the Janeway character performs rather like Taggert in Galaxy Quest; he is a role model to the Thermians as Janeway is to Hattingh. However, it is evident in the letter that Hattingh can differentiate between fact and fiction and states that Janeway is fictional – something which Mathesar cannot do with regard to the characters in Galaxy Quest. He had to be tricked into believing that the show is a fake so that Saris would not kill him but all the while he survives his punishment by keeping faith that Taggert will save him just like in the 'historical documents'.

Hattingh appears to admire Kate Mulgrew's ability to portray a strong female lead rather than believe in the character of Janeway. In general, the narrative does not intrude into Hattingh's life as much as it does for those fans who dress up like their favourite character. Therefore, *Star Trek* does not dominate her perception of personal identity as Peter Chvany argues it does for those Klingon enthusiasts who have become new self-styled 'American ethnics'.

III

Galaxy Quest and the series that inspired it examine perceptions of the frontier as both a physical and personal boundary. As a film that parodied SF fandom stereotypes, *Galaxy Quest* succeeded in deconstructing existing images of the cult fan as a lonely, insular individual and instead demonstrated that cult fans form a supportive community that share in their passion for the SF text. The documented reality that served as the Thermians' blueprint for a new society also gave its human fans confidence to express their own personalities. They were able to transgress personal boundaries set by the society in which they lived and assume a more active and resilient identity. Space as the final frontier was the canvas on which the fans could map out their new personas; it helped them become who they ideally wanted to be. Yet, as I have explained, space in the American imagination is linked to some very complex historical ideologies such as expansion, self-improvement and exceptionalism that serve only to exclude those deemed unfit. This sits awkwardly with *Star Trek*'s ethos, which posits that everyone should be included in a utopian future. Hence, I have tried to show that fans of *Star Trek*, unlike their filmic counterparts, are able to interact with the textual narrative on a more multilayered level and are therefore aware of these veiled meanings attached to space and the frontier.

Unlike the Thermians, who believe in everything that *Galaxy Quest* represented, the *Star Trek* fans I have looked at recognise that only certain aspects of the series can be useful to copy or admire. International fans appear to appreciate American cultural images such as the self-made man, but they transform them, making them accessible to all people. The future of the human race is more important than national identities. Crossing the frontier in *Galaxy Quest* gave SF fans a chance to realise their potential; believing in the reality of the programme inspired them to be better individuals. For those fans who expressed their feelings through writing letters, crossing boundaries was only part of the act. The real achievement was to believe in themselves so that they could find the courage to make changes in their own lives. Star Trek could help a little in doing this but what the series really represented to them was the dream of a better future. To achieve that, they would have to work in the real world and not the fictional one seen on-screen.

EPILOGUE

BRINGING
THE MEMORY
TO LIFE

'Five-card stud, nothing wild. And the sky's the limit.'
Picard to his crew in the final episode, 'All Good
Things...' (1994)

This book has not set out to question the capacity in which *Star Trek*
affects the daily lives of its fans, nor has it sought to criticise or examine their various and intricate fan activities so often taken as being
representative of cult fan behaviour in general. Rather, this book has
attempted to highlight the underlying American cultural myths and
narratives that make up and support the fictional future history of
the *Star Trek* universe. At the same time, we have been able to see how
and why the series is so popular with its fans through an analysis of
their letters, which not only share the same themes identified in the
fictional text but also serve to create and maintain a supportive and
sympathetic fan community. By engaging with the text through its
characteristically American utopian, communal and self-improvement narratives, fans are able to express and confess their most personal life experiences; writing and reading fan letters has become a
cathartic and collective act of self-help at a time when many critics
would consider American society to be at its most divided.

FROM FAN PROTEST TO FAN SUPPORT

In 2003, I visited the Gene Roddenberry *Star Trek* Television Series
Collection held at the University of California, Los Angeles. Within

the collection there are hundreds of pictures, scripts, memos and fan letters sent to Roddenberry and the studio right from the very first month *Star Trek* aired on US TV screens. In many of the letters, fans speak of their affection for the new and 'politically minded' science fiction series.[1] Describing themselves as self-confessed 'nuts', they are keen to see the series succeed and take over from where contemporary series such as *Lost in Space* (1965–1968) and *Bewitched* (1964–1972) had failed to ignite their imaginations.[2] Yet, as pointed out at the very beginning of the Introduction, as soon as the series had aired fans were concerned about it being cancelled.

Written during the first season, letters in the collection concentrate on how to save the series from possible termination; in fact, fans wrote to Gene Roddenberry with many ingenious and humorous ideas to grab the attention of studio executives. Kay Anderson in 1966 wrote to say that she would buy hundreds of Playtex bras and cut out their labels, mailing them off to Playtex to show them the success of advertising during *Star Trek*'s programme breaks and encourage them to continue doing so. If this did not work then she would move on to the Plymouth car lot and tear off the sale stickers on the windscreens, sending them to the Chrysler Corp. saying that she had bought several cars because of *Star Trek*.[3] Similarly, S. D. Landers wrote to inform the producers that they were going to start smoking menthol cigarettes to support the show and prevent its cancellation – perhaps a step too far for fans in these health-conscious times?[4] Unlike the fervent letter campaigns described in the Introduction and the fan letters discussed in Part Two, these letters signal a distinct awareness of the economic impact that large groups of fans could have on the making and breaking of a television series. Fans were keen to point out to network sponsors that they were a valid and potentially strong viewing group that had to be catered for. Perhaps this was a trend to which current fans should have returned before *Star Trek: Enterprise* was cancelled by executives at UPN.[5] Besides the economic concerns fans had for the series in the late 1960s, it is important to remember the significance that the letter as a form of fan expression had on both the franchise and the fan community as a whole. As soon as fans realised that they had a voice, they continued to use the letter format as their mouthpiece. Edited collections and fan memoirs carried on this tradition in the period when *Star Trek* was off-air; fan communities were built around common interests and the desire to see a new series on the television.

The letters I have looked at both acknowledge and move beyond the original aim of letters in the late 1960s. These newer letters talk of how *Star Trek* has affected fans' lives, how its vision of a utopian future where all people can work together and maintain paradise provides the inspiration to continue facing hardship in their daily routines. Picking up on the narratives that drive the show's utopian ethos, the fan letters I examined balance the contradictory notions of community and individualism by stressing the importance of Roddenberry's vision of the future. By working together and improving oneself both physically and mentally, utopia is achievable. *Star Trek*'s own brand of American myth is described in many letters as the blueprint to humanity's self-help plan. Only through adherence to such goals can all people, not only Americans, start to move beyond devastating events and experiences such as war, severe illness or the death of a loved one. However, as many critics have pointed out, *Star Trek*'s reliance on American cultural narratives destabilises the series' pretences of being a liberal and humanist vision of the future; the future has to be American in order for it to be a reality. To some extent this is true, and an unavoidable criticism of *Star Trek*. In Chapters Four and Eight, I have shown how, as did the didactic and ideologically dominant Puritan American Jeremiad, the *Star Trek* text manipulates history – especially when it uses America's potentially exclusive belief in its exceptional past as a guide.

Nonetheless, I have also argued that the fictional reality of the series carries significant personal meaning for millions of fans worldwide; these individual meanings become the impetus for personal change, not the actual text itself. Fans are aware of the many thematic contradictions that the series produces yet they do not wish to blindly copy them to the last detail. As Terry Eagleton asserts, 'the most intriguing texts for criticism are not those which can be *read*, but those which are "writable" (*scriptible*) [sic] – texts which encourage the critic to carve them up ... produce his or her semi-arbitrary play of meaning athwart the work itself.'[6] The *Star Trek* text is but one channel of support and counsel; actually communicating with the community of fans through letter writing is the other important channel through which fans enact change. Benedict Anderson, in writing about the concept of nationhood, describes the nation as an 'imagined community' where individual members 'will never know most of their fellow-members, meet them, or even hear them, yet in the minds of each lives the image of their communion'.[7] The same can be said of the *Star Trek* fans who write letters describing their personal experiences, sharing them with fellow enthusiasts; they may never meet but through their familiarity with the *Star Trek* text they can begin to understand and relate to the larger community. At the same time, they use other people's lives as inspiration for their own, trying to improve and help themselves so as to make the future a better place than the present.

FROM FAN EPISTOLARY TO FAN ORALITY

This book has examined expressions of fan identity in written form, acknowledging the themes of utopia, community and self-improvement shared between *Star Trek* and the fan letter. As I have maintained, analyses of fan activity in general have tended to focus on the more extreme forms of fan writing, namely slash fiction and personal reworkings of the fictional text such as new scripts and 'filk music'. However, through an exploration of American fan letters, I have shown that not all fans express their opinions and passion for the series through textual poaching; instead, they express notions of identity and emotion through the intricate and delicate channels of personal revelation based around the *Star Trek* text. Writing, sharing and revealing personal traumas and experiences has created what I have called a 'network of support'; fans learn lessons from both the *Star Trek* text and fellow fans, adapting them to suit their own lives. Furthermore, it may well prove interesting to examine letters and comments published on the Internet, since there are literally thousands of personal websites, weblogs and online diaries that could contain their own networks of support.[8] The Internet, as opposed to the handwritten letter, can provide an instant source of reassurance; fans wishing to share personal thoughts and experiences in relation to the *Star Trek* text can log on and communicate with fans thousands of miles away in seconds. Physically writing the letter, submitting it for publication, and waiting for a response ensures that fans must hold on so as to participate in the network – bearing in mind that in the meantime their personal situation may have changed. This initial observation suggests to me that handwritten fan letters fulfil a different purpose to those comments posted on the Internet. The personal stories and tales of extreme trauma, recounted over long periods of time, symbolise Star Trek's life-long appeal and attraction for fans. The lengthy writing and waiting process ingrained in the fan letter reflects the perpetual attachment that many fans have to the Star Trek text. Those fans who have grown up having spent years overcoming trauma, illness or bereavement describe how they have done so alongside the continued growth and development of the series.

If the Internet is another direction one can go in researching the fan letter, then the Star Trek convention represents a physically different, if not thematically similar, space that allows for a sense of community. Whilst visiting the Roddenberry collection in March 2003, I also attended the annual Grand Slam Star Trek Convention in Pasadena. Previous studies of the Star Trek convention have compared it to a religious pilgrimage, where fans travel to meet other fans, discuss their mutual love for the series and analyse its 'sacred' text within complex debates over authenticity and Roddenberry's vision.[9] I would not disagree that the convention represents some form of secular pilgrimage. It was distinctly obvious at the Grand Slam event that the level of fan devotion to the text is intense, particularly when certain stars come on stage and talk to the audience. Older stars, such as William Shatner and Leonard Nimoy, joked with the crowd by recounting times when Star Trek's quality had been called into question by non-fans or when later series such as Star Trek: Voyager or Enterprise declared themselves to be proper Trek. Shatner and Nimoy consider themselves to be authentic Star Trek, somehow more representative of Gene Roddenberry's vision, unlike other actors and series such as Scott Bakula or Enterprise (when Nimoy reasserted his claims at being the 'original' Vulcan the audience responded with laughter and applause). However, with debates over authenticity and the sacred aside, what was fascinating about the convention space was how fans used it as a place for sharing their personal stories of hardship and trauma just like those fans writing letters.

The audience's affection for actress Nichelle Nichols provided the greatest example of this phenomenon. Appearing on stage, Nichols recounted her years on *Star Trek*. Her stories, so often told in interviews and previous conventions, become part of what fans expect to hear. Their convention experience relies on Nichols retelling her stories so much, especially the one about Martin Luther King as described in my Introduction, that they become a form of oral tradition. Jan Vansina sees oral traditions as being 'documents of *the present*, because they are told in the present. Yet they also embody a message from the past, so they are expressions *of the past* at the same time.'[10] Fans construct their own memories from those repeated stories and experiences and take inspiration from them just as much as they do from the official *Star Trek* text. The mythos has expanded to include the mutually reassuring and interdependent stories that surround the actors, actresses and fans. When Nichols asked for questions from the crowd, she only received requests from fans eager to hear again how she was cornered by Dr King or inspired Whoopi Goldberg to become an actress and comedian; once they got them, the fans dutifully responded with cheers and applause. This call and response continued when an African-American woman got up to thank Nichols for being her role model when she was growing up. Almost in tears, the fan shared with Nichols and the audience how much *Star Trek* and Lt. Uhura supported and inspired her during very hard times in her childhood.

In Chapter Seven, I identified fan letters that described how fans used *Star Trek* to change their lives, the inherently American theme of self-improvement was both recognised and utilised as a way to understand the effects the series had on personal experience. Within that chapter I also drew comparisons between letters of self-help and the narrative format of the talk show, indicating that when fans attempt to share feelings they also attempt to gain strength from the receptive fan community and the polysemic nature of the *Star Trek* text. Likewise, in terms of the convention setting, the fan's desire to share her personal experiences with Nichols and the audience reflects the openness and supportiveness of the talk show format as seen in *The Oprah Winfrey Show* (1986–), as well as the belief in individual agency so important to American society. In effect, the oral and confessional characteristics of the *Star Trek* convention may well follow Jane Shattuc's claim about *Oprah* in that it reveals 'a profound political change: the authority of everyday lived experience, whether in reactionary or progressive form'.[11] Moving from the self-edifying nature of fan epistolary to the empowerment of knowledge gained through fan orality, it would be the logical next step to progress from this work and investigate how oral histories within Star Trek fandom reflect, maintain and subvert notions of American identity.

Memory too has been an important function in the fans' interaction with the Star Trek text: they write about moments when the series helped them overcome difficulties in the past or they remember the exact time that they first saw Star Trek. At the convention, memory played an important part in the fans' sharing of oral history: Nichelle Nichols' own personal memories became enmeshed with the fans' lived experience of the Star Trek text. Perhaps one way we can look at Star Trek fandom is through the concept of 'prosthetic memory', what Alison Landsberg describes as 'a new form of memory largely made possible by the commodification of mass culture ... [which] can make people feel themselves a part of larger histories, of narratives that go beyond the confines of the nuclear family and that transcend the heretofore insurmountable barriers of race and ethnicity'.[12] In studying the ethnically mixed audience that sat listening to Nichols and the female fan talking about race and Star Trek, and those African-American Vietnam War veterans that wrote about their hopes and dreams for America in their fan letters, the recitation and memorialisation of Star Trek history and fan experience can be seen as part of contemporary America's desire to renegotiate the past. Landsberg believes prosthetic memory can help achieve what America always set out to be, a utopia. Building and sharing memories through the universalising text of Star Trek might represent the future that Roddenberry was trying to depict. In bringing the memory to life, fans are not only writing about how they have invested in Star Trek in the past and are living with Star Trek in the present, but also how they might possibly invest in humanity for the future.

NOTES

INTRODUCTION

1. There was much debate between fans and the press over the decision to add the prefix Star Trek to the title of the new series after two seasons without such associations. For the purposes of this book, I shall refer to the series from now on as Enterprise.

2. J. M. Dillard, Star Trek 'Where No One Has Gone Before: A History in Pictures (New York, NY: Pocket Books, 1996), 6.

3. See Rick Worland, 'Captain Kirk: Cold Warrior', Journal of Popular Film & Television 16.3 (1988): 109–117; and 'From the New Frontier to the Final Frontier: Star Trek from Kennedy to Gorbachev', Film & History 24.1–2 (1994): 19–35.

4. Nichelle Nichols, Beyond Uhura: Star Trek and Other Memories (London: Boxtree Ltd, 1995), 164–5.

5. Ibid. 196–7.

6. There was a similar drive to help save Enterprise, with fans writing to the heads of CBS and UPN (the networks that financed the series) and this time a website was also launched: <http://www.saveenterprise.com>.

7. For a history of the Star Trek fanzine in this period, see Joan Marie Verba, Boldly Writing: A Trekker Fan and Zine History, 1967–1987 (Minnetonka, MN: FTL Publications, 1996).

8. See Lincoln Geraghty, 'A Report on Star Trek The Adventure, Hyde Park, London', Vector: The Critical Journal of the BSFA 228 (March/April 2003): 20–1.

9. For an analysis of The Experience, see Robin Roberts, 'Performing Science Fiction: Television, Theater, and Gender in Star Trek: The Experience', Extrapolation 42.4 (2001): 340–56.

10. George Lipsitz, Time Passages: Collective Memory and American Popular Culture (Minneapolis, MN: University of Minnesota Press, 1990), 5.

11. Ibid. 19.

12.   Ibid. 20.

13.   Yehoshua Arieli, *Individualism and Nationalism in American Ideology* (Cambridge, MA: Harvard University Press, 1964), 31–48.

14.   For a regional approach, see, for example: Paul E. Johnson, *A Shopkeeper's Millennium: Society and Revivals in Rochester, New York, 1815–1837* (New York, NY: Hill and Wang, 1978); Joseph A. Conforti, *Imagining New England: Explorations of Regional Identity from the Pilgrims to the Mid-Twentieth Century* (Chapel Hill, NC: University of North Carolina Press, 2001).

15.   Ronald G. Walters, *American Reformers, 1815–1860* (New York, NY: Hill and Wang, 1978), 39.

16.   Edward Bellamy, *Looking Backward* (Mineola, NY: Dover Publications, 1996 [1888]); L. Frank Baum, *The Wonderful Wizard of Oz* (Chicago, IL: Reilly & Lee, 1900). For an analysis of American utopian science fiction in this period, specifically utopias associated with space, see De Witt Douglas Kilgore, *Astrofuturism: Science, Race, and Visions of Utopia in Space* (Philadelphia, PA: University of Pennsylvania Press, 2003).

17.   See Benedict Anderson, *Imagined Communities: Reflections on the Origin and Spread of Nationalism* (London: Verso, 1983).

18.   See Ann Gray, 'Behind Closed Doors: Video Recorders in the Home', in H. Baehr and G. Dyer (eds.), *Boxed In: Women and Television* (London: Pandora Press, 1987), 38–51; and Dorothy Hobson, *Crossroads: Drama of a Soap Opera* (London: Methuen, 1982).

19.   See John Fiske, 'Television: Polysemy and Popularity', *Critical Studies in Mass Communication* 3.4 (1986): 391–408.

20.   See Camille Bacon-Smith, *Enterprising Women: Television Fandom and the Creation of Popular Myth* (Philadelphia, PA: University of Pennsylvania Press, 1992); and John Tulloch and Henry Jenkins, *Science Fiction Audiences: Watching Doctor Who and Star Trek* (London: Routledge, 1995).

21.   Mark Jancovich and Lucy Faire with Sarah Stubbings, *The Place of the Audience: Cultural Geographies of Film Consumption* (London: BFI, 2003), 27.

22.   See Ien Ang, *Watching Dallas: Soap Opera and the Melodramatic Imagination*, trans. Della Couling (London: Routledge, 1985 [1982]); David Morley, *The Nationwide Audience* (London: BFI, 1980); and Christine Geraghty, *Women and Soap Opera: A Study of Prime Time Soaps* (Cambridge: Polity Press, 1991).

23.   David Morley, *Television, Audiences & Cultural Studies* (London: Routledge, 1992), 89.

24.   See Henry Jenkins, *Textual Poachers: Television Fans and Participatory Culture* (New York, NY: Routledge, 1992).

25. Nicholas Abercrombie and Brian Longhurst, *Audiences: A Sociological Theory of Performance and Imagination* (London: Sage Publications, 1998), 121.

26. Sara Gwenllian-Jones and Roberta E. Pearson, 'Introduction', in Sara Gwenllian-Jones and Roberta E. Pearson (eds.), *Cult Television* (Minneapolis, MN: University of Minnesota Press, 2004), xvii.

27. David Barton and Nigel Hall, 'Introduction', in David Barton and Nigel Hall (eds.), *Letter Writing as a Social Practice* (Amsterdam: John Benjamins Publishing, 1999), 1.

28. William Merrill Decker, *Epistolary Practices: Letter Writing in America before Telecommunications* (Chapel Hill, NC: University of North Carolina Press, 1998), 6.

29. Ibid. 16.

30. Ibid. 241.

31. See Hayden White, *Metahistory: The Historical Imagination in Nineteenth Century Europe* (Baltimore, MD: Johns Hopkins University Press, 1973).

32. See Robert Jewett and John Shelton Lawrence, *The American Monomyth* (Garden City, NY: Anchor Press, 1977).

33. See Sacvan Bercovitch, *The American Jeremiad* (Madison, WI: University of Wisconsin Press, 1978).

34. See Richard Dyer, 'Entertainment and Utopia', in Rick Altman (ed.), *Genre: The Musical* (London: Routledge and Kegan Paul, 1981), 175–89.

35. See Robert D. Putnam, *Bowling Alone: The Collapse and Revival of American Community* (New York, NY: Touchstone, 2000); and Robert Wuthnow, *Sharing the Journey: Support Groups and America's New Quest for Community* (New York, NY: Free Press, 1994).

PART ONE

1. See Hayden White, *Figural Realism: Studies in the Mimesis Effect* (Baltimore, MD: Johns Hopkins University Press, 1999).

2. See Daniel L. Bernardi, *Star Trek and History: Race-ing Towards a White Future* (New Brunswick, NJ: Rutgers University Press, 1998); Jan Johnson-Smith, *American Science Fiction TV: Star Trek, Stargate and Beyond* (London: I.B.Tauris & Co. Ltd, 2005); Robin Roberts, *Sexual Generations: 'Star Trek: The Next Generation' and Gender* (Urbana, IL: University of Illinois Press, 1999).

3. Bernardi, *Star Trek and History*, 96–104.

4. Arthur M. Schlesinger Jr., *The Disuniting of America: Reflections on a Multicultural Society* (2nd edition, New York, NY: W. W. Norton, 1998 [1991]), 167–79.

5.   Bernardi, Star Trek and History, 92.

6.   Edward W. Said, *Orientalism: Western Conceptions of the Orient* (Harmondsworth: Penguin Books, 1995 [1978]), 94.

CHAPTER ONE

1.   William Blake Tyrrell, 'Star Trek as Myth and Television as Mythmaker', *Journal of Popular Culture* 10.4 (1977): 713.

2.   For a full bibliographic list, see Lincoln Geraghty, 'Reading on the Frontier: A Star Trek Bibliography', *Extrapolation* 43.3 (2002): 288–313.

3.   Audre Lorde, 'Poetry Is Not a Luxury', in Audre Lorde, *Sister Outsider* (Freedom, CA: The Crossing Press, 1984), 36.

4.   The series of fan stories was originally published in 1998 and each volume (currently standing at nine) contains the top three prize-winners of a Star Trek short story contest held every year. See Dean Wesley Smith, John J. Ordover and Paula M. Block (eds.), Star Trek *Strange New Worlds* Volume I (New York, NY: Pocket Books, 1998).

5.   Mandy Coe, 'Bred to Boldly Go', in Valerie Laws (ed.), Star Trek *The Poems* (Manchester: Iron Press, 2000), 9.

6.   Henry Jenkins, *Textual Poachers: Television Fans and Participatory Culture* (New York, NY: Routledge, 1992), 75; Michel de Certeau, *The Practice of Everyday Life* (Berkeley, CA: University of California Press, 1984), 174.

7.   An interview with David Carson, 'Generation Games', *Star Trek Monthly Magazine* (September 2001): 47.

8.   Jacqueline Lichtenberg, Sondra Marshak and Joan Winston, Star Trek *Lives!* (New York, NY: Bantam Books, 1975), 9–51.

9.   Constance Penley, *NASA/TREK: Popular Science and Sex in America* (New York, NY: Verso, 1997), 2–3.

10.   Ibid. 101–2.

11.   Jay Goulding, *Empire, Aliens, and Conquest: A Critique of American Ideology in Star Trek and Other Science Fiction Adventures* (Toronto, OT: Sisyphus Press, 1985), 39.

12.   David Gerrold, *The World of* Star Trek: *The Inside Story of TV's Most Popular Series* (3rd edition, London: Virgin Books, 1996 [1973, 1984]), x.

13.   Lorde, 'Poetry Is Not a Luxury', 37.

14.   Jenkins, *Textual Poachers*, 52.

15.   Quoted in Penley, NASA/TREK, 18.

16.   Heather Joseph-Witham, Star Trek *Fans and Costume Art* (Jackson, MS: University Press of Mississippi, 1996), 14.

17.   An interview with Barbara Adams on *The* Star Trek *Story* (BBC2, August 1996).

18.   An interview with Brent Spiner, 'Data Retrieval', *Star Trek Monthly Magazine* (March 2001): 6.

19. Rick Berman, 'Roddenberry's Vision', in Lee Ann Nicholson (ed.), *Farewell to Star Trek: The Next Generation*, TV *Guide Collector's Edition* (Toronto, OT: Telemedia Communications Inc., 1994), 2.

20. Chris Gregory, *Star Trek Parallel Narratives* (London: Macmillan Press, 2000), 16.

21. Larry Kreitzer, 'The Cultural Veneer of *Star Trek*', *Journal of Popular Culture* 30.2 (1996): 1.

22. Vivian Sobchack, *Screening Space: The American Science Fiction Film* (New Brunswick, NJ: Rutgers University Press, 1998), 277.

23. Hayden White, *Tropics of Discourse: Essays in Cultural Criticism* (Baltimore, MD: Johns Hopkins University Press, 1978), 88.

24. Gerrold, *The World of Star Trek*, 228.

25. Erich Auerbach, *Mimesis: The Representation of Reality in Western Literature* (Princeton, NJ: Princeton University Press, 1953), 73.

26. Steve Anderson, 'Loafing in the Garden of Knowledge: History TV and Popular Memory', *Film & History, Special Focus: Television as Historian, Part 1* 30.1 (2000): 20.

27. Goulding, *Empire, Aliens, and Conquest*, 40.

28. Daniel J. Boorstin, *The Discoverers* (Harmondsworth: Penguin Books, 1983), pt.12, 419–76.

29. Rom Harré and Paul F. Secord, *The Explanation of Social Behaviour* (Oxford: Basil Blackwell, 1972), 1–26.

30. Jorge Luis Borges, 'The Library of Babel', in *Fictions*, trans. Anthony Kerrigan (London: Calder Publications, 1998), 72–80.

31. Michael Jindra, '"It's About Faith in our Future": Star Trek Fandom as Cultural Religion', in Bruce David Forbes and Jeffrey H. Mahan (eds.), *Religion and Popular Culture in America* (Berkeley, CA: University of California Press, 2000), 174.

32. John Fiske, 'The Cultural Economy of Fandom', in Lisa A. Lewis (ed.), *The Adoring Audience: Fan Culture and Popular Media* (New York, NY: Routledge, 1992), 39.

33. Nick Jones, 'Video Review', *Star Trek Monthly Magazine* (January 2002): 56.

34. Michael A. Martin, 'Parallel Universes: Real Life Space Exploration vs. *Star Trek* Fantasy', *Star Trek Monthly Magazine* (February 2002): 26–32.

35. 'Continuity Conundrums', *Star Trek Monthly Magazine* (October 2001): 7.

36. 'Star Trek: To Infinity and Beyond', *Radio Times* (15–21 September 2001): 38.

37. Berman quoted in Paul Ruditis, 'Behind the Scenes of *Enterprise*', in Diane Carey, *Broken Bow: A Novel* (New York, NY: Pocket Books, 2001), 201–2.

38.   However, Pocket Books has compiled a Star Trek novel timeline which combines all of the episodes in series chronological order with every event from the novels, short stories and audiobooks published by them. This adds legitimacy to the 'historical' events that occur in the books by relating them to events and actions aired on television, and it also brings authenticity to the 'Historian's Note' which appears at the beginning of most novels. See David Bowling, Johan Ciamaglia, Ryan J. Cornelius, James R. McCain, Alex Rosenzweig, Paul T. Semones and Corey W. Tacker, with David Henderson and Lee Jamilkowski, 'The Pocket Books *Star Trek* Timeline', in Diane Carey et al., Star Trek – *Gateways #7: What Lay Beyond* (New York, NY: Pocket Books, 2001), 319–73.

39.   L. Pearson, quoted in Matt Hills, *Fan Cultures* (London: Routledge, 2002), 188 n. 15.

40.   Michael Jindra, '"It's About Faith in our Future": *Star Trek* Fandom as Cultural Religion', 174.

CHAPTER TWO

1.   J. Hawthorn (ed.), *Narrative: From Malory to Motion Pictures* (London: Edward Arnold, 1985), vii.

2.   Robert Scholes and Robert Kellogg, *The Nature of Narrative* (New York, NY: Oxford University Press, 1966), 4; see also Sarah Kozloff, 'Narrative Theory and Television', in Robert C. Allen (ed.), *Channels of Discourse, Reassembled: Television and Contemporary Criticism* (2nd edition, Chapel Hill, NC: University of North Carolina Press, 1992 [1987]), 67–100.

3.   Jill Sherwin, *Quotable* Star Trek (New York, NY: Pocket Books, 1999), 301.

4.   An interview with David Carson, 'Generation Games', *Star Trek Monthly Magazine* (September 2001): 46.

5.   Sherwin, *Quotable* Star Trek, 312.

6.   Kerwin Lee Klein, *Frontiers of Historical Imagination: Narrating the European Conquest of Native America, 1890–1990* (Berkeley, CA: University of California Press, 1997), 53.

7.   Northrop Frye, *Anatomy of Criticism: Four Essays* (Princeton, NJ: Princeton University Press, 1957), 282–93, 251–62, 263–8, 268–70, 270–81; Klein, *Frontiers of Historical Imagination*, 53–4.

8.   Kenneth Burke, *A Grammar of Motives* (Berkeley, CA: University of California Press, 1962), 507–17.

9.   Marshall McLuhan, *Understanding Media: The Extensions of Man* (New York, NY: Routledge and Kegan Paul Ltd, 1962), 7–21.

10.   Hayden White, *The Content of the Form: Narrative Discourse and Historical*

Representation (Baltimore, MD: Johns Hopkins University Press, 1987), xi.

11. Klein, *Frontiers of Historical Imagination*, 54.

12. Roland Barthes, *Mythologies*, trans. Annette Lavers (London: Vintage, 1993 [1972]), 66.

13. The last nine episodes of DS9 in 1999 concerned the final developments of the 'Dominion War'; they also signalled the farewell to the major characters. This meant that all nine had to adequately finish off storylines that had been going on for a number of years; there was no time for introducing new plots or characters from 'Penumbra' to 'What You Leave Behind'.

14. See Michèle Barrett and Duncan Barrett, Star Trek: *The Human Frontier* (Cambridge: Polity Press, 2001), 135–204.

15. Paul A. Cantor, 'The Simpsons: Atomistic Politics and the Nuclear Family', in William Irwin, Mark T. Conrad and Aeon J. Skoble (eds.), *The Simpsons and Philosophy: The D'Oh! of Homer* (Chicago and La Salle, IL: Open Court, 2001), 162.

16. Klein, *Frontiers of Historical Imagination*, 54.

17. Richard Reynolds, *Super Heroes: A Modern Mythology* (London: B.T. Batsford, 1992), 37–8.

18. Thomas M. Disch, *The Dreams Our Stuff is Made Of: How Science Fiction Conquered the World* (New York, NY: Free Press, 1998), 97–114.

19. Janet H. Murray, *Hamlet on the Holodeck: The Future of Narrative in Cyberspace* (Cambridge, MA: MIT Press, 1997), 30.

20. Ibid. 38.

CHAPTER THREE

1. Jon Wagner, 'Intimations of Immortality: Death/Life Mediations in Star Trek', in Jennifer E. Porter and Darcee L. McLaren (eds.), Star Trek and Sacred Grounds: Explorations of Star Trek, Religion, and American Culture (Albany, NY: State University of New York Press, 1999), 119.

2. Susan L. Schwartz, 'Enterprise Engaged: Mythic Enactment and Ritual Performance', in Ross Kraemer, William Cassidy and Susan L. Schwartz, *Religions of Star Trek* (Boulder, CO: Westview Press, 2001), 131.

3. Lane Roth, 'Death and Rebirth in Star Trek II: The Wrath of Khan', Extrapolation 28.2 (1987): 155–66.

4. Richard Slotkin, 'Myth and the Production of History', in Sacvan Bercovitch and Myra Jehlen (eds.), *Ideology and Classic American Literature* (Cambridge: Cambridge University Press, 1986), 70.

5. Jeffrey Richards, 'Fires Were Started', in David Ellwood (ed.), *The Movies as History: Visions of the Twentieth Century* (Stroud: Sutton Publishing, 2000), 26.

6.   Robert Jewett and John Shelton Lawrence, *The American Monomyth* (Garden City, NY: Anchor Press, 1977), 19.

7.   Ibid. xx.

8.   Ibid.

9.   Orlando Patterson, *Freedom Volume 1: Freedom in the Making of Western Culture* (London: I.B.Tauris & Co. Ltd, 1991), 294.

10.   J. P. Telotte, *Science Fiction Film* (New York, NY: Cambridge University Press, 2001), 48.

11.   Louis A. Woods and Gary L. Harmon, 'Jung and *Star Trek*: The Coincidentia Oppositorum and Images of the Shadow', *Journal of Popular Culture* 28.2 (1994): 169.

12.   See Mike Hertenstein, *The Double Vision of Star Trek: Half-Humans, Evil Twins and Science Fiction* (Chicago, IL: Cornerstone Press, 1998), 7–16.

13.   Steven A. Galipeau, *The Journey of Luke Skywalker: An Analysis of Modern Myth and Symbol* (Chicago and La Salle, IL: Open Court, 2001), 33–4.

14.   Telotte, *Science Fiction Film*, 49.

15.   Jewett and Lawrence, *The American Monomyth*, 6.

16.   Mark P. Lagon, '"We Owe It to Them to Interfere": *Star Trek* and U.S. Statecraft in the 1960s and the 1990s', *Extrapolation* 34.3 (1993): 262.

17.   Jay Goulding, *Empire, Aliens, and Conquest: A Critique of American Ideology in Star Trek and Other Science Fiction Adventures* (Toronto, OT: Sisyphus Press, 1985), 80–1.

18.   Jewett and Lawrence, *The American Monomyth*, xx.

19.   Mary Henderson, *Star Wars: The Magic of Myth* (New York, NY: Bantam Books, 1997), 6.

20.   Charles Champlin, *George Lucas: The Creative Impulse* (New York, NY: Harry N. Abrams, Inc., 1992), 41.

21.   Fredric Jameson, 'Postmodernism and Consumer Society', in Hal Foster (ed.), *The Anti-Aesthetic: Essays on Postmodern Culture* (Port Townsend, WA: Bay Press, 1983), 117.

22.   Ibid. 116.

23.   Adam Roberts, *Science Fiction: The New Critical Idiom* (London: Routledge, 2000), 85, 90.

24.   Telotte, *Science Fiction Film*, 105.

25.   William Blake Tyrrell, 'Star Trek as Myth and Television as Mythmaker', *Journal of Popular Culture* 10.4 (1977): 712.

26.   Galipeau, *The Journey of Luke Skywalker*, 60.

27.   Gene Roddenberry offered his own definitions of science fiction and fantasy in Susan Sackett's *Letters to Star Trek* (New York, NY: Ballantine, 1977), 186. In response to the frequently asked question 'how does science fiction differ from fantasy?' Roddenberry remarked:
      Science fiction differs from fantasy by involving itself in

extrapolations of present knowledge and generally staying true to physical laws as we understand them at present. Science fiction can also be an extrapolation of *conditions* as we know them now, that is, social, religious, economic, etc. It can be a contemporary story or go backward or forward in time ... Fantasy, on the other hand, need abide by no recognized rules. Its features need not be derived from anything we know at all, and it can easily come out of superstition, mythology and so on.

As Roddenberry intimates, *Star Trek*'s methods of storytelling very much rely on a contemporary extrapolation of society. Such a reliance on his so-called *conditions* provides the link to a reality that underpins and fortifies the history of the future and fictional universe of *Star Trek*.

28. Goulding, *Empire, Aliens, and Conquest*, 67.

29. Jon Wagner and Jan Lundeen, *Deep Space and Sacred Time: Star Trek in the American Mythos* (Westport, CT: Praeger, 1998), 6.

30. Brooks Landon, 'Bet On It: Cyber/video/punk/performance', in Larry McCaffery (ed.), *Storming the Reality Studio* (Durham, NC: Duke University Press, 1991), 239.

CHAPTER FOUR

1. Ziauddin Sardar, 'Introduction', in Ziauddin Sardar and Sean Cubitt (eds.), *Aliens R Us: The Other in Science Fiction Cinema* (London: Pluto Press, 2002), 1.

2. Richard Weiss, *The American Myth of Success: From Horatio Alger to Norman Vincent Peale* (Urbana, IL: University of Illinois Press, 1988 [1969]), 29.

3. See Benjamin Franklin, *The Autobiography of Benjamin Franklin* (Mineola, NY: Dover Publications, 1996 [1868]); David M. Larson, 'Benjamin Franklin 1706–1790', in Paul Lauter (ed.), *The Heath Anthology of American Literature*. Volume 1 (2nd edition, Lexington, MA: D.C. Heath and Company, 1994), 710.

4. John G. Cawelti, *Apostles of the Self-Made Man: Changing Concepts of Success in America* (Chicago, IL: University of Chicago Press, 1965), 4–5. See also Irvin G. Wyllie, *The Self-Made Man in America: The Myth of Rags to Riches* (New York, NY: Free Press, 1954); Barry Alan Shain, *The Myth of American Individualism: The Protestant Origins of American Political Thought* (Princeton, NJ: Princeton University Press, 1994); Jeffery Louis Decker, *Made in America: Self-Styled Success from Horatio Alger to Oprah Winfrey* (Minneapolis, MN: University of Minnesota Press, 1997).

5. Cawelti, *Apostles of the Self-Made Man*, 5. Cf. Michael Zuckerman, 'The Selling of the Self: From Franklin to Barnum', in Barbara B. Oberg

and Harry S. Stout (eds.), *Benjamin Franklin, Jonathan Edwards, and the Representation of American Culture* (New York, NY: Oxford University Press, 1993), 152–67.

6.   Cawelti, *Apostles*, 5–6. See also Robert F. Sayre, *The Examined Self: Benjamin Franklin, Henry Adams, Henry James* (Princeton, NJ: Princeton University Press, 1964). Cf. Christopher J. Galdieri, 'Alexis de Tocqueville's *Democracy in America* and the American *Enterprise*', *Extrapolation* 42.1 (2001): 65–74.

7.   See Sacvan Bercovitch, *The Puritan Origins of the American Self* (New Haven, CT: Yale University Press, 1975), particularly the final chapter on the myth of America and how the Puritan method of responding to the problems of the time is replicated through from the Great Awakening to the American Renaissance, 136–86; also Bercovitch, *The American Jeremiad* (Madison, WI: University of Wisconsin Press, 1978), 176–210, highlights how the jeremiad infused symbolic meaning into the term America and how that meaning was interpreted by literary critics throughout history; Richard H. King, *Civil Rights and the Idea of Freedom* (2nd edition, Athens, GA: University of Georgia Press, 1996 [1992]), 100.

8.   Douglas Tallack, *Twentieth-Century America: The Intellectual and Cultural Context* (London: Longman, 1991), 12.

9.   Edward Bellamy, *Looking Backward* (New York, NY: Dover Publications, 1996 [1888]), 2.

10.   Bercovitch, *The American Jeremiad*, xi.

11.   Background to the jeremiad comes from the introduction to the Book of Jeremiah, *The Compact NIV Study Bible, The New International Version* (London: Hodder and Stoughton, 1995), 1096–9.

12.   Bercovitch, *The American Jeremiad*, 3–30; Perry Miller, *Errand into the Wilderness* (Cambridge, MA: The Belknap Press of Harvard University Press, 1956), 1–15.

13.   David Minter, 'The Puritan Jeremiad as a Literary Form', in Sacvan Bercovitch (ed.), *The American Puritan Imagination: Essays in Revaluation* (Cambridge: Cambridge University Press, 1974), 46–7.

14.   Cotton Mather, *Magnalia Christi Americana; or, The Ecclesiastical History of New England*, Vols. 1 and 2, ed. Thomas Robbins (Hartford, CT: n.n., 1853 [1702]).

15.   Mason I. Lowance, Jr., 'Cotton Mather's *Magnalia* and the Metaphors of Biblical History', in Sacvan Bercovitch (ed.), *Typology and Early American Literature* (Amherst, MA: University of Massachusetts Press, 1972), 143.

16.   Minter, 'The Puritan Jeremiad', 52.

17.   Bercovitch, *The American Jeremiad*, 5.

18. Sacvan Bercovitch, 'The American Puritan Imagination: An Introduction', in Sacvan Bercovitch (ed.), *The American Puritan Imagination*, 8.

19. John Winthrop, 'Modell of Christian Charity', in Karen Ordahl Kupperman (ed.), *Major Problems in American Colonial History* (Lexington, MA: D.C. Heath and Company, 1993 [1630]), 126.

20. Bercovitch, *The American Jeremiad*, 6–7.

21. Vivian Sobchack, *Screening Space: The American Science Fiction Film* (New Brunswick, NJ: Rutgers University Press, 1998), 277.

22. Ibid. 276–7.

23. Ian Maher, 'The Outward Voyage and the Inward Search: Star Trek Motion Pictures and the Spiritual Quest', in Jennifer E. Porter and Darcee L. McLaren (eds.), *Star Trek and Sacred Grounds: Explorations of Star Trek, Religion, and American Culture* (Albany, NY: State University of New York Press, 1999), 165.

24. Ibid. 171.

25. Perry Miller, *Errand into the Wilderness*, 1–15; Cf. the response in Sacvan Bercovitch, 'New England's Errand Reappraised', in John Higham and Paul K. Conkin (eds.), *New Directions in American Intellectual History* (Baltimore, MD: Johns Hopkins University Press, 1979), 90–1.

26. Jon Roper, *The American Presidents: Heroic Leadership from Kennedy to Clinton* (Edinburgh: Edinburgh University Press, 2000),138.

27. Ibid. 142.

28. Ronald W. Reagan, 'Inaugural Address, January 20, 1981', in *Public Papers of the Presidents of the United States: Ronald Reagan, 1981 – January 20 to December 31, 1981* (Washington DC: US Government Printing Office, 1982 [1981]), 2–3.

29. Roper, *The American Presidents*, 145.

30. Frances Fitzgerald, *Way Out There in the Blue: Reagan, Star Wars and the End of the Cold War* (New York, NY: Simon & Schuster, 2000), 25.

31. See Frederick Merk, *Manifest Destiny and Mission in American History* (Cambridge, MA: Harvard University Press, 1995 [1963]).

32. Ronald W. Reagan, 'Remarks at the Annual Convention of the National League of Cities in Los Angeles, California, November 29, 1982', in *Public Papers of the Presidents of the United States: Ronald Reagan, 1982, Book II – July 3 to December 31, 1982* (Washington DC: US Government Printing Office, 1983 [1982]), 1521.

33. Paul D. Erickson, *Reagan Speaks: The Making of an American Myth* (New York, NY: New York University Press, 1985), 89.

34. Ronald W. Reagan, 'Farewell Address to the Nation, January 11, 1989', in *Public Papers of the Presidents of the United States: Ronald Reagan, 1988–89, Book II – July 2 1988 to January 19, 1989* (Washington DC: US

Government Printing Office, 1989 [1991]), 1722 [further quotations come from this source].

35. An interview with Nicholas Meyer, 'The Darling Buds of Meyer', *Star Trek Monthly Magazine* (December 2002): 40.

36. See Robert Berkhofer Jr., *The White Man's Indian: Images of the Native American from Columbus to the Present* (New York, NY: Vintage Books, 1978); Francis Jennings, *The Invasion of America: Indians, Colonialism, and the Cant of Conquest* (New York, NY: W. W. Norton and Company, 1975); Peter Hulme, *Colonial Encounters: Europe and the Native Caribbean, 1492–1797* (New York, NY: Meuthen Press, 1986); Reginald Horsman, *Race and Manifest Destiny: The Origins of American Racial Anglo-Saxonism* (Cambridge, MA: Harvard University Press, 1981).

37. Bercovitch, 'The American Puritan Imagination: An Introduction', 7.

PART TWO

1. Henry Jenkins, 'Star Trek Rerun, Reread, Rewritten: Fan Writing as Textual Poaching', *Critical Studies in Mass Communication* 5.2 (1988): 85–107; and '"Strangers No More, We Sing": Filking and the Social Construction of the Science Fiction Fan Community', in Lisa A. Lewis (ed.), *The Adoring Audience: Fan Culture and Popular Media* (New York, NY: Routledge, 1992), 208–36; Michel de Certeau, *The Practice of Everyday Life* (Berkeley, CA: University of California Press, 1984).

2. 'Filk music' is a term that describes science fiction folk singing. To clarify what I mean by 'typical fan', I should point out that the fans I look at distinguish themselves from more passionate fans by invoking various discourses in their form of textual interaction: the fan letter. Letter-writing allows fans to express a particular kind of sociological and emotional discourse through a particular type of 'imagined community'. The reasons behind this form of fan expression, as opposed to the extreme versions I have already described, seem to be connected to issues relating to inclusion, belonging, and being seen as 'normal'/accepted in the public sphere.

3. See Helen Taylor, *Scarlett's Women: Gone with the Wind and its Female Fans* (London: Virago Press, 1989); and Ien Ang, *Watching Dallas: Soap Opera and the Melodramatic Imagination*, trans. Della Couling (London: Routledge, 1985 [1982]).

4. Geoff King and Tanya Krzywinska, *Science Fiction Cinema: From Outerspace to Cyberspace* (London: Wallflower Press, 2000), 58.

5. For the purposes of this, however, I want to focus on those fans who have had their letters published in print rather than online. This is for two reasons. First, the publications I have looked at are products of the fan community, the magazine and newsletter are bought by

subscription and therefore cater for a specific market. The edited books were projects that specifically asked for fans who wanted to write letters, two of the books being published prior to the advent of the Internet. Second, the Internet is simply too vast to be able to read every single fan response, most of which pertain to the television text rather than the fans' actual emotions, whereas the letters printed on paper are a result of a more focused effort to write their feelings by fans who want to communicate with other fans.

CHAPTER FIVE

1. Daniel L. Bernardi, *Star Trek and History: Race-ing Towards a White Future* (New Brunswick, NJ: Rutgers University Press, 1998), 29–30.

2. Ibid. 30.

3. Russell Jacoby, *The End of Utopia: Politics and Culture in an Age of Apathy* (New York, NY: Basic Books, 1999), xi.

4. Rick Altman, *Film/Genre* (London: BFI Publishing, 1999), 190–1.

5. Anthony Easthope, 'The Personal and the Political in Utopian Science Fiction', in Philip John Davies (ed.), *Science Fiction, Social Conflict and War* (Manchester: Manchester University Press, 1990), 50.

6. Fredric Jameson, 'Cognitive Mapping', in Cary Nelson and Lawrence Grossberg (eds.), *Marxism and the Interpretation of Culture* (Urbana, IL: University of Illinois Press, 1988), 355, quoted in Easthope, 'The Personal and the Political in Utopian Science Fiction', 50.

7. Richard Dyer, 'Entertainment and Utopia', in Rick Altman (ed.), *Genre: The Musical* (London: Routledge and Kegan Paul, 1981), 177.

8. This phrase is taken from a letter received from Elliott Slack printed in *Star Trek Explorer: The Magazine of the Official UK Star Trek Fan Club* 3 (2001): 5.

9. See L. Frank Baum, *The Wonderful Wizard of Oz* (Chicago, IL: Reilly & Lee, 1900). The sequels are listed with publication date only: *The Marvelous Land of Oz* (1904), *Ozma of Oz* (1907), *Dorothy and the Wizard in Oz* (1908), *The Road to Oz* (1909), *The Emerald City of Oz* (1910), *The Patchwork Girl of Oz* (1913), *Tik-Tok of Oz* (1914), *The Scarecrow of Oz* (1915), *Rinkitink in Oz* (1916), *The Lost Princess of Oz* (1917), *The Tin Woodman of Oz* (1918), *The Magic of Oz* (1919), *Glinda of Oz* (1920).

10. Jack Zipes, *Fairy Tales and the Art of Subversion: The Classical Genre for Children and the Process of Civilization* (New York, NY: Routledge, 1983), 129.

11. Jack Zipes, *Fairy Tale as Myth/Myth as Fairy Tale* (Lexington, KY: The University Press of Kentucky, 1994), 138.

12. Zipes, *Fairy Tales and the Art of Subversion*, 126; see also Fred Erisman, 'L. Frank Baum and the Progressive Dilemma', *American Quarterly* 20

(1968): 617–23, and Henry M. Littlefield, 'The Wizard of Oz: Parable on Populism', *American Quarterly* 16 (1964): 47–58.

13. Jack Zipes, *When Dreams Come True: Classical Fairy Tales and their Tradition* (New York, NY: Routledge, 1999), 182.

14. See Alison Lurie, *Not in Front of the Grown-Ups: Subversive Children's Literature* (London: Cardinal, 1990), 28–9; and *Boys and Girls Forever: Children's Classics from Cinderella to Harry Potter* (New York, NY: Penguin Books, 2003), 25–45.

15. Michael Patrick Hearn, 'L. Frank Baum and the "Modernized Fairy Tale"', *Children's Literature in Education* 10.2 (1979): 57.

16. Perry Nodelman, quoted in Peter Hunt and Millicent Lenz, *Alternative Worlds in Fantasy Fiction* (London: Continuum, 2001), 26–7.

17. Christine Geraghty, 'Soap Opera and Utopia', in John Storey (ed.), *Cultural Theory and Popular Culture: A Reader* (2nd edition, London: Prentice Hall, 1998 [1994]), 320. In this article, Geraghty uses Dyer's model to analyse women's fiction, enabling us to have an understanding of why 'escape' and 'fulfilment' also remain persistent characteristics of soap operas.

18. This table is created from the five problems and solutions proposed by Dyer in 'Entertainment and Utopia', 183–4, and summarised by Geraghty in 'Soap Opera and Utopia', 320.

19. Letter received from Danielle Ruddy, printed in Nikki Stafford (ed.), *Trekkers: True Stories by Fans for Fans* (Toronto, ON: ECW Press, 2002), 83–6.

20. Letter received from Gerald Gurian, printed in Nikki Stafford (ed.), *Trekkers: True Stories by Fans for Fans*, 126–33.

21. Letter received from Mark Emanuel Mendoza, printed in Nikki Stafford (ed.), *Trekkers: True Stories by Fans for Fans*, 30–1.

22. Letter received from Shamira, printed in Nikki Stafford (ed.), *Trekkers: True Stories by Fans for Fans*, 11–14.

23. Gerald Gurian, 126.

24. Letter received from Douglas W. Mayo, printed in Nikki Stafford (ed.), *Trekkers: True Stories by Fans for Fans*, 5–8.

25. Letter received from Dan Harris, printed in Nikki Stafford (ed.), *Trekkers: True Stories by Fans for Fans*, 167–8.

26. Letter received from Jason Lighthall, printed in Nikki Stafford (ed.), *Trekkers: True Stories by Fans for Fans*, 2–4.

27. Ibid. 4.

28. Letter received from Marco Di Lalla, printed in Nikki Stafford (ed.), *Trekkers: True Stories by Fans for Fans*, 168–71.

29. Ibid. 169.

30. Letter received from Gregory Newman, printed in Nikki Stafford (ed.),

Trekkers: True Stories by Fans for Fans, 9–10. From here on, the following extracts are taken Newman's letter.

31. H. Bruce Franklin, *Vietnam and Other American Fantasies* (Amherst, MA: University of Massachusetts Press, 2000), 136. Cf. H. Bruce Franklin, 'Star Trek in the Vietnam Era', *Film & History* 24.1–2 (1994): 36–46; and Gary Westfahl, *Science Fiction, Children's Literature, and Popular Culture: Coming of Age in Fantasyland* (Westport, CT: Greenwood Press, 2000), particularly his chapter 'Opposing War, Exploiting War: The Troubled Pacifism of Star Trek', 69–78.

32. An interview with DeForest Kelly on *Trekkies*, dir. Roger Nygard (Paramount Pictures, 1998).

33. 'The City on the Edge of Forever' received the Hugo Award for best Dramatic Presentation in 1968, and its writer also won the Writers' Guild of America Award. Being set in 1930s America, the plot centred on the relationship between Kirk and a woman called Edith Keeler who believed that America should not join the Second World War. After realising that his presence in the past was changing the timeline, keeping America out of the war because of Keeler's peacekeeping efforts and allowing Hitler victory, Kirk decided to let her die in order to restore the proper timeline. In 'A Private Little War', Kirk and his crew discover that the Klingons are providing weapons to some of the inhabitants of a peaceful planet. Kirk decides to intervene and give weapons to the rest of the primitive aliens so as to redress the imbalance and take revenge on the Klingons.

34. The plot of 'The Omega Glory' was discussed in Chapter One. 'Let That Be Your Last Battlefield' is a famous episode from the last season of the original series. Two aliens arrive on the ship; one alien's face is split down the middle, half black and half white, while the second's is half white and half black. They both hate each other but fail to recognise that the intense racial hatred that fuelled their peoples' war has resulted in them being the only remaining survivors, in fact, both blame the other for the devastation and beam down to the surface of their war-torn planet to continue their fight.

35. Franklin, *Vietnam and Other American Fantasies*, 148.

36. Tom Engelhardt, *The End of Victory Culture: Cold War America and the Disillusioning of a Generation* (Amherst, MA: University of Massachusetts Press, 1998), 248.

37. Ibid. 249.

CHAPTER SIX

1. Zygmunt Bauman, *Community: Seeking Safety in an Insecure World* (Cambridge: Polity Press, 2001), 1.

2.   Ibid. 2.

3.   Robert D. Putnam, *Bowling Alone: The Collapse and Revival of American Community* (New York, NY: Touchstone, 2000).

4.   Robert D. Putnam, 'Bowling Alone: America's Declining Social Capital', *Journal of Democracy* 6.1 (1995): 70.

5.   Ibid. 65–6.

6.   Ibid. 71.

7.   Robert Wuthnow, *Sharing the Journey: Support Groups and America's New Quest for Community* (New York, NY: Free Press, 1994), 45.

8.   Ibid. 3–6.

9.   Putnam, 'Bowling Alone: America's Declining Social Capital', 72.

10. Extreme examples of *Star Trek* fans contributing to the local community can be found in *Trekkies* (1998). The documentary shows fans that belong to Klingon- and Federation-based clubs meeting in one another's homes and discussing fund-raising and charity events to help with local action groups such as town clean-up and 'support your hospital'. *Trekkies* shows fans dressed as Klingons collecting money from the public for a children's charity. As we have seen, examples in the letters put forward more universal and wide-ranging actions society has to undertake: eradicating poverty, hunger, greed, discrimination, etc.

11. Joli Jenson, 'Fandom as Pathology: The Consequences of Characterization', in Lisa A. Lewis (ed.), *The Adoring Audience*, 16.

12. Lawrence Grossberg, 'Is there a Fan in the House?: The Affective Sensibility of Fandom', in Lisa A. Lewis (ed.), *The Adoring Audience*, 65.

13. Camille Bacon-Smith, *Enterprising Women: Television Fandom and the Creation of Popular Myth* (Philadelphia, PA: University of Pennsylvania Press, 1992), 261. See also Bacon-Smith, 'Suffering and Solace: The Genre of Pain', in Will Brooker and Deborah Jermyn (eds.), *The Audience Studies Reader* (London: Routledge, 2003), 192–8.

14. Bacon-Smith, *Enterprising Women*, 268.

15. A step on from this would be the slash fiction I discussed in Chapter One. Many of the female fans who write slash would perhaps see hurt-comfort fiction as a precursor to their more explicit stories concerning Kirk and Spock's potential erotic relationship.

16. Bacon-Smith, *Enterprising Women*, 269.

17. Kirby Farrell, *Post-Traumatic Culture: Injury and Interpretation in the Nineties* (Baltimore, MD: Johns Hopkins University Press, 1998), x.

18. Ibid. 2.

19. Ibid. 21.

20. Ibid. 19, 21.

21. Ibid. 26.

22. Letter received from Kenneth Westfall, printed in Susan Sackett (ed.), *Letters to Star Trek* (New York, NY: Ballantine, 1977), 21–2.

23. Fred Turner, *Echoes of Combat: The Vietnam War in American Memory* (New York, NY: Anchor Books, 1996), 80.

24. Ibid. 81.

25. Marita Sturken, *Tangled Memories: The Vietnam War, the AIDS Epidemic, and the Politics of Remembering* (Berkeley, CA: University of California Press, 1997), 17.

26. Judith Lewis Herman, *Trauma and Recovery* (New York, NY: Basic Books, 1992), quoted in Turner, *Echoes of Combat*, 81–2.

27. Lincoln Enterprises is the name of an organisation that was created by Gene Roddenberry to receive, and reply to, the thousands of fan letters, autograph requests and general enquiries that flooded the studio every month during the series' three-year run and after it had been taken off air. It continues to this day to deal with all fan mail concerning the original cast members, including autograph requests, and it is managed by Gene's wife, Majel Barrett-Roddenberry. Subsequent series' fan mail goes directly to a department at Paramount Studios.

28. Herman quoted in Turner, *Echoes of Combat*, 81.

29. Colleen I. Murray, 'Death, Dying, and Bereavement', in Patrick C. McKenry and Sharon J. Price (eds.), *Families and Change: Coping with Stressful Events* (Thousands Oaks, CA: Sage Publications, 1994), 173.

30. There have been many official publications that follow the 'life lesson' idea in *Star Trek*. These books offer ingenious tips on succeeding in life and changing your fortunes by adhering to codes and maxims revealed in *Star Trek* movies and episodes: Dave Marinaccio, *All I Really Needed to Know I Learned from Watching* Star Trek (New York, NY: Crown Publishing, 1995); and *All the Other Things I Really Needed to Know I Learned from Watching* Star Trek: The Next Generation (New York, NY: Pocket Books, 1998); Richard Raben and Hiyaguha Cohen, *Boldly Live As You've Never Lived Before: (Unauthorized and Unexpected) Life Lessons from* Star Trek (New York, NY: Morrow, William & Co., 1995); Wess Roberts and Bill Ross, *Make It So: Leadership Lessons from* Star Trek: The Next Generation (New York, NY: Pocket Books, 1995).

31. Letter received from Virginia Walker, printed in Sackett (ed.), *Letters to Star Trek*, 15–17.

32. Virginia Walker, printed in Sackett (ed.), *Letters to Star Trek*, 16.

33. Murray, 'Death, Dying, and Bereavement', 188.

34. Virginia Walker, printed in Sackett (ed.), *Letters to Star Trek*, 16.

35. Sackett (ed.), *Letters to Star Trek*, 15.

36. William Blake Tyrrell, 'Star Trek as Myth and Television as Mythmaker', *Journal of Popular Culture* 10.4 (1977): 717.

37. Michael Jindra, 'Star Trek Fandom as a Religious Phenomenon', *Sociology of Religion* 55.1 (1994): 50.

38. Letter received from Sandra Bunner, printed in *Star Trek Monthly Magazine* (January 2002): 64.

39. Letter received from Andrea Dearden, printed in *Star Trek Monthly Magazine* (Summer 2001): 95.

40. Letter received from Philip Arkinstall, printed in *Star Trek Monthly Magazine* (March 2001): 63.

41. David Gerrold, *The World of Star Trek: The Inside Story of TV's Most Popular Series* (3rd edition, London: Virgin Books, 1996 [1973, 1984]), 228.

42. Daniel L. Bernardi, *Star Trek and History: Race-ing Towards a White Future* (New Brunswick, NJ: Rutgers University Press, 1998), 7.

43. Letter received from Mark Bird, printed in Nikki Stafford (ed.), *Trekkers: True Stories by Fans for Fans* (Toronto, ON: ECW Press, 2002), 172–3.

44. Ibid. 173.

45. Bourbon includes the name of her Klingon alter ego in the letter: K'Lannagh O'Sullivan, House of E'Toh.

46. Letter received from Avril Storm Bourbon, printed in Stafford (ed.), *Trekkers: True Stories by Fans for Fans*, 174–6.

47. Robert W. Habenstein, 'The Social Organization of Death', in David L. Sills (ed.), *International Encyclopedia of the Social Sciences, Volume 4* (New York, NY: Macmillan, 1968), 26, quoted in Peter Uhlenberg, 'Death and the Family', in Michael Gordon (ed.), *The American Family in Social-Historical Perspective* (New York, NY: St Martin's Press, 1983), 169.

48. 'Heart of Glory' was the first TNG episode to address the Klingons in any significant way. Fans of the aggressive but honourable aliens were delighted to see the Worf character given some screen time and that the Klingons were becoming an important part of the *Star Trek* universe once again. Many seeds for successive Klingon storylines were planted in this episode and new insights into Klingon culture, the Death Howl being one of them, were revealed for the first time.

49. Tyrrell, 'Star Trek as Myth and Television as Mythmaker', 717.

50. See Gary Alan Fine, *Shared Fantasy: Role-Playing Games as Social Worlds* (Chicago, IL: University of Chicago Press, 1983); Kurt Lancaster, *Interacting with Babylon 5: Fan Performances in a Media Universe* (Austin, TX: University of Texas Press, 2001).

51. Putnam sees television as being one of the four main reasons for the erosion of American social capital, therefore it is ironic that as a television series *Star Trek* has brought people together as a community (in this case a community based on Klingon culture) and given them common ground through which they can exercise their individual

liberties. See Putnam, 'Bowling Alone: America's Declining Social Capital', 74–5.

52. Robert Bellah, 'Civil Religion in America', in R. Richey and D. Jones (eds.), *American Civil Religion* (New York, NY: Harper & Row, 1974), 40.

53. Dennis Klass, 'John Bowlby's model of grief and the problems of identification', *Omega: The Journal of Death and Dying* 18.1 (1987): 31, quoted in Murray, 'Death, Dying, and Bereavement', 188.

CHAPTER SEVEN

1. Compare this to the immensely successful *Chicken Soup* series – popular volumes of collected personal stories aimed at inspiring different people at particular times, offering help and guidance for those who feel lost. See Jack Canfield and Mark Victor Hansen (eds.), *Chicken Soup for the Soul: 101 Stories to Open the Heart and Rekindle the Spirit* (Deerfield Beach, FL: Health Communications Incorporated, 1993). Since the publication of the first volume of 'inspirational' stories there have been 57 sequels to date, resulting in 80 million copies being sold in 32 languages around the world. Other *Chicken Soup* volumes range from those aimed at mothers, teenagers, children, the recently bereaved and teachers to some aimed at quite specific groups including pet lovers, those who enjoy Christmas, Jewish mothers, baseball fans and NASCAR (American motor sports) enthusiasts. A history of the *Chicken Soup* volumes is accessible on the website available at: <http://www.chickensoup.com/> (Accessed 13 April 2004).

2. Roland Barthes, *The Pleasure of the Text*, trans. Richard Miller (New York, NY: Hill and Wang, 1975), 14.

3. Mark Jancovich, 'Screen Theory', in Joanne Hollows and Mark Jancovich (eds.), *Approaches to Popular Film* (Manchester: Manchester University Press, 1995), 126.

4. Ibid. 144–5.

5. Sonia Livingstone and Peter Lunt, *Talk on Television: Audience Participation and Public Debate* (London: Routledge, 1994), 43.

6. Ibid. 66–7.

7. Joshua Gamson, *Freaks Talk Back: Tabloid Talk Shows and Sexual Nonconformity* (Chicago, IL: University of Chicago Press, 1998), 104.

8. Jane Shattuc, *The Talking Cure: TV Talk Shows and Women* (New York, NY: Routledge, 1997), 136.

9. Jon Dovey, *Freakshow: First Person Media and Factual Television* (London: Pluto Press, 2000), 107.

10. Fred Pelka, 'Hating the Sick: Health Chauvinism and Its Cure', *The Humanist* 54.4 (July/August 1997): 17, quoted in Hanley E. Kanar, 'No Ramps in Space: The Inability to Envision Accessibility in *Star Trek*:

Deep Space Nine', in Elyce Rae Helford (ed.), *Fantasy Girls: Gender in the New Universe of Science Fiction and Fantasy Television* (Lanham, MD: Rowman and Littlefield Publishers, 2000), 247.

11.   Kanar, 'No Ramps in Space: The Inability to Envision Accessibility in *Star Trek: Deep Space Nine*', 261.

12.   Ibid. 248.

13.   Leah R. Van de Berg, 'Liminality: Worf as Metonymic Signifier of Racial, Cultural, and National Differences', in Taylor Harrison, Sarah Projansky, Kent A. Ono and Elyce Rae Helford (eds.), *Enterprise Zones: Critical Positions on Star Trek* (Boulder, CO: Westview Press, 1996), 51–68. In the episode 'Ethics', Worf is seriously injured when a support beam breaks and causes a heavy container to fall on him. He is paralysed from the waist down. This news crushes Worf's Klingon pride, and he refuses to allow anyone, including his son Alexander, to see him. Worf, believing his life to be already over, asks Riker to assist in his ceremonial suicide, citing the belief that no Klingon should live as an object of pity or shame. But, thanks to advanced Federation medicine and a mysterious Klingon biochemical reaction, Worf recovers on the operating table. This combination of miracle and science saves Worf from living as an object of pity.

14.   Letter received from Mayo, printed in Nikki Stafford (ed.), *Trekkers: True Stories by Fans for Fans* (Toronto, ON: ECW Press, 2002), 5–8.

15.   Ibid. 7.

16.   Letter received from Nicola Corbett, printed in Star Trek Explorer: The Magazine of the Official UK Star Trek Fan Club 2.3 (2000): 5.

17.   Robert D. Putnam, *Bowling Alone: The Collapse and Revival of American Community* (New York, NY: Touchstone, 2000), 326.

18.   Anonymous letter, printed in Jacqueline Lichtenberg, Sondra Marshak, and Joan Winston, Star Trek Lives! (New York, NY: Bantam Books, 1975), 19.

19.   Putnam, *Bowling Alone*, 326.

20.   Ibid. Information taken from Lisa Berkman and Thomas Glass, 'Social Integration, Social Networks, Social Support, and Health', in Lisa F. Berkman and Ichiro Kawachi (eds.), *Social Epidemiology* (New York, NY: Oxford University Press, 2000), 137–74.

21.   Letter received from Lighthall, printed in Nikki Stafford (ed.), *Trekkers: True Stories by Fans for Fans*, 4.

22.   Letter received from Di Lalla, printed in Nikki Stafford (ed.), *Trekkers: True Stories by Fans for Fans*, 168–71.

23.   Ibid. 171.

24.   Letter received from Jeanna F. Gallo, printed in Nikki Stafford (ed.), *Trekkers: True Stories by Fans for Fans*, 91–93.

25.   Letter received from Kathy Warren, printed in Nikki Stafford (ed.), *Trekkers: True Stories by Fans for Fans*, 78–83.

26.   Jacqueline Lichtenberg, Sondra Marshak, and Joan Winston, *Star Trek Lives!*, 11.

27.   Ibid. 42.

28.   Wayne's role in *Sands of Iwo Jima* (1949) is exemplary of the mythic image he so often portrayed. See Richard Slotkin, *Gunfighter Nation: The Myth of the Frontier in Twentieth-Century America* (Norton, OK: Oklahoma University Press, 1998), 519–20.

29.   Lou Harry, *It's Slinky!: The Fun and Wonderful Toy* (Philadelphia, PA: Running Press, 2000), 49.

30.   Richard Drinnon, *Facing West: The Metaphysics of Indian-Hating and Empire-Building* (Norman, OK: Oklahoma University Press, 1997), 455–67.

31.   George C. Herring, *America's Longest War: The United States and Vietnam, 1950–1975* (3rd edition, New York, NY: McGraw-Hill, 1996 [1979, 1986]), 236; Tom Engelhardt, *The End of Victory Culture: Cold War America and the Disillusioning of a Generation* (Amherst, MA: University of Massachusetts Press, 1998), 215–27.

32.   See Richard Slotkin, 'Unit Pride: Ethnic Platoons and the Myths of American Nationality', *American Literary History* 13.3 (2001): 469–98, for a comparison of *Star Trek*'s use of the war image in its episodes and the Hollywood platoon as an idealised version of American society pulling together. For Slotkin, whereas *Star Trek*'s original mission of space exploration has its roots in the genre of the Western film, its wars 'come from the combat film and are fought by multiethnic, multiracial, and multigendered military units' (493) contributing to the myth of oneness in American society.

33.   William Shatner and Chip Walter, *Star Trek: I'm Working on That: A Trek from Science Fiction to Science Fact* (New York, NY: Pocket Books, 2002), 9.

PART THREE

1.   Henry Jenkins, 'Interactive Audiences?', in Dan Harries (ed.), *The New Media Book* (London: BFI, 2002), 157.

2.   See Henry Jenkins and John Tulloch, 'Beyond the *Star Trek* Phenomenon: Reconceptualizing the Science Fiction Audience', in John Tulloch and Henry Jenkins, *Science Fiction Audiences: Watching Doctor Who and Star Trek* (London: Routledge, 1995), 3–24.

3.   Jenkins, 'Interactive Audiences?' 159.

4.   Nancy K. Baym, 'Talking About Soaps: Communicative Practices in a Computer-Mediated Fan Culture', in Cheryl Harris and Alison

Alexander (eds.), *Theorizing Fandom: Fans, Subculture and Identity* (Cresskill, NJ: Hampton Press, 1998), 115.

5.　　See Nathan Hunt, 'The Importance of Trivia: Ownership, Exclusion and Authority in Science Fiction Fandom', in Mark Jancovich, Antonio Lázaro Reboll, Julian Stringer and Andy Willis (eds.), *Defining Cult Movies: The Cultural Politics of Oppositional Taste* (Manchester: Manchester University Press, 2003), 185–201.

6.　　See Will Brooker, 'Internet Fandom and the Continuing Narratives of *Star Wars, Blade Runner* and *Alien*', in Annette Kuhn (ed.), *Alien Zone II: The Spaces of Science Fiction Cinema* (London: Verso, 1999), 50–72; and *Using the Force: Creativity, Community and Star Wars Fans* (New York, NY: Continuum, 2002).

7.　　Matt Hills, 'Putting Away Childish Things: Jar Jar Binks and the "Virtual Star" as an Object of Fan Loathing', in Thomas Austin and Martin Barker (eds.), *Contemporary Hollywood Stardom* (London: Arnold, 2003), 89. For more on *Star Wars* fans' attempts at establishing cultural status, see also Matt Hills, 'Star Wars in Fandom, Film Theory, and the Museum', in Julian Stringer (ed.), *Movie Blockbusters* (London: Routledge, 2003), 178–89.

CHAPTER EIGHT

1.　　For the first two seasons of Enterprise, the Star Trek name was absent from the show. In fact, this was the first Star Trek series from Paramount not to have the traditional moniker. It was felt by producers that dropping the Star Trek would signal to audiences that this was a fresh take on the future, stamping a sense of originality and uniqueness onto a Star Trek product without making it obvious. However, due to falling ratings and a perceived lack of interest in the show because people were not aware that it was Star Trek, the famous signature was added at the start of Season Three. UPN communications director Diane Kuri emphasised that 'by formally changing the show's title, we will be able to further capitalise on and form a stronger connection to the famous and highly successful Star Trek franchise.' See 'Star Trek is Back', *Star Trek Monthly Magazine* (December 2003): 7. However, I believe that this shift was not entirely based on marketing strategies; it is pretty obvious that Enterprise was always a Star Trek show. Instead, this shift signals a return to Star Trek's traditional roots – emphasising to fans that Enterprise is not that new at all.

2.　　Thomas Richards, Star Trek in Myth and Legend (London: Orion Books, 1998), 173.

3.　　The Westerns *Wagon Train* and *Rifleman* were television serials that Roddenberry saw as being influential on Star Trek; one clearly emphasises the voyage aspect of the space series and the other the more sedentary, more violent aspects of the series set in a contested area of space. See J. M. Dillard, Star Trek 'Where No One Has Gone Before': A History in Pictures (New York, NY: Pocket Books, 1996), 152.

4. Chris Gregory, Star Trek Parallel Narratives (London: Macmillan Press, 2000), 69.

5. Ibid.74.

6. Karin Blair, 'Star Trek Old and New: From the Alien Embodied to the Alien Imagined', in George McKay (ed.), Yankee Go Home (And Take Me With You): Americanization and Popular Culture (Sheffield: Sheffield Academic Press, 1997), 88.

7. Some examples of these books are Marco Palmieri (ed.), The Lives of Dax (New York, NY: Pocket Books, 1999); Andrew J. Robinson, Star Trek: Deep Space Nine #27 – A Stitch in Time (New York, NY: Pocket Books, 2000); S. D. Perry, Avatar Book One of Two and Avatar Book Two of Two (New York, NY: Pocket Books, 2001); the Mission: Gamma series: David R. George III's Twilight, Heather Jarman's This Gray Spirit, Michael A. Martin and Andy Mangels' Cathedral, Robert Simpson's Lesser Evil (New York, NY: Pocket Books, 2002); and the Klingon-based novels by J. G. Hertzler and Jeffrey Lang, The Left Hand of Destiny, Book One and Book Two (New York, NY: Pocket Books, 2003); S. D. Perry's Rising Son and Unity (New York, NY: Pocket Books, 2003) continued to celebrate DS9's tenth anniversary with a story about Jake Sisko trying to contact his father through the Bajoran Wormhole.

8. L. Pearson, quoted in Matt Hills, Fan Cultures (London: Routledge, 2002), 226, n. 15.

9. Karen Anijar, Teaching Toward the 24th Century: Star Trek as Social Curriculum, Garland Reference Library of Social Science (New York, NY: Falmer Press, 2000), 194–5.

10. Nick Jones, 'Retcon Tricks', Star Trek Monthly Magazine (February 2002): 19.

11. John Harlow, 'Amazons lead Hollywood raid on antiquity', Sunday Times (20 January 2002): Section I, 27.

12. Donna Minkowitz, 'Beam Us Back, Scotty!', The Nation (25 March 2002): 37.

13. Ibid. 36.

14. In the build-up to the third season of Enterprise in September 2003, the Star Trek website posted a timeline that charts the history of space exploration. Included in this timeline are key dates in the history of Star Trek's future narrative, many of which are pictured in the opening credits sequence. See 'Key Events in Exploration History'. Available at: <http://www.

startrek.com/startrek/view/features/documentaries/article/462. html> (Accessed 10 September 2003). Below are a few extracts: '**1799** – Henry Spencer of Baltimore, Maryland, builds a sailing ship, a schooner named Enterprise. **1903** – The Wright Brothers build and fly the first motorized airplane in Kitty Hawk, North Carolina, forever giving mankind 'wings'. **1957** – Earth's Space Age, and the so-called space race, begins when the USSR puts an artificial satellite, Sputnik-1, into orbit around the planet. Although unverified, it has been reported that in October of this year a Vulcan scientific party observes Earth and the Sputnik launch. After three weeks of surreptitious intelligence gathering, the party is forced to land on the planet. The fate of the four Vulcans remains a mystery. **1976** – NASA unveils Enterprise (Space Shuttle OV-101), the prototype for its new fleet of reusable Earth-orbiting shuttles. Flight testing begins the following year. **2063** – In the post-war era, Zefram Cochrane converts an intercontinental ballistic missile (ICBM) into the first faster-than-light, or warp, spaceship – the *Phoenix*. On April 5, the Phoenix's test flight attracts the attention of other space travelers [sic] and 'first contact' is soon made between humans and Vulcans. *c.***2143** – Starfleet pilot Jonathan Archer meets engineer Charles 'Trip' Tucker III while the two officers are working together on tests for the warp-capable NX-Alpha and Beta ships. Henry Archer, Jonathan's father, was the main designer of the NX ship engine. **2151** – With veteran Starfleet pilot Jonathan Archer at the helm, the first Warp 5 capable ship, the Enterprise NX-01, is sent on its first mission. The actual launch is pushed forward to April 15 when a diplomatic crisis escalates. The ship's assignment: to return a mysterious Klingon who landed on Earth at Broken Bow, Oklahoma, back to his homeworld.'

15.   Sarah Neely, 'Cool Intentions: The Literary Classic, the Teenpic and the "Chick Flick"', in Deborah Cartmell, I. Q. Hunter and Imelda Whelehan (eds.), *Retrovisions: Reinventing the Past in Film and Fiction* (London: Pluto Press, 2001), 74.

16.   Deborah Cartmell and I.Q. Hunter, 'Introduction: Retrovisions: Historical Makeovers in Film and Literature', in Deborah Cartmell, I.Q. Hunter, and Imelda Whelehan (eds.), *Retrovisions: Reinventing the Past in Film and Fiction*, 7.

17.   Deborah L. Madsen, *American Exceptionalism* (Edinburgh: Edinburgh University Press, 1998), 166.

18.   Letter received from Bryn Hughes, 'Russians Ruled Out', *Radio Times* (10–16 August 2002): 8.

19.   Letter received from Hugh Henderson, 'Yanks for the Memory', *Star Trek Monthly Magazine* (November 2002): 20.

20.   Email response received from 'Sleader', 'Minor Issue', *Back in Time: Enterprise Fan Forum*, posted 6 April 2002. Available at: <http://bitent. cjb.net/fbackintimeenterprisefrm1.showMessage?topicID=62.topic> (Accessed 1 August 2003).

21.   Daniel L. Bernardi, *Star Trek and History: Race-ing Towards a White Future* (New Brunswick, NJ: Rutgers University Press, 1998), 96–104.

CHAPTER NINE

1.   It is interesting to note that *Star Trek* is not mentioned in connection with *Galaxy Quest* in any of its DVD/video release packaging or marketing material. Also, interviews and documentaries featured on the 2001 DVD release neither mention nor posit *Star Trek* and its fans as inspiration for the movie or as its obvious target audience. What is stressed as the basis for *Galaxy Quest*'s possible appeal for its perceived audience is the concept that a group of actors from a once-popular TV show have to assume their fictional identities to save the day for real. According to producer Mark Johnson, this concept 'had great comic potential' (see inside production notes, *Galaxy Quest* DVD, 2001). For the purposes of this chapter, it is important to point out here the fact that fans are not seen as the 'comic potential' for the movie intimates that they are not the subject of ridicule. Rather, their development as individuals represents the serious thrust of the film's message.

2.   For an equally positive and enlightening reading of the film, see Roz Kaveney, *From Alien to The Matrix: Reading Science Fiction Film* (London: I.B.Tauris & Co. Ltd, 2005).

3.   William Shatner and other stars of *Star Trek* have watched and enjoyed *Galaxy Quest*. Shatner's quote is taken from an interview he gave on the *Star Trek* website on 11 August 2001, my excerpt was printed on the *Galaxy Quest* website along with other star comments. Available at: <http://www.questarian.com/Databank/gq-trek_talks.htm> (Accessed 4 December 2003).

4.   Nichelle Nichols, *Beyond Uhura: Star Trek and Other Memories* (London: Boxtree Ltd, 1995), 187.

5.   Paul Wells, 'To Affinity and Beyond: Woody, Buzz and the New Authenticity', in Thomas Austin and Martin Barker (eds.), *Contemporary Hollywood Stardom* (London: Arnold, 2003), 101.

6.   Peter A. Chvany, 'Do We Look Like Ferengi Capitalists to You? *Star Trek*'s Klingons as Emergent Virtual American Ethnics', in Henry Jenkins, Tara McPherson and Jane Shattuc (eds.), *Hop on Pop: The Politics and Pleasures of Popular Culture* (Durham, NC: Duke University

Press, 2003), 106–7.

7.   Lisabeth Shatner, *Captain's Log: William Shatner's Personal Account of the Making of* Star Trek V: The Final Frontier (London: Titan Books, 1989),132–7; and Judith and Garfield Reeves-Stevens, *The Art of* Star Trek (New York, NY: Pocket Books, 1995), 256.

8.   See 'The Questarian' website, available at: <http://www.questarian. com/AR/gq-Altered_Reality.htm> (Accessed 4 December 2003).

9.   Robert Jewett and John Shelton Lawrence, *The American Monomyth* (Garden City, NY: Anchor Press, 1977); Michael Coyne, *The Crowded Prairie: American National Identity in the Hollywood Western* (London: I.B.Tauris & Co. Ltd, 1997), 7.

10.   Geoff King believes that the actors' position in *Galaxy Quest* as participants in a real space drama is 'a scenario in which continued parody of the television show [*Star Trek*] gains increased dimension and comic effect'. A similar effect can be seen in *¡Three Amigos!* and to some extent in *Spaceballs* (1987), although the latter parody, aimed at *Star Wars*, is more 'a thinly developed play' on the original plot; King sees this as 'a hook for the deployment of a variety of broad parodic gags'. See King, *Film Comedy* (London: Wallflower Press, 2002), 128. See also Dan Harries, *Film Parody* (London: BFI, 2000) for a comprehensive analysis of parody in film.

11.   Richard Slotkin, *Gunfighter Nation: The Myth of the Frontier in Twentieth-Century America* (Norton, OK: Oklahoma University Press, 1998), 635.

12.   Frederick Jackson Turner, *The Frontier in American History* (3rd edition, Tucson, AZ: University of Arizona Press, 1994 [1920]), 4.

13.   De Witt Douglas Kilgore, *Astrofuturism: Science, Race, and Visions of Utopia in Space* (Philadelphia, PA: University of Pennsylvania Press, 2003), 2.

14.   For a record of their mission, see John Bakeless (ed.), *The Journals of Lewis and Clark* (New York, NY: Mentor Press, 1964); Howard E. McCurdy, *Space and the American Imagination* (Washington DC: Smithsonian Institute Press, 1997), 143.

15.   Vivian Sobchack, *Screening Space: The American Science Fiction Film* (New Brunswick, NJ: Rutgers University Press, 1998), 276.

16.   Daniel L. Bernardi, *Star Trek and History: Race-ing Towards a White Future* (New Brunswick, NJ: Rutgers University Press, 1998), 72.

17.   Christine Wertheim, '*Star Trek: First Contact*: The Hybrid, the Whore and the Machine', in Ziauddin Sardar and Sean Cubitt (eds.), *Aliens R Us: The Other in Science Fiction Cinema* (London: Pluto Press, 2002), 75. Wertheim actually makes a mistake here; Riker and Geordie are not the ones to be interrupted whilst admiring the Phoenix; Data and Picard are caught 'cooing' over the artefact. In this scene, it is interesting to note that Picard says that after seeing it displayed in

the Smithsonian Institute (rather like the Enterprise model on display today), touching the Phoenix makes it all the more real to him.

18. Piers D. Britton and Simon J. Barker, *Reading Between Designs: Visual Imagery and the Generation of Meaning in* The Avengers, The Prisoner, *and* Doctor Who (Austin, TX: University of Texas Press, 2003), 31.

19. Michael A. G. Michaud, *Reaching for the High Frontier: The American Pro-Space Movement, 1972–84* (New York, NY: Praeger, 1986),128–9; see also Susan Sackett, *Inside* Trek: *My Secret Life with Star Trek Creator Gene Roddenberry* (Tulsa, OK: Hawk Publishing Group, 2002), 50–1.

20. Ironically, the Space Shuttle Enterprise never went into space; it was used as a dummy by NASA scientists. It was originally going to be called Constitution. Again after fan intervention, the Space Shuttle Enterprise's future has been secured: it has been relocated to the new National Air and Space Museum's Steven F. Udvar-Hazy Center to the east of Dulles Airport outside Washington DC. In *Star Trek*, the shuttle Enterprise has become intertwined with its historical version of space exploration; officially being the first of eight spacecraft to bear the name. The famous Enterprise captained by Kirk is a *Constitution* class vessel. Of course, the most recent series is also called *Enterprise*.

21. Rupert Wilkinson, *American Tough: The Tough-Guy Tradition and American Character* (Westport, CT: Greenwood Press, 1984), 53.

22. In a deleted scene included on the special 2001 DVD release of *Galaxy Quest*, a similar thing happens with the Thermians. While they show Taggert and his crew around the engine room, a number of Thermians ask Tech. Sgt. Chen to help them with an engineering problem they cannot solve. Of course, as Chen the problem would be easy to solve but as Fred Kwan the actor he has no idea what to say. In his attempt to retain his fictional persona, and get the answer, Kwan prods the Thermians for their own theories on what to do, merely saying 'and' and 'so' when the Thermian engineer posits an idea. This method drives the Thermians to come up with their own solution thus confirming to themselves and the audience that they had the power within themselves all along. By way of retaining the fictional reality of the *Galaxy Quest* TV show – and for comic effect – the Thermians praise Kwan for his 'genius' as Tech. Sgt. Chen even though he did not offer any advice.

23. Robert M. Farr and Serge Moscovici (eds.), *Social Representations* (Cambridge and Paris: Cambridge University Press and Maison des Sciences de l'Homme, 1984).

24. Martha Augoustinos and Iain Walker, *Social Cognition: An Integrated Introduction* (London: Sage Publications, 1995), 135.

25. Serge Moscovici, 'Foreword', in Claudine Herzlich, *Health and Illness:*

A Social Psychological Analysis, trans. Douglas Graham (London: Academic Press, 1973), xiii.

26.   Nikki Stafford (ed.), *Trekkers: True Stories by Fans for Fans* (Toronto, ON: ECW Press, 2002).

27.   Letter received from Mark Emanuel Mendoza, 'Real Life: The Final Frontier', in Stafford (ed.), *Trekkers: True Stories by Fans for Fans*, 30–1.

28.   Ibid. 33.

29.   Interview in 'Higher Intelligence', *People* (24 December 2001): 92.

30.   Mendoza, 'Real Life', 32.

31.   Letter received from James Kaye, 'Future Perfect', *Star Trek Monthly Magazine* (February 2001): 96.

32.   Kilgore, *Astrofuturism*, 2.

33.   Letter received from Samantha Hattingh, 'Fame', *Star Trek Monthly Magazine* (April 2001): 63.

EPILOGUE

1.   Letter from Robin Weises (30 March 1967), Gene Roddenberry *Star Trek* Television Series Collection, 1966–1969 (Collection 62): Box 28, folder 5. Arts Library Special Collections, Young Research Library, University of California, Los Angeles. Letter references hereafter will give box and folder number.

2.   Letter from Maureen Dyshere and Katherine Thompson (11 July 1967): Box 28, folder 2.

3.   Letter from Kay Anderson (4 December 1966): Box 28, folder 1.

4.   Letter from S. D. Landers (16 December 1966): Box 28, folder 1.

5.   See '*Star Trek: Enterprise* Cancelled!' Available at: <http://www.startrek.com/startrek/view/news/article/9469.html> (Accessed 7 February 2005).

6.   Terry Eagleton, *Literary Theory: An Introduction* (Oxford: Blackwell, 1983), 137 (author's emphasis).

7.   Benedict Anderson, *Imagined Communities: Reflections on the Origin and Spread of Nationalism* (London: Verso, 1983), 6.

8.   A recent article in the *Journal of American Studies* may possibly signal the academic turn to analysing the significance of the Internet in American culture. In Viviane Serfaty, 'Online Diaries: Towards a Structural Approach', *Journal of American Studies* 38.3 (2004): 457–71, the author examines the links between weblogs (blogs) and Emerson's concept of self-reliance. The two represent America's constant attempts at exploring notions of the self and the nation's continued process of becoming.

9.   See Jennifer E. Porter, 'To Boldly Go: *Star Trek* Convention Attendance as Pilgrimage', in Jennifer E. Porter and Darcee L. McLaren (eds.), *Star*

Trek and Sacred Grounds: Explorations of Star Trek, Religion, and American Culture (Albany, NY: State University of New York Press, 1999), 245–70.

10. Jan Vansina, Oral Tradition as History (London: James Currey, 1985), xii (author's emphasis).

11. Jane Shattuc, The Talking Cure: TV Talk Shows and Women (New York, NY: Routledge, 1997), 109.

12. Alison Landsberg, Prosthetic Memory: The Transformation of American Remembrance in the Age of Mass Culture (New York, NY: Columbia University Press, 2004), 152.

FILMOGRAPHY

STAR TREK EPISODES
'Amok Time' dir. Joseph Pevney, 1967
'The Andorian Incident' dir. Roxann Dawson, 2001
'The Apple' dir. Joseph Peveny, 1967
'All Good Things...' dir. Winrich Kolbe, 1994
'The Best of Both Worlds' parts 1 & 2 dir. Cliff Bole, 1990
'Broken Bow' dir. James L. Conway, 2001
'The Cage' dir. Robert Butler, 1964
'Caretaker' dir. Winrich Kolbe, 1995
'The City on the Edge of Forever' dir. Joseph Pevney, 1967
'The Corbomite Maneuver' dir. Joseph Sargent, 1966
'Critical Care' dir. Terry Windell, 2000
'Crossover' dir. David Livingston, 1994
'Distant Origin' dir. David Livingston, 1997
'Emissary' dir. David Carson, 1993
'The Emperor's New Cloak' dir. LeVar Burton, 1998
'The Enemy Within' dir. Leo Penn, 1966
'Errand of Mercy' dir. John Newland, 1967
'Ethics' dir. Chip Chalmers, 1992
'Flashback' dir. David Livingston, 1996
'The Gamesters of Triskelion' dir. Gene Nelson, 1968
'Heart of Glory' dir. Rob Bowman, 1988
'Imperfection' dir. David Livingston, 2000
'Jetrel' dir. Kim Friedman, 1995
'The Killing Game' parts 1 & 2 dir. David Livingston and Victor Lobl, 1998
'Let That Be Your Last Battlefield' dir. Jud Taylor, 1969
'Lineage' dir. Peter Lauritson, 2001
'Melora' dir. Winrich Kolbe, 1993
'Mirror Mirror' dir. Marc Daniels, 1967

'The Omega Glory' dir. Vincent McEveety, 1968
'One Small Step...' dir. Robert Picardo, 1999
'Parallels' dir. Robert Wiemer, 1993
'Pen Pals' dir. Winrich Kolbe, 1989
'Penumbra' dir. Steve Posey, 1999
'A Piece of the Action' dir. James Komack, 1968
'Plato's Stepchildren' dir. David Alexander, 1968
'A Private Little War' dir. Marc Daniels, 1968
'Repentance' dir. Mike Vejar, 2001
'Resurrection' dir. LeVar Burton, 1997
'Return of the Archons' dir. Joseph Pevney, 1967
'Rightful Heir' dir. Winrich Kolbe, 1993
'Sacred Ground' dir. Robert Duncan McNeill, 1996
'Shattered Mirror' dir. James L. Conway, 1996
'Space Seed' dir. Marc Daniels, 1967
'Sub Rosa' dir. Jonathan Frakes, 1994
'A Taste of Armageddon' dir. Joseph Pevney, 1967
'Through the Looking Glass' dir. Winrich Kolbe, 1995
'Tomorrow is Yesterday' dir. Michael O'Herlihy, 1967
'Trials and Tribble-ations' dir. Jonathan West, 1996
'The Trouble with Tribbles' dir. Joseph Pevney, 1967
'What You Leave Behind' dir. Allan Kroeker, 1999
'Where No Man Has Gone Before' dir. James Goldstone, 1966
'Whom Gods Destroy' dir. Herb Wallerstein, 1969
'Year of Hell' parts 1 & 2 dir. Allan Kroeker and Mike Vejar, 1997
'Yesterday's Enterprise' dir. David Carson, 1990

TELEVISION

Bewitched, ABC, 1964–1972
Buck Rogers, Universal, 1939, 1950
Crossroads, ITV, 1964–1988
Dallas, CBS, 1978–1991
Doctor Who, BBC, 1963–1989, 1996, 2005–present
Flash Gordon, Universal, 1936, 1959
Frasier, NBC/Paramount, 1993–2004
The Fugitive, ABC/Quinn Martin, 1963–1967
Futurama, Fox/Twentieth Century Fox, 1999–2003
Hart to Hart, ABC, 1979–1984
Hercules: The Legendary Journeys, MCA/Universal, 1994–1999
Home Improvement, Buena Vista Television/Touchstone Television, 1991–1999
Lost in Space, CBS, 1965–1968
Nationwide, BBC, 1969–1983

The Oprah Winfrey Show, Harpo Productions Inc./Syndicated, 1986–present

Quantum Leap, NBC/Universal, 1989–1993

Saturday Night Live, NBC/Paramount, 1975–present

The Simpsons, Fox/20th Century Fox, 1989–present

Smallville: Superman the Early Years, WB, 2001–present

South Park, Comedy Central, 1997–present

'Star Mitzvah' _Frasier_, dir. Sheldon Epps, 2002

Star Trek, NBC, 1966–1969

Star Trek: Enterprise [_Enterprise_], Paramount/UPN, 2001–2005

Star Trek: Deep Space Nine, Paramount, 1993–1999

Star Trek Story, BBC2, August 2001

Star Trek: The Animated Series, NBC, 1973–1974

Star Trek: The Next Generation, Paramount, 1987–1994

Star Trek: Thirty Years and Beyond, BBC2/Paramount, 1996

Star Trek: Voyager, Paramount/UPN, 1995–2001

'Where No Fan Has Gone Before' _Futurama_, dir. Pat Shinagawa, 2002

Xena: Warrior Princess, MCA/Universal, 1995–2001

FILM

Alien, dir. Ridley Scott, 20th Century Fox, 1979

Anger Management, dir. Peter Segal, Happy Madison Productions/Revolution Studios, 2003

Batman, dir. Tim Burton, Warner Bros., 1989

The Cable Guy, dir. Ben Stiller, Columbia Pictures, 1996

The Empire Strikes Back, dir. Irvin Kershner, 20th Century Fox, 1980

Galaxy Quest, dir. Dean Parisot, Dreamworks, 1999

Gone with the Wind, dir. Victor Fleming, MGM, 1939

The Magnificent Seven, dir. John Sturges, MGM/United Artists, 1960

Return of the Jedi, dir. Richard Marquand, 20th Century Fox, 1983

Sands of Iwo Jima, dir. Allan Dwan, Republic, 1949

The Searchers, dir. John Ford, Warner Bros., 1956

The Seven Samurai, dir. Akira Kurosawa, Paramount Pictures, 1954

Shane, dir. George Stevens, Paramount Pictures, 1953

Spaceballs, dir. Mel Brooks, Brooksfilms Ltd/MGM, 1987

Star Trek II: The Wrath of Khan, dir. Nicholas Meyer, Paramount Pictures, 1982

Star Trek III: The Search for Spock, dir. Leonard Nimoy, Paramount Pictures, 1984

Star Trek IV: The Voyage Home, dir. Leonard Nimoy, Paramount Pictures, 1986

Star Trek V: The Final Frontier, dir. William Shatner, Paramount Pictures, 1989

Star Trek VI: The Undiscovered Country, dir. Nicholas Meyer, Paramount Pictures, 1991

Star Trek: First Contact, dir. Jonathan Frakes, Paramount Pictures, 1996

Star Trek Generations, dir. David Carson, Paramount Pictures, 1994

Star Trek: Insurrection, dir. Jonathan Frakes, Paramount Pictures, 1998

Star Trek Nemesis, dir. Stuart Baird, Paramount Pictures, 2002

Star Trek: The Motion Picture, dir. Robert Wise, Paramount Pictures, 1979

Star Wars, dir. George Lucas, 20th Century Fox, 1977

Star Wars Episode I: The Phantom Menace, dir. George Lucas, 20th Century Fox, 1999

Star Wars Episode II: Attack of the Clones, dir. George Lucas, 20th Century Fox, 2002

Star Wars Episode III: Revenge of the Sith, dir. George Lucas, 20th Century Fox, 2005

Superman, dir. Richard Donner, Warner Bros., 1978

¡Three Amigos!, dir. John Landis, HBO/LA Films, 1986

THX 1138, dir. George Lucas, Warner Bros., 1971

Toy Story, dir. John Lasseter, Disney/Pixar, 1995

Toy Story 2, dir. John Lasseter, Disney/Pixar, 1999

Trekkies, dir. Roger Nygard, Paramount Pictures, 1998

The Wizard of Oz, dir. Victor Fleming, MGM, 1939

BIBLIOGRAPHY

Abercrombie, Nicholas, and Brian Longhurst, *Audiences: A Sociological Theory of Performance and Imagination* (London: Sage Publications, 1998)

Altman, Rick (ed.), *Genre: The Musical* (London: Routledge and Kegan Paul, 1981)

Altman, Rick, *Film/Genre* (London: BFI Publishing, 1999)

Anderson, Benedict, *Imagined Communities: Reflections on the Origin and Spread of Nationalism* (London: Verso, 1983)

Anderson, Steve, 'Loafing in the Garden of Knowledge: History TV and Popular Memory', *Film & History, Special Focus: Television as Historian*, Part 1 30.1 (2000): 14–23

Ang, Ien, *Watching Dallas: Soap Opera and the Melodramatic Imagination*, trans. Della Couling (London: Routledge, 1985 [1982])

Anijar, Karen, *Teaching Toward the 24th Century: Star Trek as Social Curriculum*, Garland Reference Library of Social Science (New York, NY: Falmer Press, 2000)

Arieli, Yehoshua, *Individualism and Nationalism in American Ideology* (Cambridge, MA: Harvard University Press, 1964)

Auerbach, Erich, *Mimesis: The Representation of Reality in Western Literature* (Princeton, NJ: Princeton University Press, 1953)

Augoustinos, Martha, and Iain Walker, *Social Cognition: An Integrated Introduction* (London: Sage Publications, 1995)

Bacon-Smith, Camille, *Enterprising Women: Television Fandom and the Creation of Popular Myth* (Philadelphia, PA: University of Pennsylvania Press, 1992)

———, 'Suffering and Solace: The Genre of Pain', in Will Brooker and Deborah Jermyn (eds.), *The Audience Studies Reader* (London: Routledge, 2003), 192–8

Bakeless, John (ed.), *The Journals of Lewis and Clark* (New York, NY: Mentor Press, 1964)

Barrett, Michèle, and Duncan Barrett, *Star Trek: The Human Frontier* (Cambridge: Polity Press, 2001)

Barthes, Roland, The Pleasure of the Text, trans. Richard Miller (New York, NY: Hill and Wang, 1975)

_____, Mythologies, trans. Annette Lavers (London: Vintage, 1993 [1972])

Barton, David, and Nigel Hall, 'Introduction', in David Barton and Nigel Hall (eds.), Letter Writing as a Social Practice (Amsterdam: John Benjamins Publishing, 1999), 1–14

Barton, David, and Nigel Hall (eds.), Letter Writing as a Social Practice (Amsterdam: John Benjamins Publishing, 1999)

Baum, L. Frank, The Wonderful Wizard of Oz (Chicago, IL: Reilly & Lee, 1900)

Bauman, Zygmunt, Community: Seeking Safety in an Insecure World (Cambridge: Polity Press, 2001)

Baym, Nancy K., 'Talking About Soaps: Communicative Practices in a Computer-Mediated Fan Culture', in Cheryl Harris and Alison Alexander (eds.), Theorizing Fandom: Fans, Subculture and Identity (Cresskill, NJ: Hampton Press, 1998), 111–29

Bellah, Robert, 'Civil Religion in America', in R. Richey and D. Jones (eds.), American Civil Religion (New York, NY: Harper & Row, 1974), 21–44

Bellamy, Edward, Looking Backward (Mineola, NY: Dover Publications, 1996 [1888])

Bercovitch, Sacvan, 'The American Puritan Imagination: An Introduction', in Sacvan Bercovitch (ed.), The American Puritan Imagination: Essays in Revaluation (Cambridge: Cambridge University Press, 1974), 1–16

_____, The Puritan Origins of the American Self (New Haven, CT: Yale University Press, 1975)

_____, The American Jeremiad (Madison, WI: University of Wisconsin Press, 1978)

_____, 'New England's Errand Reappraised', in John Higham and Paul K. Conkin (eds.), New Directions in American Intellectual History (Baltimore, MD: Johns Hopkins University Press, 1979), 85–104

Bercovitch, Sacvan (ed.), Typology and Early American Literature (Amherst, MA: University of Massachusetts Press, 1972)

_____, The American Puritan Imagination: Essays in Revaluation (Cambridge: Cambridge University Press, 1974)

Bercovitch, Sacvan, and Myra Jehlen (eds.), Ideology and Classic American Literature (Cambridge: Cambridge University Press, 1986)

Berkhofer Jr., Robert, The White Man's Indian: Images of the Native American from Columbus to the Present (New York, NY: Vintage Books, 1978)

Berkman, Lisa, and Thomas Glass, 'Social Integration, Social Networks, Social Support, and Health', in Lisa F. Berkman and Ichiro Kawachi (eds.), Social Epidemiology (New York, NY: Oxford University Press, 2000), 137–74

Berman, Rick, 'Roddenberry's Vision', in Lee Ann Nicholson (ed.), Farewell to

Star Trek: The Next Generation, *TV Guide Collector's Edition* (Toronto, OT: Telemedia Communications Inc., 1994), 2–3

Bernardi, Daniel L., *Star Trek and History: Race-ing Towards a White Future* (New Brunswick, NJ: Rutgers University Press, 1998)

Blair, Karin, 'Star Trek Old and New: From the Alien Embodied to the Alien Imagined', in George McKay (ed.), *Yankee Go Home (And Take Me With You): Americanization and Popular Culture* (Sheffield: Sheffield Academic Press, 1997), 78–88

Boorstin, Daniel, *The Discoverers* (Harmondsworth: Penguin Books, 1983)

Borges, Jorge Luis, *Fictions*, trans. Anthony Kerrigan (London: Calder Publications, 1998 [1962])

Bowling, David, Johan Ciamaglia, Ryan J. Cornelius, James R. McCain, Alex Rosenzweig, Paul T. Semones and Corey W. Tacker, with David Henderson and Lee Jamilkowski, 'The Pocket Books *Star Trek* Timeline', in Diane Carey et al., *Star Trek – Gateways #7: What Lay Beyond* (New York, NY: Pocket Books, 2001), 319–73

Britton, Piers D., and Simon J. Barker, *Reading Between Designs: Visual Imagery and the Generation of Meaning in* The Avengers, The Prisoner, *and* Doctor Who (Austin, TX: University of Texas Press, 2003)

Brooker, Will, 'Internet Fandom and the Continuing Narratives of *Star Wars, Blade Runner* and *Alien*', in Annette Kuhn (ed.), *Alien Zone II: The Spaces of Science Fiction Cinema* (London: Verso, 1999), 50–72

_____, *Using the Force: Creativity, Community and Star Wars Fans* (New York, NY: Continuum, 2002)

Brooker, Will, and Deborah Jermyn (eds.), *The Audience Studies Reader* (London: Routledge, 2003)

Bukatman, Scott, *Terminal Identity: The Virtual Subject in Postmodern Science Fiction* (Durham, NC: Duke University Press, 1993)

Burke, Kenneth, *A Grammar of Motives* (Berkeley, CA: University of California Press, 1962)

Canfield, Jack, and Mark Victor Hansen (eds.), *Chicken Soup for the Soul: 101 Stories to Open the Heart and Rekindle the Spirit* (Deerfield Beach, FL: Health Communications Incorporated, 1993)

Cantor, Paul A., 'The Simpsons: Atomistic Politics and the Nuclear Family', in William Irwin, Mark T. Conrad and Aeon J. Skoble (eds.), *The Simpsons and Philosophy: The D'Oh! of Homer* (Chicago and La Salle, IL: Open Court, 2001), 160–78

Carey, Diane, *Broken Bow: A Novel* (New York, NY: Pocket Books, 2001)

Carey, Diane, Peter David, Keith R. A. DeCandido, Christine Golden, Robert Greenberger and Susan Wright, *Star Trek – Gateways #7: What Lay Beyond* (New York, NY: Pocket Books, 2001)

Cartmell, Deborah and I. Q. Hunter, 'Introduction: Retrovisions: Historical

Makeovers in Film and Literature', in Deborah Cartmell, I. Q. Hunter and Imelda Whelehan (eds.), *Retrovisions: Reinventing the Past in Film and Fiction* (London: Pluto Press, 2001), 1–7

Cartmell, Deborah, I. Q. Hunter, and Imelda Whelehan (eds.), *Retrovisions: Reinventing the Past in Film and Fiction* (London: Pluto Press, 2001)

Cawelti, John G., *Apostles of the Self-Made Man: Changing Concepts of Success in America* (Chicago, IL: University of Chicago Press, 1965)

Champlin, Charles, *George Lucas: The Creative Impulse* (New York, NY: Harry N. Abrams, Inc., 1992)

Chvany, Peter A., 'Do We Look Like Ferengi Capitalists to You? Star Trek's Klingons as Emergent Virtual American Ethnics', in Henry Jenkins, Tara McPherson and Jane Shattuc (eds.), *Hop on Pop: The Politics and Pleasures of Popular Culture* (Durham, NC: Duke University Press, 2003), 105–21

Coe, Mandy, 'Bred to boldly go', in Valerie Laws (ed.), Star Trek: The Poems (Manchester: Iron Press, 2000), 9

Conforti, Joseph A., *Imagining New England: Explorations of Regional Identity from the Pilgrims to the Mid-Twentieth Century* (Chapel Hill, NC: University of North Carolina Press, 2001)

'Continuity Conundrums', *Star Trek Monthly Magazine* (October 2001): 7

Cox, Greg, *Star Trek: The Eugenics Wars, The Rise and Fall of Khan Noonien Singh – Volume One* (New York, NY: Pocket Books, 2001)

_____, *Star Trek: The Eugenics Wars, The Rise and Fall of Khan Noonien Singh – Volume Two* (New York, NY: Pocket Books, 2002)

Coyne, Michael, *The Crowded Prairie: American National Identity in the Hollywood Western* (London: I.B.Tauris & Co. Ltd, 1997)

'Data Retrieval', *Star Trek Monthly Magazine* (March 2001): 6

de Certeau, Michel, *The Practice of Everyday Life* (Berkeley, CA: University of California Press, 1984)

Decker, Jeffery Louis, *Made in America: Self-Styled Success from Horatio Alger to Oprah Winfrey* (Minneapolis, MN: University of Minnesota Press, 1997)

Decker, William Merrill, *Epistolary Practices: Letter Writing in America before Telecommunications* (Chapel Hill, NC: University of North Carolina Press, 1998)

Dillard, J. M., Star Trek 'Where No One Has Gone Before': A History in Pictures (New York, NY: Pocket Books, 1996)

Disch, T. M., *The Dreams Our Stuff is Made Of: How Science Fiction Conquered the World* (New York, NY: Free Press, 1998)

Dovey, Jon, *Freakshow: First Person Media and Factual Television* (London: Pluto Press, 2000)

Drinnon, Richard, *Facing West: The Metaphysics of Indian-Hating and Empire-Building* (Norman, OK: Oklahoma University Press, 1997)

Dyer, Richard, 'Entertainment and Utopia', in Rick Altman (ed.), *Genre: The Musical* (London: Routledge and Kegan Paul, 1981), 175–89

Eagleton, Terry, *Literary Theory: An Introduction* (Oxford: Blackwell, 1983)

Easthope, Anthony, 'The Personal and the Political in Utopian Science Fiction', in Philip John Davies (ed.), *Science Fiction, Social Conflict and War* (Manchester: Manchester University Press, 1990), 50–67

Ellwood, David (ed.), *The Movies as History: Visions of the Twentieth Century* (Stroud: Sutton Publishing, 2000)

Engelhardt, Tom, *The End of Victory Culture: Cold War America and the Disillusioning of a Generation* (Amherst, MA: University of Massachusetts Press, 1998)

Erickson, Paul D., *Reagan Speaks: The Making of an American Myth* (New York, NY: New York University Press, 1985)

Erisman, Fred., 'L. Frank Baum and the Progressive Dilemma', *American Quarterly* 20 (1968): 617–23

Farr, Robert M., and Serge Moscovici (eds.), *Social Representations* (Cambridge and Paris: Cambridge University Press and Maison des Sciences de l 'Homme, 1984)

Farrell, Kirby, *Post-Traumatic Culture: Injury and Interpretation in the Nineties* (Baltimore, MD: Johns Hopkins University Press, 1998)

Fine, Gary Alan, *Shared Fantasy: Role-Playing Games as Social Worlds* (Chicago, IL: University of Chicago Press, 1983)

Fiske, John, 'Television: Polysemy and Popularity', *Critical Studies in Mass Communication* 3.4 (1986): 391–408

_____, 'The Cultural Economy of Fandom', in Lisa A. Lewis (ed.), *The Adoring Audience: Fan Culture and Popular Media* (New York, NY: Routledge, 1992), 30–49

Fitzgerald, Frances, *Way Out There in the Blue: Reagan, Star Wars and the End of the Cold War* (New York, NY: Simon & Schuster, 2000)

Franklin, Benjamin, *The Autobiography of Benjamin Franklin* (Mineola, NY: Dover Publications, 1996 [1868])

Franklin, H. Bruce, 'Star Trek in the Vietnam Era', *Film & History* 24.1–2 (1994): 36–46

_____, *Vietnam and Other American Fantasies* (Amherst, MA: University of Massachusetts Press, 2000)

Frye, Northrop, *Anatomy of Criticism: Four Essays* (Princeton, NJ: Princeton University Press, 1957)

Galdieri, Christopher J., 'Alexis de Tocqueville's *Democracy in America* and the American Enterprise', *Extrapolation* 42.1 (2001): 65–74

Galipeau, Steven A., *The Journey of Luke Skywalker: An Analysis of Modern Myth and Symbol* (Chicago and La Salle, IL: Open Court, 2001)

Gamson, Joshua, *Freaks Talk Back: Tabloid Talk Shows and Sexual Nonconformity* (Chicago, IL: University of Chicago Press, 1998)

'Generation Games', *Star Trek Monthly Magazine*, September (2001): 44–7

George III, David R., *Star Trek Deep Space Nine – Mission Gamma: Twilight* (New York, NY: Pocket Books, 2002)

Geraghty, Christine, *Women and Soap Opera: A Study of Prime Time Soaps* (Cambridge: Polity Press, 1991)

_____, 'Soap Opera and Utopia', in John Storey (ed.), *Cultural Theory and Popular Culture: A Reader* (2nd edition, London: Prentice Hall, 1998 [1994]), 319–27

Geraghty, Lincoln, 'Reading on the Frontier: A Star Trek Bibliography', *Extrapolation* 43.3 (2002): 288–313

_____, 'A Report on Star Trek: The Adventure, Hyde Park-London', *Vector: The Critical Journal of the BSFA* #228 (March/April 2003): 20–1

Gerrold, David, *The World of Star Trek: The Inside Story of TV's Most Popular Series.* (3rd edition, London: Virgin Books, 1996 [1973, 1984])

Goulding, Jay, *Empire, Aliens, and Conquest: A Critique of American Ideology in Star Trek and Other Science Fiction Adventures* (Toronto, OT: Sisyphus Press, 1985)

Gray, Ann, 'Behind Closed Doors: Video Recorders in the Home', in H. Baehr and G. Dyer (eds.), *Boxed In: Women and Television* (London: Pandora Press, 1987), 38–51

Gregory, Chris, *Star Trek Parallel Narratives* (London: Macmillan Press, 2000)

Grossberg, Lawrence, 'Is there a Fan in the House? The Affective Sensibility of Fandom', in Lisa A. Lewis (ed.), *The Adoring Audience: Fan Culture and Popular Media* (New York, NY: Routledge, 1992), 50–65

Gwenllian-Jones, Sara, and Roberta E. Pearson (eds.), *Cult Television* (Minneapolis, MN: University of Minnesota Press, 2004)

_____, 'Introduction', in Sara Gwenllian-Jones and Roberta E. Pearson (eds.), *Cult Television* (Minneapolis, MN: University of Minnesota Press, 2004), ix-xx

Habenstein, Robert W., 'The Social Organization of Death', in David L. Sills (ed.), *International Encyclopedia of the Social Sciences, Volume 4* (New York, NY: Macmillan, 1968), 19–28

Harlow, John, 'Amazons lead Hollywood raid on antiquity', *Sunday Times* (20 January 2002): Section I, 27.

Harré, Rom, and Paul F. Secord, *The Explanation of Social Behaviour* (Oxford: Basil Blackwell, 1972)

Harries, Dan, *Film Parody* (London: BFI, 2000)

Harries, Dan (ed.), *The New Media Book* (London: BFI, 2002)

Harrison, Taylor, Sarah Projansky, Kent A. Ono and Elyce Rae Helford (eds.), *Enterprise Zones: Critical Positions on Star Trek* (Boulder, CO: Westview Press, 1996)

Harry, Lou, *It's Slinky!: The Fun and Wonderful Toy* (Philadelphia, PA: Running

Press, 2000)

Hawthorn, J. (ed.), *Narrative: From Malory to Motion Pictures* (London: Edward Arnold, 1985)

Hearn, Michael Patrick, 'L. Frank Baum and the "Modernized Fairy Tale"', *Children's Literature in Education* 10.2 (1979): 57–67

Helford, Elyce Rae (ed.), *Fantasy Girls: Gender in the New Universe of Science Fiction and Fantasy Television* (Lanham, MD: Rowman and Littlefield Publishers, 2000)

Henderson, Mary, *Star Wars: The Magic of Myth* (New York, NY: Bantam Books, 1997)

Herman, Judith Lewis, *Trauma and Recovery* (New York, NY: Basic Books, 1992)

Herring, George C. *America's Longest War: The United States and Vietnam, 1950–1975* (3rd edition, New York, NY: McGraw-Hill, 1996 [1979, 1986])

Hertenstein, Mike, *The Double Vision of Star Trek: Half-Humans, Evil Twins and Science Fiction* (Chicago, IL: Cornerstone Press, 1998)

Hertzler, J. G., and Jeffrey Lang, *Star Trek Deep Space Nine – The Left Hand of Destiny, Book One* (New York, NY: Pocket Books, 2003)

_____, *Star Trek Deep Space Nine – The Left Hand of Destiny, Book Two* (New York, NY: Pocket Books, 2003)

Herzlich, Claudine, *Health and Illness: A Social Psychological Analysis*, trans. Douglas Graham (London: Academic Press, 1973)

'Higher Intelligence', *People* (24 December 2001): 92.

Hills, Matt, *Fan Cultures* (London: Routledge, 2002)

_____, 'Putting Away Childish Things: Jar Jar Binks and the "Virtual Star" as an Object of Fan Loathing', in Thomas Austin and Martin Barker (eds.), *Contemporary Hollywood Stardom* (London: Arnold, 2003), 74–89

_____, 'Star Wars in Fandom, Film Theory, and the Museum', in Julian Stringer (ed.), *Movie Blockbusters* (London: Routledge, 2003), 178–89

Hobson, Dorothy, *Crossroads: Drama of a Soap Opera* (London: Methuen, 1982)

Hollows, Joanne, and Mark Jancovich (eds.), *Approaches to Popular Film* (Manchester: Manchester University Press, 1995)

Horsman, Reginald, *Race and Manifest Destiny: The Origins of American Racial Anglo-Saxonism* (Cambridge, MA: Harvard University Press, 1981)

Hulme, Peter, *Colonial Encounters: Europe and the Native Caribbean, 1492–1797* (New York, NY: Methuen Press, 1986)

Hunt, Nathan, 'The Importance of Trivia: Ownership, Exclusion and Authority in Science Fiction Fandom', in Mark Jancovich, Antonio Lázaro Reboll, Julian Stringer, and Andy Willis (eds.), *Defining Cult Movies: The Cultural Politics of Oppositional Taste* (Manchester: Manchester University Press, 2003), 185–201

Hunt, Peter, and Millicent Lenz, *Alternative Worlds in Fantasy Fiction* (London: Continuum, 2001)

Jacoby, Russell, *The End of Utopia: Politics and Culture in an Age of Apathy* (New York, NY: Basic Books, 1999)

Jameson, Fredric, 'Postmodernism and Consumer Society', in Hal Foster (ed.), *The Anti-Aesthetic: Essays on Postmodern Culture* (Port Townsend, WA: Bay Press, 1983), 111–25

―――, 'Cognitive Mapping', in Cary Nelson and Lawrence Grossberg (eds.), *Marxism and the Interpretation of Culture* (Urbana, IL: University of Illinois Press, 1988), 347–57

Jancovich, Mark, 'Screen Theory', in Joanne Hollows and Mark Jancovich (eds.), *Approaches to Popular Film* (Manchester: Manchester University Press, 1995), 123–50

Jancovich, Mark, and Lucy Faire, with Sarah Stubbings, *The Place of the Audience: Cultural Geographies of Film Consumption* (London: BFI, 2003)

Jancovich, Mark, Antonio Lázaro Reboll, Julian Stringer and Andy Willis (eds.), *Defining Cult Movies: The Cultural Politics of Oppositional Taste* (Manchester: Manchester University Press, 2003)

Jarman, Heather, *Star Trek Deep Space Nine – Mission Gamma: This Gray Spirit* (New York, NY: Pocket Books, 2002)

Jaspars, Jos, and Colin Fraser, 'Attitudes and Social Representations', in Robert M. Farr and Serge Moscovici (eds.), *Social Representations* (Cambridge and Paris: Cambridge University Press and Maison des Sciences de l'Homme, 1984), 101–23

Jenkins, Henry, 'Star Trek Rerun, Reread, Rewritten: Fan Writing as Textual Poaching', *Critical Studies in Mass Communication* 5.2 (1988): 85–107

―――, *Textual Poachers: Television Fans and Participatory Culture* (New York, NY: Routledge, 1992)

―――, '"Strangers No More, We Sing": Filking and the Social Construction of the Science Fiction Fan Community', in Lisa A. Lewis (ed.), *The Adoring Audience: Fan Culture and Popular Media* (New York, NY: Routledge, 1992), 208–36

―――, 'Interactive Audiences?', in Dan Harries (ed.), *The New Media Book* (London: BFI, 2002), 157–70

Jenkins, Henry, Tara McPherson and Jane Shattuc (eds.), *Hop on Pop: The Politics and Pleasures of Popular Culture* (Durham, NC: Duke University Press, 2003)

Jenkins, Henry and John Tulloch, 'Beyond the Star Trek Phenomenon: Reconceptualizing the Science Fiction Audience', in John Tulloch and Henry Jenkins, *Science Fiction Audiences: Watching Doctor Who and Star Trek* (London: Routledge, 1995), 3–24

Jennings, Francis, *The Invasion of America: Indians, Colonialism and the Cant of Conquest* (New York, NY: W.W. Norton and Company, 1975)

Jenson, Joli, 'Fandom as Pathology: The Consequences of Characterization', in

Lisa A. Lewis (ed.), *The Adoring Audience: Fan Culture and Popular Media* (New York, NY: Routledge, 1992), 9–29

Jewett, Robert, and John Shelton Lawrence, *The American Monomyth* (Garden City, NY: Anchor Press, 1977)

Jindra, Michael, 'Star Trek Fandom as a Religious Phenomenon', *Sociology of Religion* 55.1 (1994): 27–51

_____, '"It's About Faith in our Future": Star Trek Fandom as Cultural Religion', in Bruce David Forbes and Jeffrey H. Mahan (eds.), *Religion and Popular Culture in America* (Berkeley, CA: University of California Press, 2000), 165–79

Johnson, Paul E., *A Shopkeeper's Millennium: Society and Revivals in Rochester, New York, 1815–1837* (New York, NY: Hill and Wang, 1978)

Johnson-Smith, Jan, *American Science Fiction TV: Star Trek, Stargate and Beyond* (London: I.B.Tauris & Co. Ltd, 2005)

Jones, Nick, 'Video Review', *Star Trek Monthly Magazine*, January (2002): 56

_____, 'Retcon Tricks', *Star Trek Monthly Magazine*, February (2002): 18–21

Joseph-Witham, Heather, *Star Trek Fans and Costume Art* (Jackson, MS: University Press of Mississippi, 1996)

Kanar, Hanley E., 'No Ramps in Space: The Inability to Envision Accessibility in Star Trek: Deep Space Nine', in Elyce Rae Helford (ed.), *Fantasy Girls: Gender in the New Universe of Science Fiction and Fantasy Television* (Lanham, MD: Rowman and Littlefield Publishers, 2000), 245–64

Kaveney, Roz, *From Alien to The Matrix: Reading Science Fiction Film* (London: I.B.Tauris & Co. Ltd, 2005)

Kelly, DeForest, Personal Interview, *Trekkies*, dir. Roger Nygard, Paramount Pictures (1998)

Kilgore, De Witt Douglas, *Astrofuturism: Science, Race and Visions of Utopia in Space* (Philadelphia, PA: University of Pennsylvania Press, 2003)

King, Geoff, *Film Comedy* (London: Wallflower Press, 2002)

King, Geoff, and Tanya Krzywinska, *Science Fiction Cinema: From Outerspace to Cyberspace* (London: Wallflower Press, 2000)

King, Richard H., *Civil Rights and the Idea of Freedom* (2nd edition, Athens, GA: University of Georgia Press, 1996 [1992])

Klass, Dennis, 'John Bowlby's model of grief and the problems of identification', *Omega: The Journal of Death and Dying* 18.1 (1987): 13–32

Klein, Kerwin Lee, *Frontiers of Historical Imagination: Narrating the European Conquest of Native America, 1890–1990* (Berkeley, CA: University of California Press, 1997)

Kozloff, Sarah, 'Narrative Theory and Television', in Robert C. Allen (ed.), *Channels of Discourse, Reassembled: Television and Contemporary Criticism* (2nd edition, Chapel Hill, NC: University of North Carolina Press, 1992 [1987]), 67–100

Kreitzer, Larry, 'The Cultural Veneer of *Star Trek*', *Journal of Popular Culture* 30.2 (1996): 1–28

Kupperman, Karen Ordahl (ed.), *Major Problems in American Colonial History* (Lexington, MA: D.C. Heath and Company, 1993)

Lagon, Mark P., '"We Owe it to Them to Interfere": *Star Trek* and U.S. Statecraft in the 1960s and the 1990s', *Extrapolation* 34.3 (1993): 251–64

Lancaster, Kurt, *Interacting with Babylon 5: Fan Performances in a Media Universe* (Austin, TX: University of Texas Press, 2001)

Landon, Brooks, 'Bet On It: Cyber/video/punk/performance', in Larry McCaffery (ed.), *Storming the Reality Studio* (Durham, NC: Duke University Press, 1991), 239–44

Landsberg, Alison, *Prosthetic Memory: The Transformation of American Remembrance in the Age of Mass Culture* (New York, NY: Columbia University Press, 2004)

Larson, David M., 'Benjamin Franklin 1706–1790', in Paul Lauter (ed.), *The Heath Anthology of American Literature*, Volume 1 (2nd edition, Lexington, MA: D.C. Heath and Company, 1994), 708–11

Laws, Valerie (ed.), *Star Trek: The Poems* (Manchester: Iron Press, 2000)

Lewis, Lisa A. (ed.), *The Adoring Audience: Fan Culture and Popular Media* (New York, NY: Routledge, 1992)

Lichtenberg, Jacqueline, Sondra Marshak and Joan Winston, *Star Trek Lives!* (New York, NY: Bantam Books, 1975)

Lipsitz, George, *Time Passages: Collective Memory and American Popular Culture* (Minneapolis, MN: University of Minnesota Press, 1990)

Littlefield, Henry M., 'The Wizard of Oz: Parable on Populism', *American Quarterly* 16 (1964): 47–58

Livingstone, Sonia, and Peter Lunt, *Talk on Television: Audience Participation and Public Debate* (London: Routledge, 1994)

Lorde, Audre, 'Poetry Is Not a Luxury', in Audre Lorde, *Sister Outsider* (Freedom, CA: The Crossing Press, 1984), 36–9

Lowance, Jr., Mason I., 'Cotton Mather's *Magnalia* and the Metaphors of Biblical History', in Sacvan Bercovitch (ed.), *Typology and Early American Literature* (Amherst, MA: University of Massachusetts Press, 1972), 139–60

Lurie, Alison, *Not in Front of the Grown-Ups: Subversive Children's Literature* (London: Cardinal, 1990)

_____, *Boys and Girls Forever: Children's Classics from Cinderella to Harry Potter* (New York, NY: Penguin Books, 2003)

McCurdy, Howard E., *Space and the American Imagination* (Washington D.C.: Smithsonian Institute Press, 1997)

McKay, George (ed.), *Yankee Go Home (And Take Me With You): Americanization and Popular Culture* (Sheffield: Sheffield Academic Press, 1997)

McLuhan, Marshall, *Understanding Media: The Extensions of Man* (New York, NY: Routledge and Kegan Paul Ltd, 1964)

Madsen, Deborah L., *American Exceptionalism* (Edinburgh: BAAS, Edinburgh University Press, 1998)

Maher, Ian, 'The Outward Voyage and the Inward Search: Star Trek Motion Pictures and the Spiritual Quest', in Jennifer E. Porter and Darcee L. McLaren (eds.), Star Trek and Sacred Grounds: Explorations of Star Trek, Religion and American Culture (Albany, NY: State University of New York Press, 1999), 165–91

Marinaccio, Dave, *All I Really Needed to Know I Learned from Watching* Star Trek (New York, NY: Crown Publishing, 1995)

_____, *All the Other Things I Really Needed to Know I Learned from Watching* Star Trek: The Next Generation (New York, NY: Pocket Books, 1998)

Martin, Michael A., 'Parallel Universes: Real Life Space Exploration vs. *Star Trek* Fantasy', Star Trek Monthly Magazine, February (2002): 26–32

Martin, Michael A., and Andy Mangels, *Star Trek Deep Space Nine – Mission Gamma: Cathedral* (New York, NY: Pocket Books, 2002)

Mather, Cotton, *Magnalia Christi Americana; or, The Ecclesiastical History of New England*, Thomas Robbins (ed.), Volumes 1 and 2 (Hartford, CT: n.n., 1853 [1702])

Merk, Frederick, *Manifest Destiny and Mission in American History* (Cambridge, MA: Harvard University Press, 1995 [1963])

Michaud, Michael A. G., *Reaching for the High Frontier: The American Pro-Space Movement, 1972–84* (New York, NY: Praeger, 1986)

Miller, Perry, *Errand into the Wilderness* (Cambridge, MA: Belknap Press of Harvard University Press, 1956)

Minkowitz, Donna, 'Beam Us Back, Scotty!', The Nation (25 March 2002): 36–7

Minter, David, 'The Puritan Jeremiad as a Literary Form', in Sacvan Bercovitch (ed.), *The American Puritan Imagination: Essays in Revaluation* (Cambridge: Cambridge University Press, 1974), 45–55

Morley, David, *The Nationwide Audience* (London: BFI, 1980)

_____, *Television, Audiences & Cultural Studies* (London: Routledge, 1992)

Moscovici, Serge, 'Forward', in Claudine Herzlich, *Health and Illness: A Social Psychological Analysis*, trans. Douglas Graham (London: Academic Press, 1973), ix-xiv

_____, 'The Phenomenon of Social Representations', in Robert M. Farr and Serge Moscovici (eds.), *Social Representations* (Cambridge and Paris: Cambridge University Press and Maison des Sciences de l'Homme, 1984), 3–69

Murray, Colleen I., 'Death, Dying and Bereavement', in Patrick C. McKenry and Sharon J. Price (eds.), *Families and Change: Coping with Stressful Events* (Thousands Oaks, CA: Sage Publications, 1994), 173–94

Murray, Janet H., *Hamlet on the Holodeck: The Future of Narrative in Cyberspace* (Cambridge, MA: MIT Press, 1997)

Neely, Sarah, 'Cool Intentions: The Literary Classic, the Teenpic and the "Chick Flick"', in Deborah Cartmell, I. Q. Hunter and Imelda Whelehan (eds.), *Retrovisions: Reinventing the Past in Film and Fiction* (London: Pluto Press, 2001), 74–86

Nichols, Nichelle, *Beyond Uhura: Star Trek and Other Memories* (London: Boxtree Ltd, 1994)

Nicholson, Lee Ann (ed.), *Farewell to Star Trek: The Next Generation*, *TV Guide Collector's Edition* (Toronto, OT: Telemedia Communications Inc., 1994)

Nobles, Gregory H., *American Frontiers: Cultural Encounters and Continental Conquest* (London: Penguin Books, 1997)

Okuda, Michael and Denise, *Star Trek Chronology: A History of the Future* (New York, NY: Pocket Books, 1993)

Okuda, Michael and Denise, with Debbie Mirek, *The Star Trek Encyclopedia: A Reference Guide to the Future* (3rd edition, New York, NY: Pocket Books, 1997)

Palmieri, Marco (ed.), *Star Trek Deep Space Nine – The Lives of Dax* (New York, NY: Pocket Books, 1999)

Patterson, Orlando, *Freedom Volume 1: Freedom in the Making of Western Culture* (London: I.B.Tauris & Co. Ltd, 1991)

Pearson, L., *I, Who: The Unauthorised Guide to Doctor Who Novels* (New York, NY: Sidewinder Press, 1999)

Pelka, Fred, 'Hating the Sick: Health Chauvinism and Its Cure', *The Humanist* 54.4 (July/August 1997): 17–20

Penley, Constance, *NASA/TREK: Popular Science and Sex in America* (New York, NY: Verso, 1997)

Perry, S. D., *Star Trek Deep Space Nine – Avatar Book One of Two* (New York, NY: Pocket Books, 2001)

_____, *Star Trek Deep Space Nine – Avatar Book Two of Two* (New York, NY: Pocket Books, 2001)

_____, *Star Trek Deep Space Nine – Rising Son* (New York, NY: Pocket Books, 2003)

_____, *Star Trek Deep Space Nine – Unity* (New York, NY: Pocket Books, 2003)

Porter, Jennifer E., and Darcee L. McLaren (eds.), *Star Trek and Sacred Grounds: Explorations of Star Trek, Religion and American Culture* (Albany, NY: State University of New York Press, 1999)

Putnam, Robert D., 'Bowling Alone: America's Declining Social Capital', *Journal of Democracy* 6.1 (1995): 65–78

_____, *Bowling Alone: The Collapse and Revival of American Community* (New York, NY: Touchstone, 2000)

Raben, Richard and Hiyaguha Cohen, *Boldly Live As You've Never Lived Before: (Unauthorized and Unexpected) Life Lessons from Star Trek* (New York, NY: Morrow, William & Co., 1995)

Reagan, Ronald W., 'Inaugural Address, January 20, 1981', in *Public Papers of the Presidents of the United States: Ronald Reagan, 1981 – January 20 to December 31, 1981* (Washington D.C.: US Government Printing Office, 1982 [1981]), 1–4

_____, 'Remarks at the Annual Convention of the National League of Cities in Los Angeles, California, November 29, 1982', in *Public Papers of the Presidents of the United States: Ronald Reagan, 1982, Book II – July 3 to December 31, 1982* (Washington D.C.: US Government Printing Office, 1983 [1982]), 1516–21

_____, 'Farewell Address to the Nation, January 11, 1989', in *Public Papers of the Presidents of the United States: Ronald Reagan, 1988–89, Book II – July 2 1988 to January 19, 1989* (Washington D.C.: US Government Printing Office, 1991 [1989]), 1718–23

Reeves-Stevens, Judith and Garfield, *The Art of Star Trek* (New York, NY: Pocket Books, 1995)

Reynolds, Richard, *Super Heroes: A Modern Mythology* (London: B.T. Batsford, 1992)

Richards, Jeffrey, 'Fires Were Started', in David Ellwood (ed.), *The Movies as History: Visions of the Twentieth Century* (Stroud: Sutton Publishing, 2000), 26–35

Richards, Thomas, *The Meaning of Star Trek* (New York, NY: Doubleday, 1997)

_____, *Star Trek in Myth and Legend* (London: Orion Books, 1998)

Roberts, Adam, *Science Fiction: The New Critical Idiom* (London: Routledge, 2000)

Roberts, Robin, *Sexual Generations: 'Star Trek: The Next Generation' and Gender* (Urbana, IL: University of Illinois Press, 1999)

_____, 'Performing Science Fiction: Television, Theater and Gender in Star Trek: The Experience', *Extrapolation* 42.4 (2001): 340–56

Roberts, Wess, and Bill Ross, *Make It So: Leadership Lessons from Star Trek: The Next Generation* (New York, NY: Pocket Books, 1995)

Robinson, Andrew J., *Star Trek: Deep Space Nine #27 – A Stitch in Time* (New York, NY: Pocket Books, 2000)

Roper, Jon, *The American Presidents: Heroic Leadership from Kennedy to Clinton* (Edinburgh: Edinburgh University Press, 2000)

Roth, Lane, 'Death and Rebirth in Star Trek II: The Wrath of Khan', *Extrapolation* 28.2 (1987): 155–66

Ruditis, Paul, 'Behind the Scenes of Enterprise', in Diane Carey, *Broken Bow: A Novel* (New York, NY: Pocket Books, 2001), 199–232

Sackett, Susan (ed.), *Letters to Star Trek* (New York, NY: Ballantine, 1977)

_____, *Inside Trek: My Secret Life with Star Trek Creator Gene Roddenberry* (Tulsa, OK:

Hawk Publishing Group, 2002)

Said, Edward W., *Orientalism: Western Conceptions of the Orient* (Harmondsworth: Penguin Books, 1995 [1978])

Sardar, Ziauddin, 'Introduction', in Ziauddin Sardar and Sean Cubitt (eds.), *Aliens R Us: The Other in Science Fiction Cinema* (London: Pluto Press, 2002), 1–17

Sardar, Ziauddin and Sean Cubitt (eds.), *Aliens R Us: The Other in Science Fiction Cinema* (London: Pluto Press, 2002)

Sayre, Robert F., *The Examined Self: Benjamin Franklin, Henry Adams, Henry James* (Princeton, NJ: Princeton University Press, 1964)

Schlesinger Jr., Arthur M., *The Disuniting of America: Reflections on a Multicultural Society* (2nd edition, New York, NY: W. W. Norton, 1998 [1991])

Scholes, Robert, and Robert Kellogg, *The Nature of Narrative* (New York, NY: Oxford University Press, 1966)

Schwartz, Susan L., 'Enterprise Engaged: Mythic Enactment and Ritual Performance', in Ross Kraemer, William Cassidy and Susan L. Schwartz, *Religions of* Star Trek (Boulder, CO: Westview Press, 2001), 129–58

Serfaty, Viviane, 'Online Diaries: Towards a Structural Approach', *Journal of American Studies* 38.3 (2004): 457–71

Shain, Barry Alan, *The Myth of American Individualism: The Protestant Origins of American Political Thought* (Princeton, NJ: Princeton University Press, 1994)

Shatner, Lisabeth, *Captain's Log: William Shatner's Personal Account of the Making of* Star Trek V: The Final Frontier (London: Titan Books, 1989)

Shatner, William, Personal Interview. Available at: <http://www.questarian.com/Databank/gq-trek_talks.htm> [Accessed 4th December 2003]

Shatner, William, and Chip Walter, *Star Trek: I'm Working on That: A Trek from Science Fiction to Science Fact* (New York, NY: Pocket Books, 2002)

Shattuc, Jane, *The Talking Cure: TV Talk Shows and Women* (New York, NY: Routledge, 1997)

Sherwin, Jill, *Quotable* Star Trek (New York, NY: Pocket Books, 1999)

Simpson, Robert, Star Trek Deep Space Nine – *Mission Gamma: Lesser Evil* (New York, NY: Pocket Books, 2002)

Slotkin, Richard, 'Myth and the Production of History', in Sacvan Bercovitch and Myra Jehlen (eds.), *Ideology and Classic American Literature* (Cambridge: Cambridge University Press, 1986), 70–90

——, *Gunfighter Nation: The Myth of the Frontier in Twentieth-Century America.* Norton, OK: Oklahoma University Press, 1998)

——, 'Unit Pride: Ethnic Platoons and the Myths of American Nationality', *American Literary History* 13.3 (2001): 469–98

Smith, Dean Wesley, John J. Ordover and Paula M. Block (eds.), Star Trek Strange

New Worlds (New York, NY: Pocket Books, 1998)

Sobchack, Vivian, Screening Space: The American Science Fiction Film (New Brunswick, NJ: Rutgers University Press, 1998)

Stafford, Nikki (ed.), Trekkers: True Stories by Fans for Fans (Toronto, ON: ECW Press, 2002)

'Star Trek: Enterprise Cancelled!' Available at: <http://www.startrek.com/startrek/view/news/article/9469.html> [Accessed 7 February 2005]

'Star Trek is Back', Star Trek Monthly Magazine, December (2003): 7

'Star Trek: To Infinity and Beyond', Radio Times, 15–21 September (2001): 38–42

Stowe, Harriet Beecher, Uncle Tom's Cabin, or, life among the lowly (London: Dent, 1961 [1852])

Stringer, Julian (ed.), Movie Blockbusters (London: Routledge, 2003)

Sturken, Marita, Tangled Memories: The Vietnam War, the AIDS Epidemic and the Politics of Remembering (Berkeley, CA: University of California Press, 1997)

Tallack, Douglas, Twentieth-Century America: The Intellectual and Cultural Context (London: Longman, 1991)

Taylor, Helen, Scarlett's Women: Gone with the Wind and its Female Fans (London: Virago Press, 1989)

Telotte, J.P., Science Fiction Film (New York, NY: Cambridge University Press, 2001)

The Compact NIV Study Bible, The New International Version (London: Hodder and Stoughton, 1995)

'The Darling Buds of Meyer', Star Trek Monthly Magazine, December (2002): 38–40

Tocqueville, Alexis de, Democracy in America (Oxford: Oxford University Press, 1946 [1835])

Tulloch, John, and Henry Jenkins, Science Fiction Audiences: Watching Doctor Who and Star Trek (London: Routledge, 1995)

Turner, Fred, Echoes of Combat: The Vietnam War in American Memory (New York, NY: Anchor Books, 1996)

Turner, Frederick Jackson, The Frontier in American History (3rd edition, Tucson, AZ: University of Arizona Press, 1994 [1920])

Tyrrell, William Blake, 'Star Trek as Myth and Television as Mythmaker', Journal of Popular Culture 10.4 (1977): 711–19

Uhlenberg, Peter, 'Death and the Family', in Michael Gordon (ed.), The American Family in Social-Historical Perspective (New York, NY: St Martin's Press, 1983), 169–77

Van de Berg, Leah R., 'Liminality: Worf as Metonymic Signifier of Racial, Cultural and National Differences', in Taylor Harrison, Sarah Projansky, Kent A. Ono and Elyce Rae Helford (eds.), Enterprise Zones: Critical Positions on Star Trek (Boulder, CO: Westview Press, 1996), 51–68

Vansina, Jan, *Oral Tradition as History* (London: James Currey, 1985)

Verba, Joan Marie, *Boldly Writing: A Trekker Fan and Zine History, 1967–1987* (Minnetonka, MN: FTL Publications, 1996)

Wagner, Jon, 'Intimations of Immortality: Death/Life Mediations in *Star Trek*', in Jennifer E. Porter and Darcee L. McLaren (eds.), *Star Trek and Sacred Grounds: Explorations of Star Trek, Religion and American Culture* (Albany, NY: State University of New York Press, 1999), 119–38

Wagner, Jon and Jan Lundeen, *Deep Space and Sacred Time: Star Trek in the American Mythos* (Westport, CT: Praeger, 1998)

Walters, Ronald G., *American Reformers, 1815–1860* (New York, NY: Hill and Wang, 1978)

Weiss, Richard, *The American Myth of Success: From Horatio Alger to Norman Vincent Peale* (Urbana, IL: University of Illinois Press, 1988 [1969])

Wells, Paul, 'To Affinity and Beyond: Woody, Buzz and the New Authenticity', in Thomas Austin and Martin Barker (eds.), *Contemporary Hollywood Stardom* (London: Arnold, 2003), 90–102

Wertheim, Christine, '*Star Trek: First Contact*: The Hybrid, the Whore and the Machine', in Ziauddin Sardar and Sean Cubitt (eds.), *Aliens R Us: The Other in Science Fiction Cinema* (London: Pluto Press, 2002), 74–93

Westfahl, Gary, *Science Fiction, Children's Literature and Popular Culture: Coming of Age in Fantasyland* (Westport, CT: Greenwood Press, 2000)

White, Hayden, *Metahistory: The Historical Imagination in Nineteenth Century Europe* (Baltimore, MD: Johns Hopkins University Press, 1973)

———, *Tropics of Discourse: Essays in Cultural Criticism* (Baltimore, MD: Johns Hopkins University Press, 1978)

———, *The Content of the Form: Narrative Discourse and Historical Representation* (Baltimore, MD: Johns Hopkins University Press, 1987)

———, *Figural Realism: Studies in the Mimesis Effect* (Baltimore, MD: Johns Hopkins University Press, 1999)

Wilkinson, Rupert, *American Tough: The Tough-Guy Tradition and American Character* (Westport, CT: Greenwood Press, 1984)

Winthrop, John, 'Modell of Christian Charity', in Karen Ordahl Kupperman (ed.), *Major Problems in American Colonial History* (Lexington, MA: D.C. Heath and Company, 1993 [1630]), 124–6

Woods, Louis A., and Gary L. Harmon, 'Jung and *Star Trek*: The Coincidentia Oppositorum and Images of the Shadow', *Journal of Popular Culture* 28.2 (1994): 169–84

Worland, Rick, 'Captain Kirk: Cold Warrior', *Journal of Popular Film & Television* 16.3 (1988): 109–17

———, 'From the New Frontier to the Final Frontier: *Star Trek* from Kennedy to Gorbachev', *Film & History* 24.1–2 (1994): 19–35

Wuthnow, Robert, *Sharing the Journey: Support Groups and America's New Quest for*

Community (New York, NY: Free Press, 1994)

Wyllie, Irvin G., *The Self-Made Man in America: The Myth of Rags to Riches* (New York, NY: Free Press, 1954)

Zipes, Jack, *Fairy Tales and the Art of Subversion: The Classical Genre for Children and the Process of Civilization* (New York, NY: Routledge, 1983)

_____, *Fairy Tale as Myth/Myth as Fairy Tale* (Lexington, KY: University Press of Kentucky, 1994)

_____, *When Dreams Come True: Classical Fairy Tales and their Tradition* (New York, NY: Routledge, 1999)

Zuckerman, Michael, 'The Selling of the Self: From Franklin to Barnum', in Barbara B. Oberg and Harry S. Stout (eds.), *Benjamin Franklin, Jonathan Edwards and the Representation of American Culture* (New York, NY: Oxford University Press, 1993), 152–67

INDEX